CREATION Health is a registered trademark of Florida Hospital.

No part of this publication may be reproduced, stored in a retrieval system, or transmitted in any form or by any means – electronic, mechanical, photocopying, recording or otherwise – without written permission from Florida Hospital Mission Integration & Culture.

Florida Hospital Mission Integration & Culture
496 West Central Parkway
Altamonte Springs FL 32714
407-303-7789

ISBN # 978-0-9844792-1-4

Please Note: This book contains advice and information relating to health and fitness. It is designed for your personal knowledge and to help you be a more informed consumer of medical and health services. It is not intended to be exhaustive or to replace medical advice or treatment from your physician. Your physician should address any questions about your specific symptoms, medications, or health condition. All efforts have been made to ensure the accuracy of the information contained within this book as of the date published. The authors and the publisher expressly disclaim responsibility for any adverse effects resulting from the application of the information contained herein.

For additional information or to order additional books, visit: CREATIONHealth.com.

Please note that the CREATION Health Personal Study Guide is just one part of a three-part seminar program. To see the videos and Leader's Guide that is part of the CREATION Health program, visit: CREATIONHealth.com.

CREATION Health Personal Study Guide

© 2016 by Florida Hospital Mission Integration & Culture
Published by Florida Hospital Mission Integration & Culture

International Copyright Secured

. . . .

GENERAL EDITOR:
Robyn Edgerton

RESEARCH AND EDITING:
Heather Neal, M.S.

PRODUCTION EDITOR:
Lynell LaMountain

EDITED BY:
Lynell LaMountain
Merita Ross

COPY EDITED BY:
George Guthrie, M.D., MPH, CDE, CNS
Clifford Goldstein

PROJECT COORDINATOR:
Merita Ross

DESIGN AND LAYOUT:
Carter Design, Inc., Denver, Colorado

. . . .

CONTENTS

CHOICE

one of God's greatest gifts

CREATION
HEALTH

CONTENTS

MAKE IT WORK

Further Explanation of the DVD Topics

THE BIG PICTURE

Every day, often numerous times a day, you exercise the power of choice. This sacred gift was given to us at Creation. We want to use it wisely. It's one thing to have freedom of choice; it's another to know what to do with that freedom. This part of the CREATION Health seminar is designed to help you choose wisely.

What is meant by the word "choice"? In the broadest sense, it means the option or ability to evaluate various courses of action and to select among them. Choice is the ability to exercise the power of our will. Everything we do is the result of making a choice. We often do things unconsciously, but we cannot avoid making choices. Even the choice to do nothing is, still, *a choice*.

Choice is hardwired right into our brains. The frontal lobe gives us the ability to choose. It makes up 3.5% of the brain in a cat, 7% in dogs, 17% in chimps, and between 33% and 38% in humans.[1] The frontal lobe is where our judgment, reasoning, social norms, and long-term planning take place,[2-5] all of which contribute to making healthy, life-giving choices. Human reasoning and planning capabilities are more powerful and complex than those of other species, which allow for variable relationships in our decision making.

It is important that our decisions remain consistent with our will, our beliefs, and our goals. The gift of choice comes with responsibility. We must exercise wisdom in our choices because they will ultimately determine the course of our lives.

> *"Freedom is the right to choose: the right to create for oneself the alternatives of choice. Without the possibility of choice, and the exercise of choice, a man is not a man but a member, an instrument, a thing."*
>
> **~ THOMAS JEFFERSON**

We have often heard of the *power* of choice. But there really are *powers* of choice, powers to help us make the right decisions that can impact every aspect of our lives.

As we seek to make right decisions, it's important, as much as possible, not to let circumstances control all those decisions. Whatever is happening around us or to us, we still can control even the smallest choices, such as how to spend $5.00 or five minutes. These choices, no matter how small they may seem, can positively impact our lives and the lives of those around us. More importantly, small choices accumulated over the years will result in big differences.

Choice is the first step toward improving your well-being. Before we can achieve positive changes in any area of our lives, we must choose to do so. Conscious decision making is key to experiencing the positive impact of good choices.

POWER TOOLS

Conventional wisdom and decades of psychological research have linked choice to various blessings. Providing one with the ability to choose increases an individual's sense of personal control and feelings of intrinsic motivation. This personal control and intrinsic motivation, in turn, has been associated with numerous physical and psychological benefits. Yes, indeed, choices have powerful motivating consequences. Conversely, the absence of choice and control has a variety of detrimental effects on intrinsic motivation, life satisfaction, and one's well-being.[6-7]

The benefits of exercising choice and control are well illustrated by a study of nursing home residents, published in *The Journal of Personality and Psychology* and later described by Dr. Martin E. P. Seligman in his book, *Learned Optimism*.

Researchers divided the nursing home by floors. On the first floor, the residents received extra control of their lives, and extra choices. One day, the director gave a speech to the residents: "I'd like you to know about all the things that you can do for yourself here at Shady Grove. There are omelets and scrambled eggs for breakfast, but you have to *choose* which you want the night before. There are movies on Wednesday or Thursday night, but you must sign up in advance before going. Here are some plants; *pick one out* and take it to your room, but you have to water it yourself."

The director then told the residents on the second floor: "I want you to know about what we can do for you here at Shady Grove. There are omelets or scrambled eggs for breakfast. We make omelets on Monday, Wednesday, and Friday, and scrambled eggs on the other days. There are movies on Wednesday and Thursday night. Thursday nights, residents from the left quarter go, and on Wednesday nights residents from the right quarter go. Here are some plants for your rooms. The nurse will choose one for you and take care of it."

Thus, folks on both floors had the same things, but only those on the first had choice and control while those on the second had neither.

The researchers found that those with choice and control, as opposed to those in the "no-control" group, thrived in most every way. They also found that fewer of this group had died 18 months later than in the control group.[8-10] This amazing fact strongly indicated that choice and control could save lives.

Yes, the *powers* of choice can be stronger and deeper than we often realize.

Another important power tool in making good choices is *knowledge*. Seeking knowledge should be a way of life. We cannot responsibly go through this life intellectually idle. We should always be learning something new, always increasing our store of knowledge. Read, listen to audio books, watch informative programs, use the Internet wisely; find ways that appeal to you and fit into your lifestyle that can help you grow intellectually. As a result of this growth, you will ideally be better equipped to make wise choices that impact your life in many positive ways.

Another important tool is the use of reason. We can't always have all the information we would want about any particular situation; nor can we know all there is to know about everything. Thus, we must also exercise reason. We can use what we do know about the situation and apply the principles that we live by, the rules we have to keep, the laws that we are bound by, and good old common sense. These can help us make good choices.

We can use deductive or inductive reasoning to develop various rationales that, in turn, can help to guide our decision making. Just as we need to always increase our knowledge, we also need to constantly work on improving our reasoning abilities. Take a class on logic, philosophy, debate, or classical reasoning. Meet regularly with a

> "You must take personal responsibility. You cannot change the circumstances, the seasons, or the wind, but you can change yourself." ~ JIM ROHN

group of friends and engage in stimulating and constructive debate/discussions/conversations. Practice reasoning with yourself about different things throughout the day. The more we practice these critical thinking skills, the better we will become at making good choices, even when we have relatively little information available to us.

Sometimes we make poor choices because we think we have no choice. When we find ourselves in a difficult situation, it is easy to think we have limited choices or no choices at all. This is because stress can impair our thinking ability. All too often, when we perceive ourselves in a situation where we have no control, we feel helpless.

Scientists have demonstrated that animals can develop what is called "learned helplessness" in response to persistent adversity. Martin P. Seligman demonstrated this in a series of experiments with dogs. The dogs were placed in pens where they could not escape from periodic electrical shocks delivered via the floor. Initially the dogs tried to escape when shocked. After repeated shocks and having learned there was no escaping them, the dogs quit trying to escape. They simply endured. Seligman then removed the barrier; the dogs now had an escape. Yet, amazingly enough, when shocked, they still did not try to escape! Having learned that they were helpless, the dogs remained helpless – even after their circumstances had changed.[11-12] These dogs' locus of control had shifted from being internal to being entirely external. They had "learned" that their external environment, and not their own decisions or behavior, determined their fate.

Don't let this happen to you. Resolve to always exercise your powers of choice, no matter how persistent the adversity. This determination will undoubtedly improve your circumstances, no matter how dire. An internal locus of control has been associated with many benefits, such as an increased ability to stop smoking,[13] lose weight,[14] stick to a medical regimen,[15] and attain higher academic achievement.[16]

BALANCING ACTS

Making healthy choices means choosing the good things in a balanced moderate way and avoiding what's harmful. Healthy choices help balance our life. Think of how a radio equalizer works. As we use the equalizer to balance the highs and lows of music, so we can use the power of our choices to avoid extremes.

Making good choices requires a balanced approach in all that we do. Even a good thing can be overdone. If a person exercises so much that they don't have time to spend with their family and friends, then the exercise has become out of balance and can cause problems in other areas. You can have too much of a good thing. And if we choose to include good things in our lives but fail to eliminate the negative things, we are also doing ourselves a disservice. For example, the benefits to our cardio-respiratory system when we eat oatmeal for breakfast may be minimized or eliminated if we also eat a lot of high cholesterol foods at the same meal.

When we make healthy lifestyle choices, we will make a difference in how we feel today and improve our long-term health and wellness. Eating oatmeal and reducing the amount of cholesterol and saturated fat in our diet will not only help us feel more energetic and healthy today, it helps reduce the strain on our cardio-respiratory system and adds rewarding days to our lives.

BRAIN DRAIN

The importance and power of the frontal lobe in the decision-making process *cannot be underestimated*. This is dramatically illustrated in the tragic story of Phineas Gage, a railroad foreman. Phineas was working with a tapping iron when the powder underneath exploded, launching the tapping iron through Phineas's head. The iron entered first below his left cheekbone and then exited through the top of his skull, landing twenty-five to thirty yards behind him.

Before the accident, Phineas was known for his high morals and exemplary record as a railroad foreman; after the accident, his moral decline was immediately evident. He became overly emotional and overtly angry. Phineas lost interest in spiritual things, constantly used profanity, and lost respect for social norms and customs.

Dr. John Harlow, his physician, stated that the accident destroyed Phineas's "equilibrium or balance, so to speak, between his intellectual faculty and his animal propensities." Phineas's traumatic frontal lobotomy cost him his personality, his moral standards, and his commitment to family, church, and loved ones.[17-19]

As was stated earlier, the frontal lobe helps set humans apart from the rest of the animal kingdom. It is this gift that gives us the ability to choose. It is, in many ways, the power center. It is the seat of our will/choice, and it is also the seat of our judgment, reasoning, social norms, and long-term planning,[20-23] all of which help us make healthy, life-giving choices.

The story of Phineas Gage shows how a compromised frontal lobe can change personality. These changes may be minimal at first but, accumulated over time, they can become significant, life-changing factors.

Can you see how these effects can be devastating to your happiness? Deterioration of the frontal lobe can negatively affect you emotionally, socially, financially, spiritually, and in every other facet of life.

Finally, let's look at causes of frontal lobe dysfunction. The most common ones stem from lifestyle habits. Daily activities such as eating, experiencing media, and exercising affect the frontal lobe. As a matter of fact, everything we do or don't do – that is, everything we choose – affects us either positively or negatively. Nothing is neutral in our choices.

To help ensure the health of your frontal lobe, avoid input that is excessively numbing. This input can come from many sources: media, the Internet, TV, and radio. A lot of dietary fat or large amounts of sugar, as well as alcohol, can inhibit normal, healthy blood flow and have other deteriorating effects on the frontal lobe. Caffeine impinges on the brain's communication system in a number of ways. Many illicit and even legal drugs can be detrimental to frontal lobe function.

Also, beware of hypnosis. It has many negative effects. A hypnotized person loses thought activity (weak beta brain waves), has a short-circuited frontal lobe, decreased reasoning power, increased depressive tendencies, and has placed his or her mind under the control of the hypnotist.

In short, by wisely choosing what you eat, drink, hear, or see, you can provide good input for your frontal lobe.

THE COMMON EFFECTS OF A COMPROMISED FRONTAL LOBE

- Impairment of moral principles
- Social impairment (loss of love for family)
- Lack of foresight
- Inability to do abstract reasoning
- Inability to interpret proverbs
- Diminished ability for mathematical understanding
- Loss of empathy
- Lack of restraint (boasting, hostility, aggressiveness)
- Depression

CHOOSE LIFE

Take this opportunity to choose a new beginning. Think about an area of your life you would like to improve. Today, choose to make an improvement.

In John 10:10, Christ says, "I have come that you may have life!" The Greek word for "life" in this passage is ZOË, which is understood to mean "life as God has it." Take a moment and consider the life you now have, and compare it with ZOË – God's life, a life that He longs to share with you.

Wherever you are today, you're one choice away from a new beginning, a new you, a new creation through the power of the Creator. As we close this first section, dwell on the thoughts below. They encapsulate so much that could be beneficial to you and the life God wants for you.

C — Choose the gifts given at Creation – Exercise your power of **Choice** and choose ZOË

R — Choose to **Rest** and enjoy "nature's sweet restorer"

E — Choose an **Environment** that you will flourish in

A — Choose **Activity** – for growth and strength

T — Choose to **Trust** in God and His wisdom given at Creation – a balance of the principles of CREATION.

I — Choose to connect through **Interpersonal Relationships**

O — Choose to have an **Outlook** on life that reflects the Creator's love

N — Choose to eat God's bounty – enjoy the **Nutrition** of Eden.

REINFORCE THE MESSAGE

SKILL BUILDERS

Choose the Skill Builders below that you would like to experience in your own life, then write a response on how they impacted you. Last, write further actions, if any, that you would like to take as a result of doing the Skill Builders.

Skill Builder I | **Thinking Out of the Box:** Learn to be creative and see available choices.

There is a common myth that goes like this: "I haven't had many choices, or I didn't have any choice." Healthfully exercising our ability to choose is a learned behavior. Although we often think or feel as though we have limited choices, we usually have more than we realize.

Let's do an exercise that will help us see more of the options available to us.

Think of a situation/dilemma you faced recently or are facing now in which you had to make a choice but felt that you had no choice or limited ones. This could be a deeply personal situation (we encourage you to work on those privately), or it could be an everyday kind of problem.

Write down at least three different possible courses of action. If you are having trouble thinking of three choices, ask someone to help you (if the situation you are considering is not too personal). Remember, too, that sometimes unpleasant choices must be considered along with the pleasant ones.

EVERYDAY EXAMPLES

SITUATION/DILEMMA I'M FACING:
It's Monday afternoon and my boss wants a report done by tomorrow morning. The report will take about six hours to complete.

OPTION #1: *Ask a colleague for help and split the report writing with them to reduce the amount of time I have to spend on it.*

OPTION #2: *Negotiate with my boss for more time; complete report by tomorrow afternoon instead of tomorrow morning.*

OPTION #3: *Ask/pay someone to do the report for me.*

SITUATION/DILEMMA I'M FACING:
I can't get my family together at the table for a meal.

OPTION #1: *Consult with everyone's schedule to plan a meal together two weeks from now.*

OPTION #2: *Consider reducing the amount of extracurricular activities the kids are involved in so that they have more time for family.*

OPTION #3: *Entice my family by letting them know ahead of time that I'm making their favorite foods and presenting the meal attractively.*

Courses of Action

SITUATION/DILEMMA YOU'RE FACING:

....

....

....

....

What are my options?

OPTION #1:

....

....

OPTION #2:

....

....

OPTION #3:

....

....

....

Try to develop the habit of always recognizing (especially when you encounter difficult or challenging situations) that you always have at least three choices in any situation, and then cultivate your ability to find as many of them as you can and explore the merits of each before choosing.

DESCRIBE HOW THIS IMPACTED YOU:

....

....

....

FURTHER ACTION:

....

....

....

....

> *"A wise man is strong; and a man of knowledge increases power."*
>
> ~ **PROVERBS 24:5**

Skill Builder 2 | **Knowledge Brings Power**

So, if we have so many choices, how do we make the right ones? This is an important question. Knowing that we have many courses of action to choose from is just the first step. We need to make wise choices, or the powers of choice will do us no good. One of the most important tools that will help us make good choices is, as we saw earlier, knowledge. Seeking knowledge should be a way of life. We cannot responsibly go through this life intellectually idle. We should always be learning something new, always increasing our store of knowledge with useful, meaningful information. Read, listen to audio books, watch informative programs, use the Internet wisely, and find ways that appeal to you and fit into your lifestyle that help you continually grow intellectually. As a result of this growth, you will be better equipped to make wise choices. As a result of making wiser choices, you will be blessed with an abundant life – a life of purpose, peace, and joy.

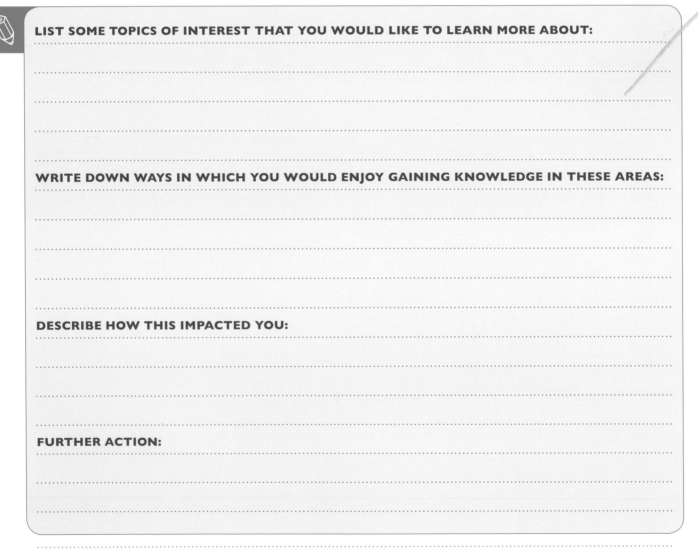

LIST SOME TOPICS OF INTEREST THAT YOU WOULD LIKE TO LEARN MORE ABOUT:

WRITE DOWN WAYS IN WHICH YOU WOULD ENJOY GAINING KNOWLEDGE IN THESE AREAS:

DESCRIBE HOW THIS IMPACTED YOU:

FURTHER ACTION:

Skill Builder 3 | Exercise Your Intellectual Muscles

As we saw earlier, another important tool when it comes to making good choices is the application of reasoning. We can't always have all the information we would want about any particular situation or decision. Nor can we know all there is to know about everything. In the face of this reality we must rely more heavily on exercising reason to help us make good choices. We can use what we do know about the situation and apply the principles that we live by, the rules we have to keep, the laws that we are bound by, and good old common sense to make good choices. We can use deductive or inductive reasoning to develop various rationales that in turn can help guide our decision making. Just as we need to always increase our knowledge base, we also need to constantly improve our reasoning abilities.

Within the next week, meet for at least thirty minutes with one or more people to discuss current events or areas of interest.

LIST SOME CURRENT EVENTS AND ISSUES THAT INTEREST YOU:

WRITE DOWN QUESTIONS AND OPINIONS ABOUT THESE EVENTS AND ISSUES:

DESCRIBE HOW THIS IMPACTED YOU:

FURTHER ACTION:

Skill Builder 4 | The Frontal Lobe

The importance and power of the frontal lobe of our brain cannot be underestimated. This God-given gift gives us the ability to choose. It is the seat of judgment, reasoning, intellect, and the will.

Directions: Read and think about the effects of your choices in light of the associated explanation and research. Put a check mark next to the appropriate effect (enhance or impair) of your lifestyle choices on your frontal lobe function.

Definition of Enhance: *Engages and challenges your frontal lobe in a practical and useful way that you can use in your daily life and your spiritual walk (is it edifying?).*

Definition of Impair: *Pacifies or bypasses your frontal lobe function in a way that takes away or weakens your ability to choose wisely.*

TELEVISION:	ENHANCE ___	IMPAIR ___	NO SIGNIFICANT EFFECT ___
MOVIES:	ENHANCE ___	IMPAIR ___	NO SIGNIFICANT EFFECT ___

> *"I know of no more encouraging fact than the unquestionable ability of man to elevate his life by a conscious endeavor."*
>
> ~ HENRY DAVID THOREAU

MUSIC:	ENHANCE ___	IMPAIR ___	NO SIGNIFICANT EFFECT ___

Music can either produce a beneficial or detrimental frontal lobe response. A meta-analysis found that active instruction in music enhances the spatial-temporal performance of children.[24]

PHYSICAL ACTIVITY/EXERCISE: ENHANCE ___   IMPAIR ___   NO SIGNIFICANT EFFECT ___

Frontal lobe research has uncovered another possible explanation of why exercise benefits those with depression: exercise improves left frontal lobe function with respect to the right. Studies suggest that the increased stimulation of the left frontal lobe that helps depression may also be responsible for a decrease in anxiety.[25] Physical activity and exercise (walking, cycling, jogging) are all great ways to enhance the frontal lobe.

 FOOD: ENHANCE ___   IMPAIR ___   NO SIGNIFICANT EFFECT ___

The more we learn about nutrition, the more we realize that optimal nutrition is vital to superior brain performance. Dietary choices can either enhance or impair brain performance. The brain uses glucose almost exclusively as its source of energy.[26] Thus, if you are on a low carbohydrate diet, your brain is not getting enough energy to function optimally. Refined sugar (like that found in soda and candy) causes a dramatic rise in blood sugar, and this is unhealthy. One study showed that five-year-old boys with little sugar in their diet had superior attention spans and more accurate responses than did their higher consuming peers. This is directly related to frontal lobe performance.[27]

 ALCOHOLIC DRINK: ENHANCE ___   IMPAIR ___   NO SIGNIFICANT EFFECT ___

In one study involving 1,300 social drinkers, researchers found a measurable decrease in abstract thinking ability. In this study individuals drank as little as one alcoholic beverage a week.[28] People with a blood alcohol level of 0.05-0.09%, less than the legal limit in most states, have at least nine times the risk of a fatal traffic accident than at 0%.[29]

ILLICIT DRUGS:	ENHANCE ___	IMPAIR ___	NO SIGNIFICANT EFFECT ___
PRESCRIPTION DRUGS:	ENHANCE ___	IMPAIR ___	NO SIGNIFICANT EFFECT ___
NICOTINE:	ENHANCE ___	IMPAIR ___	NO SIGNIFICANT EFFECT ___

Smokers are less able to perform complex mental tasks than nonsmokers.[30]

REST:	ENHANCE ___	IMPAIR ___	NO SIGNIFICANT EFFECT ___

Adequate hours of good/sound sleep, at least seven to eight hours, improve the function of the frontal lobe. People who suffer from exhaustion have low frontal lobe function. This can reduce our ability to think rationally and deductively. Lack of sleep can cause impulsive behavior and heightened emotions.

"Take a rest; a field that has rested gives a bountiful crop."

~ OVID

PRAYER:	ENHANCE ___	IMPAIR ___	NO SIGNIFICANT EFFECT ___

Prayer enhances the frontal lobe because it requires engagement of the frontal lobe. Prayer has also been shown to have potent effects in the process of healing.

Dr. Larry Dossey, a former self-proclaimed agnostic, also says that "I used to believe that we must choose between science and reason on one hand, and spirituality on the other, in how we lead our lives. Now I consider this a false choice. We can recover the sense of sacredness, not just in science, but in perhaps every area of life."[31] In his research on the topic of prayer, he cites several cases where prayer has aided in the cure of life-threatening diseases, such as cancer.[32]

MASSAGE:	ENHANCE ___	IMPAIR ___	NO SIGNIFICANT EFFECT ___

Massage can potentially enhance and balance the frontal lobes if they are imbalanced in a situation such as depression.[33]

SUNSHINE: ENHANCE ___   IMPAIR ___   NO SIGNIFICANT EFFECT ___

Animal research indicates that exposure to natural daylight results in significantly higher melatonin levels.[34] Melatonin promotes sound sleep and boosts frontal lobe functioning.

NOW LOOK BACK AT WHAT IS IMPAIRING YOUR FRONTAL LOBE.

WHAT CHANGES CAN YOU MAKE TO CHANGE AN IMPAIR TO AN ENHANCE?

....
....
....
....
....

DESCRIBE HOW THIS IMPACTED YOU:

....
....
....

FURTHER ACTION:

....
....
....

TIPS FOR SUCCESS

POWER TIPS: HOW TO MAKE BETTER CHOICES

1. **Don't be distracted by the chaos,** lack of sleep, or the demands from others. Keep focused on what the real issues are and the choices before you.

2. **Remember H.A.L.T.** What is H.A.L.T.? Do not make important decisions when you are Hungry, Angry, Lonely, or Tired.

3. **Don't be afraid to get good counsel.** The input from others, who often see things from a perspective that you can't, could prove helpful in the decision-making process.

4. **Seek to have happy, positive thoughts.** Happy thoughts help decrease activity in the right frontal lobe. This is the part of the brain that tends to be overdominant when a person is depressed.[35] Therefore, a program of overall frontal lobe enhancement, together with happy thoughts – which gently puts the brakes on the right frontal lobe relative to the left – would be expected to be helpful in enhancing the mood of someone who has an imbalance of the dominance of their frontal lobes. Balancing the brain is important for it to function at its best.

5. **Negatively charged ions in fresh air enhance mental performance.** Researchers have found that both normal children and those with learning disabilities showed measurable improvements in brain function with sunshine.[36] So get out in the fresh air and breathe deeply! Shallow breathing, which many of us do, also impacts frontal lobe function. It may allow our blood oxygen level, which is called "oxygen saturation," to go below the level necessary for optimal frontal lobe function.[37] Making a conscious effort to regularly take deep breaths may help to counter this tendency. By taking deep breaths, especially breaths of fresh air, you may boost oxygen saturation enough to improve frontal lobe function. Regular aerobic exercise will also pump well-oxygenated blood to the brain.

6. **The brain and the body should not be thought of as separate.** Just as exercise will increase blood flow to the feet or hands, it also increases blood to the brain. Blood is the vital substance of the body; increasing blood flow to the organs increases organ function. Also, stimulating an organ causes increased blood flow to that organ. Hence, engaging in thought-provoking activities stimulates the brain, thus increasing blood flow. Just as our muscles shrivel when we don't use them, so will our frontal lobe.

   One study found that imagining a certain activity stimulated 80% of the brain circuitry that would be used to physically perform the imagined task.[38] Therefore, mental practice gives strength to the brain cell connections and helps a person be prepared for when he or she will actually perform the activity. Another study found that genetically identical mice that had an intellectually stimulating environment increased the number of brain cells that are responsible for memory and learning by 15% more than those mice living in sparse surroundings.

7. **Massage is beneficial in many ways,** one of which is increased blood flow. Enhancing blood flow in general enhances blood flow to the brain, as the body naturally prioritizes brain blood flow. Researchers at the University of Miami found that fifteen-minute massages done twice a week for five weeks decreased anxiety levels and dropped the levels of the detrimental hormone cortisol.[39] The frontal lobe functions best when not under stress. Important decisions should never be made while under stressful conditions. The researchers also found the benefits of enhanced alertness and increased speed and accuracy on math computations.

8. **Exposure to sunshine stimulates the whole body and helps us sleep better.** Sunlight increases serotonin production[40] – an important brain chemical that helps prevent fatigue[41] – and as we all know, fatigue can negatively impact one's ability to make wise choices. Melatonin is another important brain chemical that sunlight impacts. This brain chemical helps us to sleep well at night, which may help us to have improved frontal lobe function the following day.

9. **Eat plenty of whole-plant complex carbohydrates,** because they are necessary for healthy frontal lobe function. The brain uses carbohydrates almost exclusively as the source of nutrients. Serotonin is a mood-enhancing brain chemical, made in the brain from dietary tryptophan, which is found in its most useful situation within whole plant foods. Increasing these foods will raise brain serotonin and can help lift our spirits. In contrast, the lower blood tryptophan availability of high-protein diets (low tryptophan to large neutral amino acid ratio) can lead to decreased function in a critical frontal lobe area that is associated with depression.[42]

   In one study, a whole-plant, carbohydrate-rich diet blocked a stress-induced rise in depression and prevented a rise in cortisol. If they were eating a protein-rich, low-carbohydrate diet before exposure to stress, the same individuals experienced heightened depression scores and cortisol increases.[43] (It is significant to note here that meat does not contain significant carbohydrates. The decreased insulin response and the competition with other large neutral amino acids keep the tryptophan in the meat from moving across the blood-brain barrier, so it is not available to make serotonin. Research shows that the serotonin and mood-enhancing benefits of a whole-food, complex-carbohydrate diet is not obtained from a predominantly meat-based diet.)

10. **Avoid behaviors known to cause debilitating diseases,** such as stroke and high blood pressure, that negatively affect the frontal lobe.[44] Instead, choose activities – such as regular exercise, healthy eating, adequate sleep, and building strong relationships – that fight these diseases.

11. **Choose to listen to uplifting, positive, happy, and peaceful music.** Choose to eliminate music that encourages negative behaviors and attitudes. If you don't know whether your music is good or bad, ask yourself: "What does this music make me think, and how does it make me feel?" If the answer is in any way negative, choose not to expose yourself to it. You will not go wrong if you choose music that makes you think on good things and that creates positive feelings.

WHO ARE YOU?

By Daniel Roberts　　　　*Used with Permission*　　　　*For further information go to wisedecisions.com*

In order to make a wise decision, you need to know as much about yourself as possible. Knowing yourself is the foundation of a wise decision and is vital when taking the first decision-making step; *"Be clear about what to decide."* There are a number of good assessments, DISC tests, interest and skill inventories, etc. on the market, and each can provide a mosaic tile of who you are. Separately they are only pieces, but put together they form a pretty good picture of you. In addition, there are two areas where, for decision-making purposes, it is especially important to know yourself:

Values: Simply put, values are what is important to you. They are not what "should" be important to you or what you think others want you to have as values. Rather, your values are what you identify with, what you admire, what you aspire to. The *Values List – Personal* is a good exercise to discover your top values. Using the list as a non-exclusive guide only, make a list of your top dozen values. Take your time. Use your values as a guide and a resource in making decisions.

> *"It is one thing to know the goal, and quite another thing to work toward it."*
>
> ~ F.J. SHEEN

Objectives: Objectives are what you want out of your life, both from your career and your personal life. Objectives are, in essence, long-term goals. In decision making it is important to know your long-term goals, your objectives, in order to be sure that the decision you are making will help you progress toward these objectives. The problem is that we want so much out of life that it's hard to focus on the most important objectives. Here is an exercise that can help: *The 25 Pieces of My Ideal Life.* (See Questions & Assessments in the back of the book.)

First, list the top twenty-five priorities you must have for your life to be ideal. These can be tangible, intangible, specific, or general… whatever you choose, it's totally up to you. Be realistic. If you're fifty-five, being a pro quarterback probably isn't achievable. Keep the list to your top twenty-five values or priorities.

Next, after you have listed your top twenty-five values, fill in the remaining columns. Be honest with yourself. You now have a guide as to what the top priorities of your ideal life are, which ones are more important to you, your progress toward them, and how hard you are working. Now that you know what you really want, be sure that both what you choose to decide and decisions you make further you toward your ideal life.

When you know yourself, your values, and what you want out of life, decisions are a lot easier to make. You are also much more likely to make a wise decision.

CRITICAL THINKING CONCEPTS FOR DECISION MAKING

By Daniel Roberts   *Used with Permission*   *For further information go to wisedecisions.com*

It is important to think clearly and carefully when making a decision. All of the effort and technique you employ will be wasted if thinking through the decision isn't done properly. A critical thinker observes his own thinking process and monitors himself for faulty logic. Here are some concepts to keep in mind:

Assumptions: These are "self-evident rules of thumb," meaning things we take for granted or assume to be correct. There is nothing wrong with assumptions and, in fact, they provide a useful service in that they give us a shortcut through unnecessary thinking. We assume the sun will rise in the morning, our spouse loves us, and our money is safe in the bank. But, in thinking through a decision, it is important to become aware of our assumptions and to determine if they are accurate.

For Example: If you are considering medicine as a career, you shouldn't just assume that doctors make a lot of money. Many do, but many do not. It depends on the type of practice, the locale, the practice group, how hard one works, etc.

If at any time during the decision you observe yourself making an assumption: "I need to work outside," "I'm not smart enough to go to law school," "I can't live anywhere but here," "My dad is always right," "The stock market always goes up," "There's a real estate bubble," etc., just stop. Ask yourself: "Is this assumption accurate?" It may be accurate or it may not be or it may be only partly accurate or accurate only part of the time. The important thing is for you to be aware and, if appropriate, do the research. Get the facts before you make the decision.

Biases and Prejudices: If you are biased in favor of or prejudiced against something that is a factor in the decision you are making, it could skew your thinking. There is nothing inherently wrong with bias and prejudice; they are simply our own opinions. But if you have a strong like or dislike for a person, political party, profession, investment, city, state, or country, or anything else that is under consideration during your decision making, stop. Ask yourself: "Is the way I feel about this affecting my objectivity? How can I put my feelings aside to stick to the facts in making my decision?"

Emotions: They play an important role in our lives. However, when it comes to thinking clearly, emotions can be a detriment. Anger, passion, and sadness all affect our judgment and cognitive ability. Think back to your own experience. Was there an occasion when you were angry and took some action or made a decision that you later regretted? And how about passion? When we are passionate about someone, an idea, or a cause, our thinking suffers. Sadness also dims our ability to think and reason.

Interestingly, though, emotions are a driving force in making our decisions. For several years I asked my critical thinking classes to list the top three most important decisions they have made in their life, then decide whether each was based primarily on emotion or logic. Consistently, on average, two-thirds to three-fourths of the decisions were reported as being based on emotion. This doesn't mean you should make decisions based on emotion alone. No, you should think logically through a major decision. Then, if you have strong feelings about your decision, reexamine it to see why. Often there is something important that was overlooked or not given sufficient credence in the decision-making process.

Stress and Depression: When the brain is overloaded by stress or dimmed by depression, the ability to think well and make wise decisions is reduced. Stress and depression, by clinical trials, have been clearly proven to reduce cognitive ability and affect memory, concentration, and judgment. In addition, it has been shown that people suffering from stress or depression have a reduced ability to develop options when making a decision.

So what do you do? The best advice is to refrain from making major career or life decisions when you are in such a state. You wouldn't run a marathon with a pulled hamstring, so don't make a major decision, one that could affect the rest of your life, when your brain isn't doing its best. Give it time, rest, let go of the decision, and come back to it a little later. Stress and depression are both treatable. If at all possible, don't make a major decision when you are under stress or depressed.

THE FIVE STEPS TO MAKING WISE DECISIONS

By Daniel Roberts   *Used with Permission*   *For further information go to wisedecisions.com*

The secret to good decision making is to have and follow a plan. A decision-making situation may seem overwhelming and confusing with issues, choices, alternatives, and risks all thrown together. By using this five-step decision-making procedure you can break the decision into steps, follow the steps, and arrive at a wise decision.

1. Be Clear about What to Decide

It is critical to know what is the ultimate problem to be solved by the decision. This is the important first step; take plenty of time to think things through carefully. Step back and take the long view. Will this decision take me further toward my goals? Will this decision be in line with my beliefs and values? Is there a larger issue that needs to be decided first? *The Decision Tree* is a tool that is useful in visualizing a series of decisions. (To complete, go to wisedecisions.com.)

Here's an example: Joe initially thought his decision was whether to buy the old fixer-upper house on Cherry Street or the new townhouse on Main. In stepping back, he saw that a decision first needed to be made as to whether to rent or to buy. In stepping back further, he saw that a decision needed to be made as to whether he wanted to live in that town. In stepping back still further, Joe realized that the most important thing he needed to decide and what he needed to know before making any other decisions was whether or not he would remain in his present job or make a career change. That was the ultimate decision to be made before considering any downstream decisions.

2. Gather Facts and Set Criteria

Determine what you need to know about the problem to be solved/decision to be made and what a successful decision would look like.

First, decide what information about the problem you will need in order to come up with and develop options to choose from. Know the time frame in which the decision needs to be made and exactly what information is needed to make the decision.

For example, if Joe's decision is whether to continue with his present career as a teacher, become a stockbroker, or go to law school, he would want to research such things as income projections, working conditions, advancement opportunities, supply and demand, and quality of life. He would also need to decide when to make the decision. If he waited until fall to decide to attend law school, he would most likely have to wait until the following fall to begin his studies.

Second, set out your criteria for a successful decision. Be clear about what minimum standards the choice you will make must meet. This will eliminate the clearly unworkable choices from consideration before you begin evaluating choices. For example, if one of Joe's criteria is to make at least $100,000 per year, the teaching option would fail. If, however, one of Joe's criteria is income stability, the stockbroker option would fail. The *Criteria Filter* is a useful tool for filtering out unacceptable options and, in addition, helping you clarify ideal factors. (To complete, go to wisedecisions.com.)

> *"Far too many people have no idea of what they can do because they have been told what they can't do."*
>
> **~ ZIG ZIGLAR**

3. Develop Options

The more options you have to choose from, the better your decision will be. Good photographers take many photographs, but pick only the best. It's the same with decision making; the more options you have to choose from, the better your decision will be.

This is a step where you should spend plenty of time to uncover all possible choices. Start by listing all the options you can think of that meet your criteria. Then combine parts and pieces of different options to come up with more options. Investigate these options, and other options may appear. Brainstorm. Think of a really crazy way to solve the problem. Imagine you were someone else, an expert, what would you do? Ask other people for their ideas. Imagine a solution and think backward to how you came up with it. Think outside of the box; often an option is right in front of us and we don't see it. Use your intuition.

4. Evaluate Options and Assess Risk

Evaluating options requires plenty of organization. Don't try to do it in your head; you need to use some simple pen and paper tools to help you see and analyze the options. Here are the most effective and easiest to use decision-making tools:

The *Ben Franklin Ledger* is the simplest and one of the most effective tools when used as Ben recommended. Divide a piece of paper in half and write "pro" on one side and "con" on the other. Next, over a period of several days, list all of the pro and con points you can think of. Then, and this is the important part, estimate the weight of each item on a 1–10 scale. Look at the list and wherever you have a pro and a con of roughly equal weight, strike them both out. When you have finished the strikeouts, what is left should guide you toward a decision. The *Modified Ben Franklin Ledger* allows you to compare the pros and cons of two separate options.

The *Measured Criteria Table* is another simple tool that will help you compare a number of options. On a sheet of paper, list down the left side the criteria factors that are important in making the decision. Then, at the top across the paper, list the options. In Joe's case he might have listed down the left side as criteria factors: income, stability, number of jobs, stress level, enjoyment, etc. Across the top, list the professions of teacher, stockbroker, and attorney. Joe would then score each profession on each criteria, on a 1–10 or 1–100 scale. By adding up the scores, he could get an idea of which profession best suited his criteria.

In a *Weighted Criteria Table* Joe could weigh the specific criterion as to how important it is to him compared to the other criteria. He might rate enjoyment as an eight on a ten-point scale and stress level as a four. Joe could then multiply each profession's score for each criteria by its weight to obtain a weighted score. The benefit of the criteria table is that the numerical scores are helpful in comparing each option.

(The above three assessments can be located in the OUTLOOK Questions & Assessments section in the back of this book.)

Assessing risk is part of making a decision. Think about and identify the risks of each option. Decide whether the risk is necessary, and take the risk only for clearly thought-out reasons. Carefully evaluate what the consequences of failure will be, and try to make an accurate estimate of the probability that the option will fail. Use this risk factor in evaluating the options.

The basic strategy for assessing risks is the commonly used Expected Value Calculation. In the basic risk evaluation formula, $EV=P/R$, and the expected value (EV) equals the prize (P) divided by the risk (R). This is usually used in evaluating investment opportunities and isn't directly applicable to most major life, career, etc. decisions. However, the concept is useful in understanding risk:

- What is the Prize – What do you hope to gain; be clear.

- What is the Risk – Don't be overly optimistic or pessimistic.

- What is the Expected Value – Be realistic.

In Joe's case, for example, there is a risk that the stock market could take a severe downturn or that he would not be accepted into law school.

> *"Planning is bringing the future into the present so you can do something about it now."*
> ~ ALAN LAKEIN

5. Make the Decision and Follow Through

You've done your homework; now is the time to commit. You probably don't have as much information or time as you would like and that's typical. Just make the decision and *commit* to implementing it. Commitment is vital and is an area related to outcome where you do have control. And:

- Decide how to measure whether the decision was successful.

- Realize that the decision and the outcome are separate and distinct.

- Don't become attached to your decision or let your ego interfere.

- Remember, you can make a new decision.

SMALL GROUP DISCUSSIONS

Directions: Review the discussion questions and choose one you would like to discuss first. Proceed through the rest of the questions as time allows.

1. Each of us has a choice, just as the Israelites had when Joshua said, "But if serving the LORD seems undesirable to you, then choose for yourselves this day whom you will serve, whether the gods your forefathers served beyond the River, or the gods of the Amorites, in whose land you are living. But as for me and my household, we will serve the LORD," Joshua 24:15. How can we apply the things we are learning in order to make better choices?

   ....

   ....

2. What mind-set does God challenge me to adopt? Look up Galatians 6:7–9, Proverbs 4:26, and Haggai 1:5–7.

   ....

   ....

3. In the story in Genesis 3:1–5 about the fall of humanity, how important is the role of free choice? According to the account, what factors did Eve use to make her choice? What can we learn from that?

   ....

   ....

4. As human beings, though we are capable of reason, we are not always dominated by it. How can we learn to balance our emotions and passions with our reason as we seek to make the right choices?

   ....

   ....

5. We all have made wrong choices and have had to face the consequences of those choices. How can we learn to accept God's forgiveness for those choices and then move on? Read Romans 5:8, 1 John 2:12.

   ....

   ....

ADDITIONAL RESOURCES

Books:

Creation Health – Secrets of Feeling Fit and Living Long,
by Des Cummings, Jr. with Monica Reed, M.D.

The CREATION Health Breakthrough, by Monica Reed, M.D.

The Creation Health Booklet Series

Health and Happiness, by Ellen G. White

Mind/Body Health: The Effects of Attitudes, Emotions, and Relationships,
by Karren, Hafen, Smith, and Frandsen

Authentic Happiness, by Dr. Martin Seligman

60 Ways to Energize Your Life,
compiled by Jan W. Kuzma, Kay Kuzma, and DeWitt S. Williams
(Small devotional book focusing on health topics)

Energized, compiled by Jan W. Kuzma, Kay Kuzma, and DeWitt S. Williams
(A full-size devotional book focusing on health topics)

Health Power: Health by Choice Not by Chance,
by Aileen Ludington, M.D. and Hans Diehl, DrHSc, MPH

Eight Sure Steps to Health and Happiness, by Lucile H. Jones

Learned Helplessness, By Dr. Martin Seligman

Choice Theory, by William Glasser

Healthy Pleasures, by Robert Ornstein and David Sobel

Feeling Fit: True Stories of People Who Turned Their Health Around, by Aileen Ludington, M.D.

Dynamic Living: How to Take Charge of Your Health,
by Aileen Ludington, M.D. and Hans Diehl, DrHSc, MPH

Dynamic Living: How to Take Charge of Your Health Workbook,
by Hans Diehl, DrHSc, Aileen Ludington, M.D., Lawson Dumbeck, MEd

Charting Your Course: A Life-Long Guide to Health and Compassion,
by Sally Coleman and David Anderson

Websites:

wisedecisions.com
(How to make wise choices. Excellent website to give you tools to help you make wise choices.)

criticalthinking.org (Website offers tools for critical thinking.)

dstress.com (Stress Reduction. Stress inhibits making good choices. This is the website of John Mason, PhD, a nationally known stress expert and author. His website includes information, tools, and products to reduce stress. A free e-newsletter is also available at the site.)

netwellness.org/healthtopics/substanceabuse/faq4.cfm
(Helping teens make wise choices.)

Other Resources:

CD, CREATION Health Music of Health and Healing

Vibrant Life magazine, vibrantlife.com

Songs That Will Encourage and Help You in Your Choices:

I Have Decided to Follow Jesus (Hymn)

Give Me Jesus (Hymn)

Holiness (Sonic Flood – Praise and Worship)

Choose Life (Christian Contemporary)

Abundantly (Jennifer LaMountain – Christian Contemporary)

*"Delight yourself also in the Lord,
and He shall give you the desires of your heart.
Commit your way to the Lord,
trust also in Him,
and He shall bring it to pass."*
~ **PSALM 37: 4–5 NKJV**

REFERENCES

1. Fuster J. *The Prefrontal Cortex, Anatomy, Physiology, and Neuropsychology of the Frontal Lobe*. 2nd edition. New York: Raven Press, 1989, 3–9, 125.

2. Stuss D, Benson D. *The Frontal Lobes*. New York: Raven Press, 1986, 243.

3. Price B, Daffner K, et al. "The Compartmental Learning Disabilities of Early Frontal Lobe Damage." *Brain* October 1990 113: 1383–1393.

4. Hawkins K, Trobst K. "Frontal Lobe Dysfunction and Aggression: Conceptual Issues and Research Findings." *Aggression and Violent Behavior* 2000 5(2): 147–157.

5. Fuster J. *The Prefrontal Cortex, Anatomy, Physiology, and Neuropsychology of the Frontal Lobe* 2nd edition. New York: Raven Press, 1989, 139.

6. Deci E, Speigel N, et al. "The Effects of Performance Standards on Teaching Styles: The Behavior of Controlling Teachers." *Journal of Educational Psychology* 1982 74: 852–859.

7. Schulz R, Hanusa B. "Long-Term Effects of Control and Predictability-Enhancing Interventions: Findings and Ethical Issues." *Journal of Personality and Social Psychology* 1978 36: 1194–1201.

8. Langer E, Rodin J. "Effects of Choice and Enhanced Personal Responsibility for the Aged: A Field Experiment in an Institutional Setting." *Journal of Personality and Social Psychology* 1976 34(2): 191–9.

9. Rodin J, Langer E. "Long-Term Effects of a Control-Relevant Intervention With the Institutionalized Aged." *Journal of Personality and Social Psychology* 1977 35(12): 897–902.

10. Seligman M, *Learned Optimism: How to Change Your Mind and Your Life*, New York, NY: Pocket Books, 1998, 169.

11. Garber J, Seligman J. *Human Helplessness*. New York: Academic Press Inc, 1980.

12. Overmier J, Seligman J. "Effects of Inescapable Shock Upon Subsequent Escape and Avoidance Responding." *Journal of Comparative and Physiological Psychology* 1967 63(1): 28–33.

13. Coan, R. "Personality Variables Associated with Cigarette Smoking." *Journal of Personality and Social Psychology* 1973 26: 86–104.

14. Balch P, Ross A. "Predicting Success in Weight Reduction as a Function of Locus of Control: A Unidimensional and Multidimensional Approach." *Journal of Consulting and Clinical Psychology* 1975 43: 119.

15. Lewis F, Morisky D, Flynn B. "A Test of Construct Validity of Health Locus of Control: Effects of Self-Reported Compliance for Hypertensive Patients." *Health Education Monographs* 1978 6: 138–148.

16. Findley M, Cooper H. "Locus of Control and Academic Achievement: A Literature Review." *Journal of Personality and Social Psychology* 1983 44: 419–427.

17. Damasio H. "The Return of Phineas Gage: Clues About the Brain from the Skull of a Famous Patient." *Science* May 20, 1994 264(5162): 1102–1105.

18. Ibid.

19. Baldwin B. "The Front-Brain." *Journal of Health and Healing* 1983 9(1): 9.

20. Price B, Daffner K, et al. "The Compartmental Learning Disabilities of Early Frontal Lobe Damage." *Brain* October 1990 113(Pt 5): 1383–1393.

21. Fuster J. *The Prefrontal Cortex, Anatomy, Physiology, and Neuropsychology of the Frontal Lobe* 2nd edition. New York: Raven Press, 1989: 126–152.

22. Baldwin B. "The Front-Brain." *Journal of Health and Healing* 1983 9(1): 9–11, 26–30.

23. Fuster J. *The Prefrontal Cortex, Anatomy, Physiology, and Neuropsychology of the Frontal Lobe* 2nd edition. New York: Raven Press, 1989: 126–152.

24. Hetland L. "Learning to Make Music Enhances Spatial Reasoning." *Journal of Aesthetic Education* Fall/Winter 2000 34(3–4): 179–238.

25. Petruzello S, Landers D. "State Anxiety Reduction and Exercise: Does Hemispheric Activation Reflect Such Changes?" *Medicine & Science in Sports & Exercise* Aug 1994 26(8): 1028–1035.

26. Brodal P. *The Central Nervous System: Structure and Function*. US: Oxford University Press, 2004, 97.

27. Prinz R, Riddle D. "Associations Between Nutrition and Behavior in 5-Year-Old Children." *Nutrition Reviews* May 1986: 151–158.

28. Parker D, Parker E, et al. "Alcohol Use and Cognitive Loss Among Employed Men and Women." *American Journal of Public Health* May 1983 73(5): 521–526.

29. Zador P. "Alcohol-Related Relative Risk of Fatal Driver Injuries in Relation to Driver Age and Sex." *Journal of Studies on Alcohol* July 1991 52(4): 302–310.

30. Bower B. "Smoke Gets in Your Brain." *Science News* Jan 16, 1993 143(3): 46–47.

31. Dossey L. *Reinventing Medicine: Beyond Mind-Body to a New Era of Healing*. San Franscisco, CA: HarperOne, 1999, as cited on http://www.dosseydossey.com/larry/default.html. Retrieved 4/8/09.

32. Dossey L. *Healing Words: The Power of Prayer and the Practice of Medicine*. New York: HarperCollins Publishers, 1993: 28–36.

33. Jones N, Field T. "Massage and Music Therapies Attenuate Frontal EEG Asymmetry in Depressed Adolescents." *Adolescence* 1999 34(135): 529–534.

34. Laakso M, Porkka-Heiskanen T, et al. "Twenty-Four House Patterns of Pineal Melatonin and Pituitary and Plasma Prolactin in Male Rats Under Natural and Artificial Lighting Conditions." *Neuroendocrinology* Sept 1988 48(3): 308–313.

35. George M, Ketter T, et al. "Brain Activity During Transient Sadness and Happiness in Healthy Women." *American Journal of Psychiatry* 1995 152(3): 341–351.

36. Morton L, Kershner J. "Differential Negative Air Ions Effects on learning Disabled and Normal-Achieving Children." *International Journal of Biometeorology* May 1990 34(1): 35–41.

REFERENCES

37. Moss M, Scholey A. "Oxygen Administration Enhances Memory Formation in Healthy Young Adults." *Psychopharmacology* April 1996 124: 255–260.

38. Stephen K, Fink G, et al. "Functional Anatomy of the Mental Representation of Upper Extremity Movements in Healthy Subjects." *Journal of Neurophysiology* Jan. 1995 73(1): 373–386.

39. Field T, Ironson G, et al. "Massage Therapy Reduces Anxiety and Enhances EEG Pattern of Alertness and Math Computations." *International Journal of Neuroscience* Sept. 1996 86 (3–4): 197–205.

40. Lambert G, Reid C, et al. "Effect of Sunlight and Season on Serotonin Turnover in the Brain." *The Lancet* Dec. 7, 2002 360: 1840–1842.

41. Rao M, Muller-Oerlinghausen B, et al. "The Influence of Phototherapy on Serotonin and Melatonin in Non-Seasonal Depression." *Pharmacopsychiatry* May 1990 23(3): 155–158.

42. Bremner J, Innis R, et al. "Positron Emission Tomography Measurement of Cerebral Metabolic Correlates of Tryptophan Depletion-Induced Depressive Relapse." *Archives of General Psychiatry* 1997 54: 364–374.

43. Markus C, Panhuysen G, et al. "Effects of Food on Cortisol and Mood in Vulnerable Subjects Under Controllable and Uncontrollable Stress." *Physiology and Behavior* Aug–Sep 2000 70(3-4): 333–342.

44. Van Swieten J, Geyskes G, et al. "Hypertension in the Elderly is Associated with White Matter Lesions and Cognitive Decline." *Annals of Neurology* Dec 1991 30(6): 825–830.

NOTES

....

....

....

....

....

....

....

....

....

....

....

....

....

....

....

....

....

....

....

....

....

> *"The greatest danger for most of us
> is not that our aim is too high and we miss it,
> but that it is too low and we reach it."*
>
> ~ MICHELANGELO

REST

the calm that refreshes you

creation®
HEALTH

CONTENTS

MAKE IT WORK

Further Explanation of the DVD Topics

THE BIG PICTURE

Rest is incredibly powerful. It refreshes, rejuvenates, regenerates, and rebuilds the mind, body, and soul. Rest empowers you to function at your best. Optimally, rest includes a good night's sleep as well as time to relax and rejuvenate daily, weekly, and annually. The true benefits of rest are misunderstood and often unappreciated. The stress and pressures of life can accumulate over time and can create a generalized "dis-ease" with life. Proper rest is a powerful antidote for this common problem.

Because our society revolves around its own concepts of "success," many people have become pressed by work and their personal desires to achieve that "success." The day is filled with many important and seemingly urgent responsibilities, so rest is easily dropped to the bottom of the list. Yet, many do not realize how much more effectively and efficiently their minds, bodies, and souls would function, and how much more likely they would reach their goals of "success" if they gave themselves the right kind of rest at the right time.

This part of our CREATION Health Seminar is designed to help you understand what proper rest is, why it is so important for your well-being, and how you can best achieve it.

Rest assured, you'll be glad you did.

"Our life is a long and arduous quest after Truth, and the soul requires inward restfulness to attain its full height."
~ MAHATMA GANDHI

"What is without periods of rest will not endure."

~ OVID

Costly Effects of Sleep Deprivation

Most everyone knows about the benefits of a healthy diet and regular exercise, but many overlook the important role of sleep. Sleep is a key to good health and should be considered – said two neurologists at Northwestern University in an editorial of the journal *Archives of Internal Medicine* – as "essential to a healthy lifestyle as exercise and nutrition."[1] If you do not improve your sleep (especially your nightly sleep) you will not get the maximum benefits from your exercise and diet.

In fact, lack of proper sleep can have many negative consequences for the brain and body, including slowed brain function and increased rates of disease and mortality. For optimal functioning, we must allow our minds and bodies the opportunity to take advantage of the restorative and rejuvenating effects of regular sleep.

A study conducted at the University of Chicago found that chronic sleep loss could hasten the onset and increase the severity of diabetes, high blood pressure, and obesity.[2] Lack of sleep is also linked to a significantly increased risk of coronary heart disease.[3] Not enough sleep can also result in excessive daytime sleepiness, reduced neurocognitive function,[4] and depression.[5] There is also evidence for a decrease in memory and learning.[6]

Research presented at the 1993 annual conference of the World Federation of Sleep Society reported that losing three hours of sleep on any given night can cut *in half* the effectiveness of an individual's immune system.[7] Lack of sleep is also associated with a decreased ability to perform tasks controlled by the frontal lobe, such as planning, concentration, motor performance, and high-level intellectual skills.[8] In schoolchildren, sleep restriction has been shown to contribute to increased attention problems;[9] in college age students, sleep restriction negatively impacted academic measures in contrast to those who had a better quality of sleep.[10] An international survey of nearly 17,500 university students from twenty-four countries found that not getting enough sleep or sleeping less than seven hours nightly was related to poorer self-reported health in young adults.[11]

One somewhat scary fact about sleep deprivation is that individuals who were sleep deprived for fourteen days reported feeling only slightly sleepy; that is – they were unaware of how impaired they really were! The cognitive performance deficits included reduced ability to pay attention and to react to stimuli such as when driving or monitoring security at airports. Other deficits involved impairment of the ability to think quickly and avoid mistakes, as well as a reduced ability to multitask.[12] The risk for other serious types of accidents is, of course, increased as well. "Large-scale disasters like Chernobyl, the Exxon Valdez crash, and the Three Mile Island incident all occurred in early pre-dawn hours, a time when vigilance is at a low point."[13] In each of these devastating, man-made tragedies, lack of sleep and rest were a major factor.

Early to Bed, Early to Rise

Getting enough good sleep is important. But how much sleep should we be getting? Studies show that for adults, seven to eight hours a night is best. In the classic Alameda County Study, which included nearly seven thousand people, researchers found that this figure was associated with the greatest longevity.[14] We have seen clearly that restricted sleep is detrimental, but too much sleep can also be detrimental to your health. Researchers discovered that subjects who reported short (six or less hours per night) or long sleep (nine or more hours) shortened their lives by an average of nine years when compared with people who slept seven to eight hours per night.[15]

New research indicates that the familiar quote from Benjamin Franklin contains a lot of wisdom. Surprising health improvements might be the morning person's real rewards. Those who go to bed early and get up early have lower rates of heart disease, diabetes, and overall lower death rates than those who stay up late and get up late.

> *"Early to bed and early to rise makes a man healthy, wealthy, and wise."*
> ~ BENJAMIN FRANKLIN

God made humans diurnal, or made to function during the day. Our bodies are designed to work best when we go to sleep early in the evening and get up early in the morning. Dr. Timothy H. Monk, one of the foremost authorities on sleep, said: "Human beings are built to be daytime creatures. It's hardwired into our circuitry… when you deliberately try to shift the sleep/wake cycle, it's like having a symphony with two conductors, each one beating out a different time… your delicate internal rhythms go haywire… you need to treat sleep as a precious and fragile thing."[16] Monk has found that early risers are more likely than night owls to stick to healthy routines and have better sleep. *Larks* (early birds) wake up, eat meals, exercise, and go to bed at pretty much the same time each day. *Night owls*, on the other hand, are not so consistent with healthy daily practices.[17]

The payoff for early birds is worth getting out of bed for. Regularity in one's life also leads to healthier eating patterns, such as a good breakfast and less night snacking. This can in turn boost your immune system, fight off colds, improve mental performance during the day, and decrease stress.

Larks and Night Owls

The National Sleep Foundation conducted a national poll in 2005 of adults, which gives us insight into why early to bed, early to rise is so beneficial. Twenty-seven percent of the respondents to the survey were categorized by the foundation as *Healthy, Lively Larks*. Members of this group were the least likely to have problems sleeping and, therefore, were the most likely to enjoy a good night's sleep. They were morning people who began their day early. They fell asleep quickly without the use of sleep aids and were least likely, of all those who responded, to have any medical conditions! Of all the respondents, they were the most likely to say that during their wake time they never or rarely felt tired, fatigued, or not up to par (73%, compared to 49% overall). Compared to the average sleeper, *Healthy, Lively Larks* are much less likely to have missed work or events and/or made errors at work at least once in the past three months because of being too sleepy (16%, compared to 28% overall).[18]

God made us all the same in some ways. How and when we should sleep for maximum benefit seems to be one of these. There is no scientifically valid basis for the idea that "we were each made differently and naturally fall into the pattern that is healthiest for us." Many years of research and hundreds of well-conducted studies show that our bodies were all created to live by the same sleep habits. As Dr. Monk states, all humans are hardwired to go to sleep when it gets dark. That's how we can maximize our health. We develop sleeping patterns because of environmental circumstances and habits that turn into conditioned responses and, over the years, these habits can become ingrained in our lives. *Night Owls* are hurting their bodies, no matter how comfortable they are with staying up late.

The good news is that becoming a morning person is doable, and the rewards for doing so are tremendous. You might be tempted to say, "I have tried to go to bed early but I can't change. I'm just a night person." Sleep habits can become firmly ingrained over a lifetime and thus, as with any longstanding habit, it will need intelligent and determined effort to change. But, rest assured – you can!

If you see the negative effects of being a *Night Owl* and the benefits of obeying your body's natural rhythms, start working on adjusting your sleep patterns. Start slowly. Don't try going from getting up at 8:30 or later every morning to getting up at 5:30 all at once. Likewise, don't try going to bed at 9:30 in the evening if your usual bedtime is 12:30 or later. Make small but incremental changes, *gradually*, over a period of weeks and months, and you will eventually become accustomed to your new schedule. Most importantly, *be consistent*. Make a plan and stick to it strictly.

The Chemistry of Sleep

Melatonin is a hormone that is a precursor to good sleep. In most people, endogenous melatonin levels are highest during the normal hours of sleep, increasing rapidly in the late evening, then peaking after midnight and decreasing toward morning.[19] Functions of melatonin include synchronizing "circadian and circannual rhythms, which stimulates immune function, and, as has recently been shown serving as a potent hydroxyl radical scavenger and antioxidant."[20] Melatonin release naturally increases in the late evening. If we arrange our schedules so that we can go to bed in sync with this natural increase, we will maximize its release and the subsequent benefits. On the other hand, if we keep the lights on and stay up in the evening, melatonin release will be reduced and it will be more difficult to enjoy quality sleep.

Ghrelin is a hormone that plays an important role in the regulation of appetite.[21] Research has found that partial sleep deprivation was associated with a decrease in plasma levels of leptin and an accompanying increase in plasma levels of ghrelin. Subjective ratings of hunger and appetite also increased. Moreover, a remarkable correlation was found between the increase in hunger and the increase in the ghrelin/leptin ratio. Thus the neuroendocrine regulation of appetite and food intake appears to be influenced by how long a person sleeps. Studies show that not enough sleep could lead to obesity.[22-23]

THE 5 STAGES OF SLEEP[30]

STAGE ONE SLEEP *is the lightest and comes as a person just dozes off. This is a light sleep where people drift in and out of sleep. The eyes move slowly and muscle activity slows. They can be awakened easily. Some may experience sudden muscle contractions after a sensation of falling.*

STAGE TWO SLEEP *is when eye movement stops and brain waves become slower although there will be an occasional burst of rapid brain waves.*

STAGE THREE SLEEP *is when an EEG (ElectroEncephaloGram) records very slow brain waves (SWS — Slow Wave Sleep) called delta waves that are interspersed with smaller, faster waves.*

STAGE FOUR SLEEP *is when most of the slow delta waves are seen. Stages 3 and 4 are called deep sleep. It is difficult to awaken someone from these levels. There is no eye movement or muscle activity during these stages. Bed wetting, sleepwalking, or night terrors happen during stage four.*

STAGE FIVE SLEEP, *the last stage, is called REM or Rapid Eye Movement sleep. Breathing is more rapid, irregular, and shallow. The eyes jerk rapidly. The arm and leg muscles are temporarily paralyzed. The EEG brain waves during this stage are similar to levels experienced by an awake individual. The REM stage is when most dreams occur. Our circadian rhythms, which are hardwired, contribute to a variety of hormonal releases, and these in turn contribute to the production of an optimal sleeping environment that will facilitate the greatest possible restoration for our bodies.*

What is the good news in all of this? We can choose to synchronize ourselves with these natural rhythms and reap the benefits. In order to do this, we should get to bed early on a regular basis.

Restricting sleep will boost ghrelin, a hormone that makes us feel hungry. At the same time, lack of sleep suppresses another hormone, leptin, which helps to make us feel full. It is probable that a lack of sleep is contributing to the increasing obesity rates in America.[24]

Ghrelin also plays an important role in carbohydrate and lipid metabolism and, possibly, heart function, immune functions, and cell proliferation. It promotes slow-wave sleep (SWS, non-REM sleep stages three and four). Ghrelin also stimulates a growth hormone (GH).[25] Researchers have found that ghrelin levels increase during the early part of the night, with highest levels in the evening and early morning before two a.m. There is then a decrease in the morning. The nocturnal increase was blunted during sleep deprivation, and ghrelin levels increased only slightly until the early morning. The secretion of ghrelin during the first hours of sleep correlated positively with peak human growth hormone concentrations.[26]

"When you were young, your mother told you that you needed to get enough sleep to grow strong and tall. She was right! Deep sleep triggers a greater release of growth hormone, which fuels growth in children and boosts muscle mass and the repair of cells and tissues in children and adults."[27]

Repairing cells and tissues assists our body in keeping well. A study using growth hormone in HIV patients showed apparent reversal of wasting syndrome, a loss of 10% or more of body weight, and restoration of lean body mass.[28]

Most of the physiologically important GH secretion occurs as several large pulses or peaks of GH release each day. The largest and most predictable of these GH peaks occurs about an hour after onset of sleep. This is partly due to the fact that the secretion of GH is strongly associated with deep non-REM sleep.[29] Deep non-REM sleep, as was noted, takes place more in the early hours of the night and diminishes as the morning approaches. This relationship again demonstrates the importance of getting to bed as early as possible in the evening. By doing so, you will maximize the secretion of GH, which will help improve and maintain your health in many ways.

Daily Rest

Daily relaxation is important in helping to refresh yourself when stress is high and the demands are great. This relaxation can take many forms. Many people report they need to do something totally different from their normal routine in order to relax.

Taking deep breaths of fresh air outside during a work break can help energize the body for the rest of the work day. Fresh air taken deeply into the lungs is a wonderful, vitalizing force. As you will learn while studying the CREATION Health principle of Environment, fresh air has many positive benefits. Fresh air is chemically different than the recirculated indoor air that most Americans breathe on a daily basis.[31] Fresh air is actually electrified. It is negatively charged, or "negatively ionized," by the oxygen molecule, which is a good thing. There are over five thousand published studies reporting on experiments with ionization. All support the conclusion that, generally speaking, an overdose of positive ions is detrimental to health while extra negative ions, the good ones, are beneficial.[32] The negatively charged oxygen reportedly brings an improved sense of well-being, increases the rate and quality of growth in both plants and animals, improves function in the lung's protective cilia, decreases anxiety through a tranquilizing and relaxing effect, lowers body temperature, lowers resting heart rate, improves learning in mammals, decreases severity of stomach ulcers, and decreases survival of bacteria and viruses in the air.[33-39] Even if you can't get into the fresh air, deep breathing can be beneficial. Long and slow abdominal breathing will reduce anxiety and improve the quality and quantity of sleep.[40]

Have you ever had an aching back or pain in your neck when you were anxious or stressed? When you have anxiety or stress in your life, one of the ways your body responds is with muscle tension. *Progressive muscle relaxation* is a method that helps relieve that tension.

In progressive muscle relaxation, you tense a group of muscles as you breathe in, and you relax them as you breathe out. You work on your muscle groups in a certain order.

If you have trouble falling asleep, this method may also help with your sleep problems.

A few minutes of progressive relaxation can renew your personal energy on a stressful day. In progressive relaxation, the individual sits in a quiet, comfortable position and starts to breathe deeply and slowly. The mind is focused on a place that brings relaxation and happiness; maybe for you it is a mountain top or favorite vacation spot. The mind seeks to enter into this place with all of the senses: touching, smelling, and hearing with the imagination as the deep breathing continues. While remaining in the imaginary restful environment, the focus then turns to tightening and then relaxing muscle groups. Begin with the hands. Then the arms, shoulders, neck, jaw, eyes, abdomen, back, legs, and feet in that order. Between each muscle group, there should be a pause to review and ensure that the other muscles are continuing to be relaxed. The next muscle group can then receive the focus until all groups have been relaxed. Once the physical and mental relaxation has been achieved, it should be enjoyed for several minutes while assuring that the muscles stay

relaxed. Progressive relaxation has been shown to be a great stress reliever.[41] For more information, visit upmc.com/services/healthy-lifestyles/chronic-stress/pages/body-awareness.aspx.

A period of meditation on something positive and encouraging might be just what you need for renewed energy. Meditating on the special personal meaning of a Bible promise can have powerful renewing and peace-promoting effects.

Relaxation can come in the form of a daily vacation, "a piece of time when you wholeheartedly pursue something *you truly enjoy*."[42] A daily vacation can be packed into as little as ten or fifteen minutes and still be stimulating and invigorating. Make your daily vacation personal; find something that you have a passion for, such as reading, playing the piano, or talking with your grandkids.

Many people can also benefit greatly by what science now calls a "power nap" of about twenty minutes or less. Power naps have been shown to have many benefits, including higher perceived alertness,[43] improved declarative,[44] procedural memory,[45] alertness and performance,[46-47] mood,[48-50] physiological activation,[51-52] and level of alertness.[53-54] Power naps have also been shown to help modulate or calm emotions.[55]

The point is, find whatever *daily relaxation* works for you, and commit to doing it for at least ten minutes each day. This is essential to feeling better and will help you perform optimally.

"How beautiful is it to do nothing, and then rest afterward."

~ PROVERB

Weekly Rest

Energizing our lives with daily, weekly, and annual vacations is essential to our health and happiness. We have an innate, God-given need for a change of pace and a time to "come apart."

This rhythm of life originated with God when He created this earth. In the beginning, He created the world in six days and then rested on the seventh day. He called it the Sabbath. And it wasn't because His physical needs demanded it. He took time to rest simply because He wanted to enjoy the life He had just created. This seven-day rhythm suggests we should honor weekly rhythms if we want to take care of our health.

During World War II, Great Britain instituted a seventy-four-hour work week, but soon found that people could not maintain the pace. After experimenting, they found that a forty-eight-hour work week with regular breaks, plus one day of rest each week, resulted in maximum efficiency.[56] During the French revolution, France experimented with a ten-day week; chaos resulted.[56]

Our world operates on a seven-day rhythm. We find this cycle in plants, animals, and humans. Medical research has demonstrated seven-day rhythms in connection with a variety of physiological functions. These include: heart rate, natural hormones in human breast milk and urine, swelling after surgery, rejection of transplanted organs, human and animal cancers and their response to treatment, inflammatory responses, and the drugs we use to treat them. For instance, a patient will tend to have an increase in swelling on the seventh and the fourteenth day after surgery. Similarly, a patient who has had a kidney transplant is more likely to reject the organ seven days and fourteen days after surgery.[57-63]

German scientists call the thing that sets a biorhythm, "zeitgeber" or "time-giver." The zeitgeber that initiates and maintains the seven-day rhythm is not yet understood, but some chronobiologists think that a regular day of rest might pace it. It is possible that we have a physiologic need to take a specific day off each week.

Taking off one whole day in seven brings renewal to the physical and spiritual life. Unlike days, months, and years, this biorhythm has no astronomical marker. There is no plausible explanation for its presence, except that it was built into our physiology by our Creator. The day can be used for many restorative things: to connect with others; it can be great for recreation, reflection, and meditation; and it can be a special time to focus on nurturing one's spiritual values. How interesting (though not surprising) that science is discovering the health benefits related to keeping God's fourth commandment!

> *"The mark of a successful man is one that has spent an entire day on the bank of a river without feeling guilty about it."*
> ~ AUTHOR UNKNOWN

Recreation

A great way to get energized is through recreation. The dictionary defines recreation as "refreshment of one's mind or body after labor through activity or play."[64] Think of it as re-creation or the process of being re-energized.

One popular form of recreation is outdoor activities. This includes activities such as bird watching, sailing, hiking, rock climbing, sports, and the list goes on. Outdoor activities often result in sunshine, fresh air, and exercise.

Hobbies are also a healthy form of recreation. These could include creative hobbies such as arts and crafts, painting, drawing, cooking, music, photography; or hobbies focused on collecting items, such as artwork, butterflies, autographs, and fossils. Other hobbies might include recreational ones, like reading and gardening, or ones focused on animals, such as beekeeping, dog breeding, training horses, and many more. The list is endless; the point is to find a hobby you enjoy and spending time doing it.

Socializing and connecting with others is another way to spend your leisure time. Friendships benefit your mind, body, and soul in many ways as will be explained in the Interpersonal Relationships section.

Take care to choose the kinds of recreation that actually refresh you because after participating in re-creation activities, you should be re-energized and better able to meet life'schallenges.

> *"A day out-of-doors, someone I loved to talk with, a good book, and some simple food and music — that would be rest."*
> ~ ELEANOR ROOSEVELT

Annual Rest

Regularly scheduled vacations are a wonderful way to put "life" back into your existence. The travel company Expedia conducted an International Vacation Deprivation Survey and found that over one-third of employed U.S. adults (34%) reported feeling better about their job and feeling more productive at it after a vacation. Respondents also reported feeling closer to their family *after* a vacation. During a twenty-year follow-up of women participants, the Framingham Heart Study found an association between infrequent vacationing and increased incidence of death from coronary causes.[65] Another study found that men who developed psychosomatic illnesses were less likely to take vacations than were men who never developed such illnesses.[66] Drs. Gump and Matthews found, in their nine-year study of more than twelve thousand men, that annual vacations were associated with a reduced risk of all-cause mortality. The specific cause of death most strongly associated with inadequate vacationing was coronary heart disease.[67]

Vacations can come in all shapes and sizes. You can get the vacation "glow" by taking your vacation time in small intervals, such as two to four days. Fatigue, neck pain, headaches, or backaches can all be a signal that it is time for a break. A vacation might be "just what the doctor ordered."

No question, our bodies are made for work and for rest. Most of us have no problem working. What we need to do is learn how to rest, and "rest assured" that getting enough sleep, enjoying weekly down time, and taking relaxing vacations are crucial components of overall good health.

You don't have to feel guilty about taking rest! Enjoy the re-creation.

REINFORCE THE MESSAGE

SKILL BUILDERS

Choose the Skill Builders below that you would like to experience in your own life, then write a response on how they impacted you. Last, write further actions, if any, that you would like to take as a result of doing the Skill Builders.

 Skill Builder 1 | **Peak Performance Sleep Log**

Every morning at breakfast fill out the chart for the previous day.

WEEK 1	SUN	MON	TUE	WED	THUR	FRI	SAT
What time did you turn your lights out?							
What time did you get up this morning?							
How many total hours did you sleep?							
How many times did you wake up during the night?							
Rate the quality of your sleep last night. 1=terrible 5=great							
Did you avoid taking a nap yesterday?	yes no	yes no	yes no	yes no	yes no	yes no	yes no
Did you avoid caffeine after 6 pm?	yes no	yes no	yes no	yes no	yes no	yes no	yes no
Did you avoid alcohol after 6 pm?	yes no	yes no	yes no	yes no	yes no	yes no	yes no
Did you do anything to reduce stress yesterday?	yes no	yes no	yes no	yes no	yes no	yes no	yes no
Did you avoid sleeping medications?	yes no	yes no	yes no	yes no	yes no	yes no	yes no
Was your bedroom quiet, dark, and cool?	yes no	yes no	yes no	yes no	yes no	yes no	yes no
Did you do anything to relax before falling asleep?	yes no	yes no	yes no	yes no	yes no	yes no	yes no
Did you eat a balanced diet yesterday?	yes no	yes no	yes no	yes no	yes no	yes no	yes no
Did you exercise yesterday?	yes no	yes no	yes no	yes no	yes no	yes no	yes no

Adapted and Used with Permission, Maas, J. Power Sleep. Harper Collins. New York, NY, 1998

SLEEP LOG INTERPRETATION:

TO BE PREPARED FOR PEAK PERFORMANCE:

- *The answers to all the yes-or-no questions should be yes*
- *You should be getting close to eight hours of sleep each night*
- *Your sleep and wake times should not change between weekdays and weekends*
- *Your sleep should be continuous, not fragmented*
- *Your sleep should be restful*

DESCRIBE HOW THIS IMPACTED YOU:

....
....
....
....

FURTHER ACTION:

....
....
....
....

Stress is the number one sleep thief, and women are the biggest sufferers.

Skill Builder 2 | Vacation or Weekend Getaway

Have you taken a vacation lately? How about a weekend getaway?
Take some time now to plan one…

Ideas: You could go somewhere new or try something unusual. On the other hand, maybe you feel the need to go to a place you have been before that you know rejuvenates you. Maybe you feel the need to visit family and reconnect with them. Whatever you choose, a much-needed getaway is beneficial to your overall well-being.

YOUR PLAN IS TO . . .

....

....

....

DESCRIBE HOW THIS IMPACTED YOU:

....

....

FURTHER ACTION:

....

....

> *"Every now and then go away, have a little relaxation,*
> *for when you come back to your work your judgment will be surer.*
> *Go some distance away because then the work appears smaller*
> *and more of it can be taken in at a glance and*
> *a lack of harmony and proportion is more readily seen."*
>
> **~ LEONARDO DA VINCI**

A great way to get energized is through recreation. Remember, the American Heritage Dictionary defines recreation as "refreshment" of one's mind or body after labor through diverting activity; play. A good way to think of it is as re-creation. Recreation is often done during one's "leisure time." Plan a specific day and time when you will participate in recreation this week.

Recreation comes in many forms, and the important thing is that you choose the forms of recreation that refresh you.

Remember, after recreation you should be more equipped to meet life's challenges, and once again you should feel "refreshed." This is a great way to determine whether it is a good form of recreation for you.

YOUR PLAN IS TO . . .

....

....

....

DESCRIBE HOW THIS IMPACTED YOU:

....

....

FURTHER ACTION:

....

....

....

Skill Builder 4 | Daily Relaxation

Choose to participate in some form of daily "vacation" or relaxation. Have a goal of spending at least ten minutes on at least four days this week to relax. Try to maintain a daily "vacation" for four days a week, or extend it to more if you can.

This daily relaxation is important in helping to refresh you when stress is high and the demands are large. Relaxation can take many forms. Many people report that they need to do something totally different from what they typically do most of the day in order to fully relax.

Ideas:

- Take short breaks to stroll outside and take deep breaths
- Do some progressive relaxation
- Meditate on the blessings in your life or an inspirational quote or Bible text
- Take a short nap if you are feeling tired
- Start a good book you have been wanting to read and take short breaks with it
- Simply choose something to do that you truly enjoy

YOUR PLAN IS TO . . .

....

....

....

DESCRIBE HOW THIS IMPACTED YOU:

....

....

....

FURTHER ACTION:

....

....

....

"The time to relax is when you don't have time for it."

~ SIDNEY J. HARRIS

Skill Builder 5 | Sabbath Rest

Choose this week to take a Sabbath Rest. Take that day to truly rest and connect with God, yourself, or others. Maybe plan a getaway to spend time in nature, or rest at home if your body needs it. You could plan an activity to help others in your community. Only you know what you need, so choose wisely what to do for your special day of rest. You will be healthier and more effective if you allow yourself such a day as frequently as possible.

YOUR PLAN IS TO . . .

....
....
....

DESCRIBE HOW THIS IMPACTED YOU:

....
....
....

FURTHER ACTION:

....
....
....

> *"Rest when you're weary. Refresh and renew yourself,*
> *your body, your mind, your spirit. Then get back to work."*
> **~ RALPH MARSTON**

47

TIPS FOR SUCCESS

POWER TIPS: HOW TO HAVE BETTER REST

Getting a good night's sleep means including activities in your day that promote good sleep. What you do during the day will greatly impact how you sleep at night. Here are a few power tips:

1. **Adequate sunlight** helps maintain a healthy circadian rhythm. Research shows that day-time sunlight helps us sleep better at night.[68] Choose a lifestyle that includes regular outdoor activities. Any activity that allows sunlight will do: sports, a walk in the park, or even washing your car. A full spectrum light of at least 10,000 lux can substitute when a person cannot get adequate amounts of sunshine because of work, season, weather, or latitude.

2. **Fresh air** is vital to circulation, and good circulation is vital to a good night's rest. Fresh air greatly improves bodily oxygenation and circulation, especially when it comes with outdoor activity. In addition, fresh outdoor air is likely to increase exposure to sunlight. Remember, negative charges in fresh air have been shown to improve one's sense of well-being, decrease anxiety through a relaxing effect, lower body temperature, and lower one's resting heart rate.

3. **Physical activity** is also important. If your body is physically tired at the end of the day, you will sleep better. Research has confirmed that regular physical activity aids nighttime sleep. Researchers from the Stanford University School of Medicine studied a group of fifty to seventy-five-year-old people who complained of sleep problems. The participants began moderate physical activity for about thirty minutes, four times per week. The researchers compared the active adults with a similar group who did no physical activity. They found that the more active group slept an average of one hour more each night, fell asleep faster, spent less time napping, and reported an overall improvement in sleep quality.[69]

    Doing physical activity outdoors is especially helpful since it exposes you to sunlight, which in the afternoon is especially helpful in preventing midday sleepiness. In order to help you sleep well, physical activity is best if done *before* evening.

4. **Your last meal of the day** should be finished at least three hours before bedtime. For your best sleep make it a "lighter" meal, too. Limit your liquid intake before bedtime. Our culture leans toward a larger dinner. We typically rush to work in the morning, and overwork during the day. As a result, dinner is many times the first opportunity to relax. It's often the best time of the day when we spend time with family and friends. Unfortunately, this practice encourages a large meal that usually includes foods more difficult to digest. Your rest will be optimal if your body is not trying to digest your dinner while you are trying to sleep. *Your digestive organs need rest too!* Restful sleep will be facilitated by a light dinner consisting of easily digestible food such as fruits, vegetables, and whole grains. Limiting your intake of liquids before bedtime will help you avoid many trips to the bathroom, a great sleep disrupter!

5. **Regular sleep patterns are key to getting great sleep.** Try going to bed at the same time each night and getting up at the same time each morning. This way your body will get into a pattern that helps you sleep better. On the weekends, don't sleep in more than thirty minutes past your normal wake-up time or you will throw off your weekly sleep pattern. A brief nap in the early afternoon on the weekend is a better option than sleeping in excessively.

6. **Keep conflict, stress, anxiety, and worry outside your bedroom.** The mind is powerful; if actively engaged, it will overpower the body's ability to sleep. Put your mind at rest before you go to bed. Don't stay up worrying about what you cannot resolve today. On the other hand, resolve interpersonal relationship issues as much as you can *before* going to bed. A clear conscience is part of a healthy lifestyle and improves your quality of sleep and the rate at which you fall asleep.

7. **Relax before bedtime.** Begin to "wind down" before bedtime. Decide when you will go to bed and then, about twenty minutes before, find an activity that is calming and relaxing.

8. **Avoid caffeine, tobacco, and other stimulants.** Each of these addictive stimulants can keep you awake at night.[70] Too much, and the wrong kind of TV, video games, and the Internet, can also stimulate your internal stress hormones and rob you of a good night's sleep.

9. **Get your sleep primarily at night.** Naps can definitely be beneficial if they don't rob you of your nighttime sleep. Use naps with discretion. Useful as they are, they shouldn't be overused. Depending on your profession, your daily and weekly schedule may be such that you can judiciously use naps three or more times a week without hurting your nighttime sleep. But for most people, perhaps two naps a week are probably all you can take on a regular basis without disrupting your nighttime sleep. If you find you are napping three or more times a week, examine your nighttime sleep habits in order to ensure you are not robbing yourself of this most critical and beneficial sleep.

10. **Take a hot bath one to two hours before your bedtime.** Research published in the journal *Sleep* found that women with insomnia who took a hot bath within one to two hours of going to bed had a better night's sleep. The bath increased their core temperature, which then quickly dropped once they got out of the bath. This helped them to sleep better.[71]

MENTAL OUTLOOK IS DAMPENED

The mental toll of skimping on slumber can be serious. The National Sleep Foundation found that more than nine out of ten people not getting enough sleep can decrease their performance at work and increase the risk of injuries. Nearly two-thirds felt that lack of sleep can muddle thinking, making it more difficult to make decisions and listen carefully, and making them prone to mistakes and to flying off the handle when faced with routine annoyances.

CREATE A GOOD SLEEP ENVIRONMENT

Creating a good sleep environment is essential. The following tips can help:

1. **Maintain a dark room.** Light can disturb your sleep. It is important to ensure that the room in which you sleep is dark, because darkness prompts melatonin release, and melatonin improves sleep. Dimming the light in your home environment for the twenty minutes before bedtime will help to create a positive sleep environment.

2. **Keep your room quiet.** Noise can wake you up, and then you struggle getting back to sleep. To block out disrupting sounds, you might want to use some form of "white noise," like a fan.

3. **Maintain a cool temperature.** Although the optimum temperature may differ slightly from one individual to the next, a cool room is best. During sleep, your body's internal temperature drops. A cooler room temperature ensures that the body is not using valuable energy and resources, which it needs for the functions of sleep and the regulation of your body's internal temperature.

4. **Use the bed only for sleep and for intimacy.** After fifteen to thirty minutes of sleeplessness, get out of bed until you are sleepy. If you work from bed while paying bills, watching TV, or doing other activities, you will gradually associate lying in bed with sleeplessness. By so doing, you will "teach" your body to remain awake when in bed. If you can't sleep, you should get out of bed and do something more conducive for sleep, like reading a book, and then don't get back into bed until you feel sleepy. If sleeplessness becomes a nightly problem, be sure to do the activities referred to above in order to help you sleep better at night.

5. **Circulate fresh air.** High air quality helps to maximize the restorative and regenerative properties of sleep. Fresh air accentuates the physiologic state of sleep by decreasing anxiety, lowering body temperature, and lowering the resting heart rate. This helps you to sleep better.

6. **Get a comfortable bed and pillow.** Having a mattress and pillow that is right for you can make a world of difference in getting a good night's sleep.

7. **Have a sleep study if you snore.** If you snore loudly, find yourself waking up in the night gasping for air, or have excessive daytime sleepiness, you should ask your doctor about having a sleep study done. Sleep apnea can have powerful negative effects on your physical, mental, and emotional health. Depression, anxiety, decreased memory, hypertension, heart disease, type 2 diabetes, and premature death have all been linked to this problem.[72-74] Take it seriously.

HOW TO BREATHE THE "RIGHT WAY"

Used with Permission, Cathleen Henning Fenton, Your Guide to Panic Disorder.
http://panicdisorder.about.com/cs/shbreathing/ht/breatheproperly.htm

Here's How:

1. Begin by lying flat on your back or standing up straight. You may also sit up straight in a chair, if that is more comfortable. Place your hand on your stomach area.

2. Breathe as you normally would, and notice whether your hand and stomach rise and fall, or if your chest rises and falls as you breathe.

3. When you are breathing properly, your chest will stay still while your stomach will rise slightly as you breathe in. When you breathe out, your chest will continue to stay still while your stomach lowers slightly.

4. Now, slowly breathe in through your nose on the count of five while gently pushing your hand up with your stomach.

5. Hold the breath for a count of five.

6. Slowly exhale through your mouth for a count of five while gently pushing down on your stomach.

7. Repeat this process for five minutes.

8. If the process causes you to begin panicking, stop. Try again later or the next day, but do the exercise for a shorter amount of time. You may need to start with one minute per day.

9. Increase the length of time each day until you can do the exercise for at least five minutes, twice daily.

10. If you continue to practice breathing this way, you will soon be doing it naturally throughout the day.

11. An additional benefit will be that once you are familiar with this exercise, you may do it while experiencing anxiety or at the beginning of a panic attack, and you will feel relief.

Tips:

1. Don't give up if you cannot do this exercise correctly right away. It takes practice. Give yourself time.

2. Remember, you are in control and can stop at any time. Take it as slowly as needed. If you feel anxious when doing the exercise, build up the length of time as gradually as possible.

3. It may help to do the exercise with someone else, if available, in case you experience anxiety or panic. The best person would be a therapist with experience in breathing techniques, but if that's not possible, a trusted friend or family member might be helpful. Just knowing someone is there can help prevent anxiety or panic.

> *"Sometimes the most important thing in a whole day is the rest we take between two deep breaths or the turning inwards in prayer for five short minutes."*
>
> **~ ETTY HILLESUM**

TEN TIPS TO HELP YOU FALL ASLEEP

By Dr. Albert   *Used with Permission*

1. Sleep in a comfortable bed.

2. Make sure your bedroom is conducive to sleep. Most people sleep best in a room that's a bit cooler than normally desired when awake.

3. Take a bath before bed.

4. Drink a glass of warm milk or a cup of herb tea.

5. Do a relaxation exercise. Breathe deeply, listen to soothing music, or let your mind wander.

6. Do some light reading.

7. Say good night to your worries and shut the bedroom door on them.

8. Make sure your last hour before bed is as peaceful as possible. Skip scary movies and save intense conversations for a better time.

9. Allow yourself to sleep or stay awake – if your body so chooses. In other words, don't try to force or control anything. You can't force sleep.

10. Get up after thirty minutes or so and do something you like or need to do. If you can't sleep, you may as well be productive.

Foods that help you snooze: bananas, rice, and combining unsweetened carbs with protein.

"Harmonize your body and mind with your natural rhythms and deep, restful sleep will soon follow."

~ MY HEALTHY LIFE

SMALL GROUP DISCUSSIONS

Directions: Review the discussion questions and choose one you would like to discuss first. Proceed through the rest of the questions as time allows.

1. What are the differences between spiritual, physical, and mental rest?

....

....

2. How many hours of sleep do you average per night? Are you happy with this amount? How could you do better?

....

....

3. What things could you do to unwind before sleeping? What works best for you?

....

....

4. If you do have a weekly day off, what can you do to help ensure that you don't allow work stresses to ruin it? What kind of defenses can you set up around it?

....

....

5. If some of you are *Night Owls*, talk with those who aren't about how they manage to get to bed earlier.

....

....

6. Talk about some of your favorite vacation spots and how they have helped you unwind and relax.

....

....

7. What are some Bible promises that you have found helpful in calming your nerves and relieving anxiety? Which promises can help you sleep better?

....

....

ADDITIONAL RESOURCES

Books:

Original Love: Experiencing Peace, Meaning and Harmony through Sabbath Rest, by Des Cummings, Jr.

Sabbath: Restoring the Sacred Rhythm of Rest, by Wayne Muller

Websites:

bettersleep.org (Great website all about sleep and rest)

Other Resources:

Get a massage in order to help you relax

Eye covers (for traveling to keep out the light when trying to rest)

Travel pillows

Bubble bath "kit" to help you relax

Aromatherapy – get some scents specifically designed to enhance sleep.

Songs to Inspire Rest:

It Is Well with My Soul (Hymn)

Nearer Still Nearer (Hymn)

I Will Rest in You (Cindy Morgan)

His Sheep Am I (Praise)

REFERENCES

1. Zee P, Turek F. "Sleep and Health: Everywhere and in Both Directions." *Archives of Internal Medicine* Sept. 18, 2006 166: 1686–1688.

2. Spiegel K, Tsali E, et al. "Sleep Curtailment in Healthy Young Men is Associated with Decreased Levels of Leptin, Elevated Ghrelin Levels, and Increased Hunger and Appetite." *Annals of Internal Medicine* Dec 7, 2004 141(11): 885–6.

3. Ayas N, White D, et al. "A Prospective Study of Sleep Duration and Coronary Heart Disease in Women." *Archives of Internal Medicine* 2003 163: 205–209.

4. Ayas N, White D, et al. "A Prospective Study of Self-Reported Sleep Duration and Incident Type 2 Diabetes in Women." *Diabetes Care* 2003 26: 380–384.

5. Patlak M, U.S. DEPARTMENT OF HEALTH AND HUMAN SERVICES, National Institutes of Health & National Heart, Lung, and Blood Institute, "Your Guide To Healthy Sleep," NIH Publication No. 06-5271, November 2005, http://www.nhlbi.nih.gov/health/public/sleep/healthy sleep.htm. Retrieved 4/28/08.

6. Stickgold R, Hobson J, et al. "Sleep, Learning, and Dreams; Off-line Memory Reprocessing." *Science* Nov. 2, 2001 294: 1052–1057.

7. Perl J. *Sleep Right in Five Nights; a Clear and Effective Guide for Conquering Insomnia.* New York: William Morrow and Company, Inc., 1993, 32.

8. Marschall-Kehrel D. "Update on Nocturia: The Best of Rest is Sleep." *Urology*, December 2004 64(6 Suppl 1): 21–4.

9. Fallone G, Acebo C, et al. "Experimental Restriction of Sleep Opportunity in Children: Effects on Teacher Ratings." *Sleep* 2005 28(12): 1561–1567.

10. Howell A, Jahrig J, et. al. "Sleep Quality, Sleep Propensity and Academic Performance." *Perceptual & Motor Skills* Oct. 2004 00(2): 525–535.

11. Steptoe A, Peacey V, et. al. "Sleep Duration and Health in Young Adults." *Archives of Internal Medicine* Sept. 18, 2006 166(16): 1689–1692.

12. Dongen H, Maislin G, et. al. "The Cumulative Cost of Additional Wakefulness: Dose-Response Effects on Neurobehavioral Functions and Sleep Physiology From Chronic Sleep Restriction and Total Sleep Deprivation." *Sleep* 2003 26(2): 117–126.

13. Nedley, N. *Proof Positive: How to Reliably Combat Disease and Achieve Optimal Health Through Nutrition and Lifestyle.* Ardmore, OK: Neil Nedley, 1998, 502.

14. Wingard D, Berkman, Brand R. "A Multivariate Analysis of Health-Related Practices; A Nine-Year Mortality Follow-up of the Alameda County Study." *American Journal of Epidemiology.* 116(5): 765–775.

15. Wingard D, Berkman L, et al. "Mortality Risk Associated with Sleeping Patterns Among Adults." *Sleep* 1983 6(2): 102–107.

16. Clarian Health, Healthy Living, Work Life, "How to Survive Shift Work." pg. 1 & 2. http://www.clarian.org/portal/patients/healthyliving?paf_gear_id=200001&paf_dm=full&paf_gm=content&task_name=articleDetail&articleId=212&sectionId=10. Retrieved 1/22/09.

REFERENCES

17. Monk T. "Morningness-Eveningness and Lifestyle Regularity." *Chronobiology International*. May 2004 21(3): 435–443.

18. National Sleep Foundation, 2005 Sleep in America Poll, http://www.kintera.org/atf/cf/ {F6BF2668-A1B4-4FE8-8D1A-A5D39340D9CB}/2005_summary_of_findings.pdf. Retrieved 2/09/09.

19. "Melatonin." The Medical Letter. November 24, 1995 37 (962): 111.

20. Melatonin. Monograph. *Altern Med Rev.* Dec. 2005 10(4): 326–36.

21. Spiegel K, Tasali E, et al. "Brief Communication: Sleep Curtailment in Healthy Young Men is Associated with Decreased Leptin Levels, Elevated Ghrelin Levels, and Increased Hunger and Appetite." *Annals of Internal Medicine* Dec. 2004 141(11): 846–850.

22. Copinschi G. "Metabolic and Endocrine Effects of Sleep Deprivation." *Essential Psychopharmacology* 2005 6(6): 341–347.

23. Taheri S, Lin L, et al. "Short Sleep Duration is Associated with Reduced Leptin, Elevated Ghrelin, and Increased Body Mass Index." *PLoS Medicine* Dec 2004 1(3) e62. doi:10.1371/ journal.pmed.0010062.

24. Kohatsu ND, et al. "Sleep Duration and Body Mass Index in a Rural Population." *Archives of Internal Medicine* Sept. 18, 2006 166: 1701–5.

25. Hubina E, Goth M, et. al. "Ghrelin – A Hormone with Multiple Functions." *Orv Hetil* Jan 19, 2005 146(25): 1345–1351.

26. Dzaja A, Dalal M, et al. "Sleep Enhances Noctural Plasma Ghrelin Levels in Healthy Subjects." *American Journal of Physiology – Endocrinology and Metabolism* June 2004 286(6): E963–967.

27. Patlak M, U.S. DEPARTMENT OF HEALTH AND HUMAN SERVICES, National Institutes of Health & National Heart, Lung, and Blood Institute, "Your Guide To Healthy Sleep," NIH Publication No. 06-5271, November 2005, http://www.nhlbi.nih.gov/health/public/sleep/ healthy sleep.htm. Retrieved 4/28/08.

28. Mulligan K. "Anabolic Effects of Recombinant Human Growth Hormone in Patients with Wasting Associated with Human Immunodeficiency Virus Infection." *Journal of Clinical Endocrinology and Metabolism* 1993 77(4): 956.

29. Obal F Jr., Krueger J. "GHRH and Sleep." *Sleep Medicine Reviews* Oct 2004 8(5): 367–377.

30. Patlak M, U.S. DEPARTMENT OF HEALTH AND HUMAN SERVICES, National Institutes of Health & National Heart, Lung, and Blood Institute, "Your Guide To Healthy Sleep," NIH Publication No. 06-5271, November 2005, http://www.nhlbi.nih.gov/health/public/sleep/ healthy sleep.htm. Retrieved 4/28/08.

31. Baldwin B. "Why is Fresh Air Fresh?" *The Journal of Health and Healing* 11(4): 26–27.

32. Soyka F. *The Ion Effect*, New York: Bantam Books, 1991, 21.

33. Baldwin B. "Why is Fresh Air Fresh?" *The Journal of Health and Healing* 11(4): 26–27.

REFERENCES

34. Duffee R, Koontz R. "Behavioral Effects of Ionized Air on Rats." *Psychophysiology* April 1965 1(4): 347–359.

35. Jordan J, Sokoloff B. "Air Ionization, Age and Maze Learning on Rats." *Journal of Gerontology* 1959 14: 344–348.

36. Reilly T, Stevenson I. "An Investigation of the Effects of Negative Air Ions on Responses to Submaximal Exercise at Different Times of the Day." *Journal of Human Ergol.* (Tokyo) June 1993 22(1): 1–9.

37. Mitchell B, King D. "Effect of Negative Ionization on Airborne Transmission of Newcastle Disease Virus. *Avian Dis*. October–December 1994 38(4): 752–732.

38. Giannini A, Jones B, et al. "Reversibility of Serotonin Irritation Syndrome with Atmospheric Anions." *Journal of Clinical Psychiatry* March 1986 47(3): 141–143.

39. Gabbay J, Bergerson O, et al. "Effect of Ionization on Microbial Air Pollution in the Dental Clinic." *Environmental Research* June 1990 52(1): 99–106.

40. Cohen L, Warneke C, et. al. "Psychological Adjustment and Sleep Quality in a Randomized Trial of the Effects of a Tibetan Yoga Intervention in Patients with Lymphoma." *Cancer* 2004 100(10): 2253–2260.

41. Carlson C, Hoyle R. "Efficacy of Abbreviated Progressive Muscle Relaxation Training: A Quantitative Review of Behavioral Medicine Research." *Journal of Consulting and Clinical Psychology* 1993 61(6): 1059–1067.

42. Bauman R. "Taking a Daily Vacation." *Vibrant Life* Jan-Feb 2002, 34.

43. Takahashi M, Nakata A, et al. "Post-Lunch Nap as a Worksite Intervention to Promote Alertness on the Job." *Ergonomics* July 15, 2004 47(9): 1003–1013.

44. Tucker M, Hirota Y, et al. "A Daytime Nap Containing Solely Non-REM Sleep Enhances Declarative but Not Procedural Memory." *Neurobiology of Learning and Memory* Sept 2006 86(2): 241–247.

45. Backhaus J, Junghanns K. "Daytime Naps Improve Procedural Motor Memory." *Sleep Medicine* Sept. 2006 7(6): 508–512.

46. Takahashi M, Arito H. "Maintenance of Alertness and Performance by a Brief Nap after Lunch Under Prior Sleep Deficit." *Sleep* Sept 15, 2000 23(6): 813–819.

47. Takahashi M, Fukuda H, et al. "Brief Naps During Post-Lunch Rest: Effects on Alertness, Performance, and Autonomic Balance." *European Journal of Applied Physiology* Jul 1998 78(2): 93–98.

48. Hayashi M, Watanabe M, et al. "The Effects of a 20 Min Nap in the Mid-Afternoon on Mood, Performance and EEG Activity." *Clinical Neurophysiology* Feb 1999 110(2): 272–279.

49. Tamaki M, Shirota A, et al. "Effects of a Daytime Nap in the Aged." *Psychiatry and Clinical Neurosciences* Apr 1999 53(2): 273–275.

REFERENCES

50. Luo Z, Inoue S. "A Short Daytime Nap Modulates Levels of Emotions Objectively Evaluated by the Emotion Spectrum Analysis Method." *Psychiatry and Clinical Neurosciences* Apr 2000 54(2): 207–212.

51. Taub J, Tanguay P, et al. "Effects of Afternoon Naps on Physiological Variables Performance and Self-Reported Activation." *Biological Psychology* Sept. 1977 5(3): 191–219.

52. Hayashi M, Horit. "The Effects of a 20-Min Nap Before Post-Lunch Dip." *Psychiatry and Clinical Neurosciences* Apr 1998 52(2): 203–204.

53. Tietzel A, Lack L. "The Short-Term Benefits of Brief and Long Naps Following Nocturnal Sleep Restriction." 2001 *Sleep* 24(3): 293–300.

54. Tietzel A, and Lack L. "The Recuperative Value of Brief and Ultra-brief Naps on Alertness and Cognitive Performance." *Journal of Sleep Research* September 2003 11(3): 213–218.

55. Luo Z, Inoue S. "A Short Daytime Nap Modulates Levels of Emotions Objectively Evaluated by the Emotion Spectrum Analysis Method." *Psychiatry and Clinical Neurosciences* Apr 2000 54(2): 207–212.

56. Ludington A, Diehl H. *"Dynamic Living; How to Take Charge of Your Health."* Hagerstown, MD: Review and Herald Publishing Association 1995, 189.

57. Baldwin B. "Seven-Day Rhythms." *The Journal of Health and Healing* 9(4): 3, 14.

58. Rawson M, Cornelissen G, et al. "Circadian and Circaseptan Components of Blood Pressure and Heart Rate During Depression." *Scripta Medica (BRNO)* April 2000 73(2): 117–124.

59. Agrimonti F, Frairia F, Fornaro D, et al. "Circadian and Circaseptan Rhythmicities in Corticosteroid Binding Activity of Human Milk." *Chronobiologia* 9: 185–193, 1982.

60. Levi F, Halberg F. "Circaseptan (About-7-Day) Bioperiodicity – Spontaneous and Reactive – and the Search for Pacemakers." *International Journal of Clinical & Laboratory Research* April 1982 12(2): 323–370.

61. Pollmann L, Hildebrandt G. "Long-Term Control of Swelling After Maxillo-Facial Surgery: A Study of Circaseptan Reactive Periodicity" *International Journal of Chronobiology* 1982 8(2): 105–114.

62. Besarab A. "Effect of Delayed Graft Function and ALG on the Circaseptan (About 7-Day) Rhythm of Human Renal Allograft Rejection." *Transplantation* 1983 35(6): 562–566.

63. Baldwin B. "Seven-Day Rhythms." *The Journal of Health and Healing* 9(4): 3, 14.

64. American Heritage Dictionary of the English Language, Fourth Edition, 2000. http://www.bartleby.com/61/10/R0091000.html. Retrieved Feb. 15, 2009.

65. Eaker E, Pinsky J, Castelli W. "Myocardial Infarction and Coronary Death among Women: Psychosocial Predictors from a 20-Year Follow-up of Women in the Framingham Study." *American Journal of Epidemiology* 1992 135(8): 854–864.

66. Vaillant G. E. "Natural History of Male Psychological Health, IV: What Kinds of Men Do Not Get Psychosomatic Illness." *Psychosomatic Medicine* 1978 40(5): 420–431.

REFERENCES

67. Gump B, and Matthews K. "Are Vacations Good for Your Health? The 9-Year Mortality Experience After the Multiple Risk Factor Intervention Trial." *Psychosomatic Medicine* 2000 62: 608–612.

68. Schenck C, Mahowald M, Sack R. "Assessment and Management of Insomnia" *JAMA*. 2003 289 (19): 2475–2479.

69. King A, et al. "Moderate-Intensity Exercise and Self-Rated Quality of Sleep in Older Adults. A Randomized Control Trial." *JAMA*. 1997: 277: 32.

70. Patlak M, U.S. DEPARTMENT OF HEALTH AND HUMAN SERVICES, National Institutes of Health & National Heart, Lung, and Blood Institute, "Your Guide To Healthy Sleep," NIH Publication No. 06-5271, November 2005, http://www.nhlbi.nih.gov/health/public/sleep/healthy sleep.htm. Retrieved 4/28/08.

71. Dorsey C. "Core Body Temperature and Sleep of Older Female Insomniacs Before and After Passive Body Heating." *Sleep* 1999 22(7): 891–898.

72. Sharafkhaneh A, Giray N, et al. "Association of Psychiatric Disorders and Sleep Apnea in a Large Cohort." *Sleep* 2005 28(11): 1405–1411.

73. Young T, Peppard P, Gottlieb D. "Epidemiology of Obstructive Sleep Apnea; A Population Health Perspective." *Am J Respir Crit Care Med* 165 2002: 1217–1239.

74. Patlak M, U.S. DEPARTMENT OF HEALTH AND HUMAN SERVICES, National Institutes of Health & National Heart, Lung, and Blood Institute, "Your Guide To Healthy Sleep," NIH Publication No. 06-5271, November 2005, http://www.nhlbi.nih.gov/health/public/sleep/healthy sleep.htm. Retrieved 4/28/08.

NOTES

ENVIRONMENT

renew your soul

CONTENTS

MAKE IT WORK

Further Explanation of the DVD Topics

THE BIG PICTURE

Environment is what lies outside of us, either immediately or in our world at large. Yet it all, to some degree, affects what's inside of us because what's outside comes inside through our skin, mouths, and minds. All our senses – sight, smell, sound, touch, and taste – can influence our mood and health. Recent research demonstrates not only the importance of our larger environment (air and water quality) but also our immediate environment (light, sound, aroma, and touch) to our overall health.

In this section of the CREATION Health seminar, we will encourage you to create the best possible environment for yourself and those around you.

Home Work

For starters, make your home an oasis, a "fertile" or "green" spot in contrast to the harshness of the world at large. Create a place that you, your family, and guests will be blessed – a place that nurtures and restores everyone who enters.

Your home reflects you. Your home should make you feel good; it should recharge and revive all who enter. It should be a place of comfort, peace, and love.

Our environment encompasses all that is around us. It impacts us through our sight, hearing, smell, touch, and taste. Work and home environments probably impact our health the most because we spend most of our time in them. So paying attention to and striving to create a healthy environment in both places gives rich rewards.

"Everyone can identify with a fragrant garden, with the beauty of sunset, with the quiet of nature, with a warm and cozy cottage."

~ THOMAS KINKADE

Sight

Our eyes see a wealth of information every day. This input can help to heal and promote our well-being, or be detrimental to us. The smiles of loved ones and friends – these can all bring healing. We see pictures or photographs that bring back good memories of special times. We see gifts of love that warm our hearts. We see nature through our windows, or the sun shining brightly or giving a warm glow at sunset. Or the enjoyable interaction with a cat, dog, or bird can evoke warm emotions.

We can also bring some of the natural world into our homes and reap benefits from plants, flowers, and fountains. When we look through our windows or go into our yards, our bodies, minds, and souls are nurtured by nature.

> *"Of all God's gifts to the sighted man, color is holiest, the most divine, the most solemn."*
> ~ JOHN RUSKIN

Organization and Clutter

Other things in our environment can either be a help or a challenge. Organization, cleanliness, and order all promote peace and health. Clutter, messes, and a lack of organization in our home can serve as stressors, or may even be a symptom of stress.

Clutter costs! For example, surveys indicate that people with cluttered desks and offices are less likely to get promoted.[1] Clutter also promotes disorder and stress in our minds, resulting in less time and energy for other tasks.

Think about it, even five minutes a day dealing with clutter adds up to over thirty hours a year of wasted time. Clutter can also result in safety hazards, such as tripping over items on the ground; it can create mold growth in damp, moist areas, and lead to dust buildup in unclean areas. It can be hazardous to children who might get ahold of something in the clutter that is dangerous.

Sometimes clutter can hurt relationships or cause hard feelings among those who resent dealing with the messes others make. Clutter can impact our social lives, too, which is important to our well-being. We might feel that the house is not clean enough to have loved ones over and, therefore, we miss out on the enrichment that socializing with those we love brings.

Clutter can contribute to depression and bad behavior. Clutter and disorganization drain energy. Take a moment to notice how you feel next time you walk into a room that is disorganized and messy, and then notice how you feel when you walk into a room that is neat, clean, and inviting.

Primary Colors and Sounds

The wonders of nature can greatly alleviate daily stress. Nature was designed this way by a loving Creator. This truth is illustrated by the two primary colors of nature: the blue sky and green vegetation. There is scientific evidence that green and blue are not only soothing and relaxing but are associated with lower levels of anxiety.[7] Blue is associated with "secure/comfortable" and "tender/soothing," which imply pleasure and low arousal.[8] It also slows the pulse rate and lowers body temperature.

A day spent in nature is a day surrounded by sound. The playful rustle of wind dancing through trees. The soothing coos of a mourning dove. The ceaseless rhythm of the ocean. The enchanting chirp of crickets on a summer's eve. Swirling water tumbling over itself in a lively brook. The peaceful patter of rain on leafy trees. Thunder rumbling across the sky. Nature is a veritable symphony of sound, and God is its conductor.

Opening our windows and letting in the sounds of nature is restful and relieves stress. Some people enjoy CDs of nature sounds, or the sounds of falling water from a tabletop fountain.

What we hear impacts us. Words of love and kindness promote health; harsh and unloving words hinder it. Many times our environment is filled with sounds that impact our health. Our lives can be cluttered with the chronic noise of beeping horns, ringing phones, loud airplanes, etc. Chronic noise exposure, whether at high or low levels, has a detrimental effect. Research shows noise elevates psychophysiological stress (resting blood pressure and overnight epinephrine and norepinephrine), decreases levels of perceived quality of life,[9] and contributes to deficits in long-term memory, speech perception, and standardized reading test scores.[10] Even low levels of noise can reduce productivity.[11] The negative effects of loud noise include hearing loss (temporary and permanent) as well as increased blood pressure, decreased concentration, and a negative effect on mood. A meta-analysis identified noise exposure as contributing to cardiovascular disease prevalence, although the relationship between noise and ischemic heart disease was inconclusive.[12]

The Medium Sends a Message

The media in our homes impacts us in a powerful way, whether we realize it or not. The TV is often on many hours a day.[2] Take a moment to consider the images it feeds our brains. Are they positive and health promoting? Research showed that after watching just a few minutes of the news, participants said they felt more anxious and sad, which subsequently led to greater fear and personal worries.[3] Typically the news is about crime, wars, and other negative things. TV viewing can also leave us non-responsive[4] and inactive, adding to weight gain problems.[5]

Also consider the movies, video games, magazines, and books in your environment. Are they filled with images that you want to model and become? This is important because the old adage, "By beholding we become changed" is true. Behavioral and cognitive studies have linked exposure to violent media with aggressive behavior. Violent video games show increased activity in areas of the brain linked to aggression and decreased responses in regions that contribute to self-control.[6]

> "You're only here for a short visit. Don't hurry, don't worry. And be sure to smell the flowers along the way."
>
> ~ WALTER HAGEN

The Nose Knows

Enjoy your sense of smell and use it to enhance the quality of your life. Take time to literally "smell the roses" and other flowers. Enjoy the smell of a wonderful Italian or Chinese meal, or whatever foods and spices you like. Bask in the fragrance of a freshly baked apple pie. Take time to get into nature and enjoy the fresh, clean air, for the sense of smell has a powerful impact on us. You might have noticed that stores use special odors that trigger emotions, thus encouraging customers to buy and spend more money.[13] For instance, customers smell the fragrance of pumpkin pie or evergreen trees as they shop for seasonal gifts or décor. You might be surprised to discover that the leathery smell of a new car is actually an artificial scent put into leather through a process called "re-tanning" to enhance the buyer's satisfaction.[14] Using scents in casinos has been shown to increase gambling.[15] London's Heathrow Airport reportedly used the scent of pine needles to reduce stress and tension for passengers.[16] In contrast, bad odors have been found to make people more aggressive.[17]

A vanilla-like odor helped to reduce anxiety by 63% in patients going for a closed MRI scan (a closed scan can make people feel claustrophobic).[18]

These examples show that our sense of smell has a powerful impact on our mood and mindset. Because smell signals are projected into the limbic area (emotion center in the brain), smell can also affect memory. This is where the field of aromatherapy comes in. It seeks to use this nose-limbic connection to enhance our sense of well-being.

Indoor Air Pollution

We can benefit from bringing nature inside, too. Research done by NASA shows that living, green, and flowering plants remove several toxic chemicals from the air in building interiors. You can enjoy these plants in your home or office, not only to improve the quality of the air but also to make it a more pleasant place. NASA found that the following ten plants are the top picks for removing formaldehyde (found in virtually all indoor environments), benzene (a commonly used solvent that is present in many common items), and carbon monoxide from the air: bamboo palm, Chinese evergreen, English ivy, gerbera daisy, Janet Craig, marginata, mass cane/corn plant, mother-in-law's tongue, pot mum, peace lily, and Warneckii.[19]

We don't often think about the quality of the air inside our homes or buildings at work. It seems obvious that air pollution is something that happens outside. Many people are surprised to learn that air pollution can be more of a concern indoors than out. In the last several years, a growing body of scientific evidence has indicated that the air within homes and buildings can be more polluted than the outdoor air in even the largest and most industrialized cities.[20]

Americans spend about 90% of their time indoors.[21] The air inside most homes is an average of two to five times more polluted than the air outside its walls.[22] "Thus, for many people, the risks to health from exposure to indoor air pollution may be greater than risks from outdoor pollution."[23] Indoor pollution is identified as one of the top five environmental risks for public health. Given this information, it's easy to see why indoor air pollution is a cause of concern and something we should pay attention to.

Where does indoor air pollution come from? It is created when we use toxic chemical products like household cleaners and pesticides; it's in home furnishings like carpets, foams, and composite wood products made from fume-emitting synthetic materials; it's in poorly vented combustion appliances like gas ranges and furnaces; it's in the fumes coming from garbage cans and indoor composting containers, to name a few.

Combine these sources with energy efficient home construction that dramatically limits the amount of fresh air exchanged between the inside and outside; air pollutant levels can quickly build to unhealthy levels.

Touch and Taste

As humans, we were created to touch and to be touched. One of the ways we can help each other is through the wonderful gift of touch. God created skin as the largest sense organ in our bodies, and skin responds positively to every loving touch. Numerous studies document how we must have touch to develop and grow. Research shows that husbands and wives who have warm contact, like a hug, have higher levels of the plasma oxytocin (a bonding and belonging hormone) and reduced blood pressure. These couples also have lower levels of the stress hormone cortisol.[24] In his book *Psychosocial Medicine: A Study of the Sick Society,* James L. Halliday writes about how infants who are deprived of regular maternal body contact can develop depression, lack of appetite, and wasting so severe that it can lead to death.[25]

Somewhere deep within the fabric of the human heart, God placed a desire to love and be loved, to touch and be touched. Well-known family therapist Virginia Satir once stated we need four hugs a day for survival, eight for maintenance, and twelve for growth. This topic is covered in more detail in the Interpersonal Relationship video and seminar.

Now, when it comes to taste, there is a banquet of options! Our Creator blessed us with an abundant variety. We can prepare our food in so many ways. Eating is meant to be a pleasure we can enjoy every day. Take time to enjoy your food, whether it's savory, sweet, tart, warm, hot, cold, fresh, raw, cooked, baked or broiled, rough or smooth. Savor every bite. Our food is our fuel, and is meant to energize us with vitality and health.

> *"There is always music amongst the trees in the garden, but our hearts must be very quiet to hear it."*
> ~ **MINNIE AUMONIER**

Pesticides

One study measured pesticide levels of urine in children and found that immediately after substituting organic food items for the children's normal diets, the concentration of pesticides found in their bodies decreased substantially to non-detectable levels until the conventional diets were reintroduced.[26]

Many people add filtration systems to their home's water supply. While filtering can be beneficial, be cautious not to "overfilter." Natural additions to our drinking water, such as dissolved minerals, give water a variety of refreshing tastes and make it healthier. Certain harmless microorganisms remove bad tastes and odors and make it more palatable. Another option for some homeowners is to drill a well, but the water should be tested to make sure it is good.

Natural Beauty

Nature has a wonderful effect on the mind. Experiencing nature, whether through passive observance or active participation, is an important component of psychological well-being, says University of Michigan researcher Rachel Kaplan.[27] Another University of Michigan researcher, Stephen Kaplan, states that the pressures of modern life contribute to the experience of mental fatigue, which can lead to less tolerance, less effectiveness, and poorer health. By providing deeply needed restorative experiences, natural settings can play a central role in reducing these devastating effects.[28]

If stressed, gaze upon the beauties of nature. Studies find that simply viewing a garden or other natural vistas can quickly reduce blood pressure and pulse rate and increase the brain activity that uplifts our mood.[29] Feasting your eyes on nature is beneficial in a variety of settings. The average anxiety level of individuals working in a building with plants was found to be lower than that of individuals working without plants. Research also shows that sunlight penetration has a significant effect on job satisfaction and adds to general well-being. Having a view of natural elements helped to buffer an employee's intention to quit his or her job.[30] Sunlight penetration was also found to increase feelings of relaxation. Results of previous studies suggest that emotional states, such as those characterized by relaxation, promote and facilitate activities requiring intense concentration.[31]

The natural world can be motivating. One study reported a dramatic increase in student performance and retail sales when undergraduate school rooms and the campus store were exposed to abundant daylight.[32] Other research showed improved science[33] and other standardized test scores, reduced discipline and classroom management problems, increased engagement and enthusiasm for learning, and greater pride and ownership in accomplishments.[34] Research also indicates that the "greener" a child's play area, the less severe his or her attention deficit symptoms.[35]

Natural Remedies

Nature has powerful healing effects. Researchers documented that patients with a view of trees outside their hospital window had shorter hospital stays, fewer negative evaluative comments from nurses in their charts, and took fewer analgesic medications than patients who had undergone the same operation but had a view of a brick wall outside their window.[36] Having windows reduced the need for health care services.[37]

A prospective study of pain medication use was conducted in eighty-nine patients undergoing elective cervical and lumbar spinal surgery who were housed on either the "bright" or "dim" side of the same hospital unit. Patients staying on the bright side of the hospital unit were exposed to an average of 46% higher-intensity sunlight. Patients exposed to an increased intensity of sunlight perceived less stress, marginally less pain, took 22% less analgesic medication per hour, and had 21% lower pain medication costs. "At discharge, patients on the bright side reported significantly less stress and a marginal decrease in pain than the patients on the dim side."[38]

In the inner city, residents of buildings with more landscaping get to know their neighbors better, socialize with them more, have stronger feelings of community, and feel safer and better adjusted than residents who live in buildings with little or no vegetation.[39] Landscaping also reduced reports of property crime and violent crime in public housing developments.[40] Another study found that the levels of aggression and violence were significantly lower in areas near nature.[41] Residents are able to cope better with the demands of living in poverty; they feel more hopeful about the future, better able to manage their most important problems,[42] and find greater satisfaction with the neighborhood when nature plays a significant role in their environment.[43] The enjoyable scenery[44-45] and the presence of hills are also associated with increased physical activity. Older people who are blessed to live near green open spaces tend to live longer.[46]

Solar Power

Sunshine is a powerful promoter of health and well-being. It is the source of energy for the earth. It provides for the growth of green plants needed for our enjoyment and food, and enables plants to create oxygen out of carbon dioxide. Sunlight promotes positive thinking by increasing serotonin, an important "happiness" brain chemical.[47] Reduced serotonin levels are connected to attention deficit hyperactivity disorder (ADHD),[48] irritability,[49] depression,[50] aggression,[51] anxiety,[52] lack of concentration,[53] chronic pain,[54] fatigue,[55] nausea,[56] obsessive-compulsive disorder,[57] fibromyalgia,[58] arthritis,[59] chronic fatigue syndrome,[60] and heat intolerance.[61] Serotonin has also been connected with eating behavior and body weight.[62]

Another important brain chemical that sunlight impacts is melatonin. This brain chemical helps us to have a good night's sleep. Adequate sunlight during the daytime leads to higher levels in the brain at night and improves sleep as well as mood.

Sunlight has been shown to kill germs.[63] Therefore, the simple practice of opening the blinds can help you be healthier, so give your bedding a sunbath to get rid of germs.

Sunlight is the best source of vitamin D. In this way, it facilitates the building of strong bones. Sunlight efficiently converts a cholesterol metabolite into vitamin D. This "sunshine vitamin" is important for many reasons, including its impact on the immune system.[64] Several recently published studies offer some of the strongest evidence yet of the power of the "sunshine vitamin" (vitamin D) against multiple sclerosis (MS),[65] rheumatoid arthritis,[66] type 1 diabetes,[67] and other autoimmune diseases.[68] Research studies confirm the inverse relationship between sunlight and blood pressure.[69-70] There is also evidence that vitamin D protects against some cancers.[71-72]

Unfortunately, sunlight has gotten a bad reputation. Yes, excessive amounts of sunlight can increase the risk of skin cancer and cataracts, but moderate amounts can be extremely beneficial. Sun in high doses does increase skin cancer risk. It is commonly understood that basal and squamous cell skin cancers (the most common types) are linked to sunburn. These are treatable and do not usually result in death or serious damage, although it is best to avoid getting a sunburn.

Sunlight, in moderate amounts, can help prevent cancer. Adequate sunlight exposure appears to protect against melanoma,[73] the most deadly of skin cancers, presumably through the increased production of protective vitamin D. One study that looked at overall cancer rates in several states concluded that although frequent sun exposure statistically causes two thousand U.S. cancer fatalities per year, it also acts to prevent another 138,000 U.S. annual cancer deaths and could, possibly, prevent thirty thousand more deaths if Americans practiced regular, moderate sunning.[74] For the best health, *it is important to get adequate sunshine without getting sunburned.*

Electric Air

Fresh air is electrified. It is negatively charged in a good way, or "negatively ionized," because of the life-giving oxygen molecule. This negatively charged oxygen has many benefits. They include: an improved sense of well-being, increased rate and quality of growth in plants and animals, improved function in the lung's protective cilia, decreased anxiety through a tranquilizing and relaxing effect, lower body temperature, improved learning in mammals, lower resting heart rate, decreased severity of stomach ulcers, and decreased survival of bacteria and viruses in the air.[75-81] This last reason is why opening a window at night to circulate fresh air in your room is a wonderful health-promoting habit. Breathing fresh air cleans out stale air from the lungs that would otherwise promote disease; fresh air also increases brain function.

> *"Forests are the lungs of our land, purifying the air and giving fresh strength to our people. Truly they make the country more livable."*
>
> ~ FRANKLIN D. ROOSEVELT

Negatively charged air is destroyed by recirculation of air in buildings, tobacco smoke, city smog, and other pollutants. Researchers have been studying the harmful effects of polluted air, which depletes the negative ions. They have documented that the common pollutant, ozone, causes eye irritation, shortness of breath, coughs, decreased lung function, and decreased physical performance.[82-83] It is important to get clean, fresh air. The wonderful thing is that protective, negatively ionized air is found in abundance in natural outdoor environments, especially in areas such as the mountains, forests, by the sea, and waterfalls. So, get outdoors and into nature!

Water, Herbs, Charcoal, and Rover

The importance of water cannot be underestimated. Falling water, whether from a waterfall, a creek, or from a rain shower, gives off negative ions. Hydrotherapy can do amazing things to stimulate our immune system and help us feel good. A hot bath can help us sleep better. In a German study conducted in Bavaria, researchers explored the positive effects of water treatment on immunity. A hydrotherapy regimen was followed for some subjects. They experienced significant increases in lymphocytes, and a significant decrease in their cortisol (a stress hormone).[84] Water has a powerful potential for healing. Hydrotherapy is an alternative practice that is used to treat almost every condition, chronic or acute. Hydrotherapy applications include hot and cold compresses, wet sheet wraps and baths, and other procedures that use the body's own immune function to fight disease.

> *"In all things of nature there is something of the marvelous."*
>
> **~ ARISTOTLE**

Many people do not have enough fluid in their systems for the best health. Often people don't drink enough water and regularly consume drinks containing caffeine, which removes fluids through its effects on the kidneys (a diuretic or "water pill"). Dehydration makes the blood thicker and more likely to clot, increasing the risk of strokes and heart attacks. One epidemiologic study demonstrated that heart attack risk decreased about 50% in people who drank at least five cups of water a day.[85] This does not apply to sodas, fruit juice, and milk products. Water is necessary for waste removal through the kidneys. Chronic dehydration may cause damage to the kidneys as well. A glass of water can ease or eliminate a tension headache. Keeping our body hydrated helps to keep our system healthy.

If a person lives in a hot or dry environment or is doing a lot of heavy work or exercise that induces sweating, they will need more than the recommended eight glasses a day. Water is absorbed fastest when taken on an empty stomach. Food and sugar slow down the absorption; thus commercial sports drinks or even fruit juices are not as good as plain water. If a person is exercising at least a couple of hours after a meal, cool water will absorb faster than warm water. A well-hydrated athlete or worker has much better endurance than a dehydrated one.

Strong evidence points to the healing benefits of herbs and other remedies readily available in nature, things such as charcoal, garlic, golden seal, tea tree oil, and aloe vera. Some might say that charcoal is one of the best-kept secrets in the world of healing.

Charcoal has the amazing ability to attract other substances to its surface and hold them there through the process of adsorption. It can adsorb many times its own weight in gases, heavy metals, poisons, and other chemicals, effectively neutralizing them. Charcoal is used in hospitals throughout the United States. The form of charcoal used for medical purposes is called activated charcoal. It is harmless and safe for internal use if used for short periods of time. Charcoal actually has the ability to draw harmful inflammatory toxins through the skin and into a poultice or compress.[86]

Another example of a healing remedy found in nature is aloe vera, well known for helping burn victims.[87] Aloe vera can help in cancer treatment,[88] can increase the absorption of vitamins C and E,[89] and is potentially helpful for wounds, edema, and pain relief in diabetics.[90] It even improves the skin.[91]

Animals are another blessing from nature that enhance well-being in numerous ways; they give unconditional love, something we don't always get from family or friends. Pets add a social dimension. They encourage individuals to get out and be active. People reach out when pets are around. They love to touch animals and be touched in return, which is an incredible health-promoting activity. Just petting a dog stimulates the immune system positively – even for a person who doesn't like dogs. Watching fish helps to calm the spirit and decreases blood pressure. The list could go on. Our relationships with animals and the benefits we gain are covered in the Interpersonal Relationships seminar.

> *"The ultimate test of man's conscience may be his willingness to sacrifice something today for future generations whose words of thanks will not be heard."*
>
> ~ GAYLORD NELSON

Environmental Issues

No question, our environment gives us peace, tranquility, food, shelter, and health. Doesn't it make you want to give back? Actually, when we give back we give to ourselves as well. Some people call it "going green." Others see it as the fight against global warming. Either way, giving back is definitely the right thing to do for future generations.

At creation, humans were appointed to be stewards of the earth – a big responsibility. The great news is that we can make a tremendous difference in the space around us. Even little things add up and make a big impact on us, our world, and on future generations. Every action we take that impacts our environment impacts our health and well-being; it impacts our outlook, it impacts how we feel about ourselves and others around us; and it can even impact us for eternity.

What are some ways to give back? An important first step is to think about everything we do in light of how it impacts our environment. Ask yourself next time you make a purchase, does this help support us and our planet for future generations? Is this product healthy for me, for my children, my yard, my home, my community, and my world?

"Between 1960 and 2007 the amount of waste each person created almost doubled from 2.7 to 4.6 pounds per day. The most effective way to stop this trend is to prevent waste in the first place. Waste prevention, also known as 'source reduction,' is the practice of designing, manufacturing, purchasing, or using materials (such as products and packaging) in ways that reduce the amount of toxicity or trash created. Reusing items is another way to stop waste at the source because it delays or avoids that item's entry into the waste collection and disposal system."[92]

A powerful perspective to adopt as a life value would be, "I will reduce, reuse, recycle, and repurchase, because it is the right thing to do."

ENVIRONMENT

REINFORCE THE MESSAGE

SKILL BUILDERS

Choose the Skill Builders below that you would like to experience in your own life, then write a response on how they impacted you. Last, write further actions, if any, that you would like to take as a result of doing the Skill Builders.

 Skill Builder 1 | **Clean Up or Organize Something in Your Environment**

Choose something in your environment that you want to clean up or organize such as a closet, drawer, etc. Then make a plan to keep it neat. For example: clean up and organize your pantry, then decide to put things away in a more orderly fashion to stay organized.

WHAT DID YOU CHOOSE TO DO:

....
....
....
....
....

DESCRIBE HOW THIS IMPACTED YOU:

....
....
....

FURTHER ACTION:

....
....
....

> *"There is no way in which to understand the world without first detecting it through the radar-net of our senses."*
> **~ DIANE ACKERMAN**

ENVIRONMENT

 Skill Builder 2 | **Choose a Room to Clean Each Day**

In order to keep your personal space cleaner, for the next week try spending five to ten minutes daily cleaning a chosen room. Start with jobs that cover the most area the fastest (vacuum, mop, or dust). Begin by clearing clutter from the larger and more obvious areas (kitchen table, living room coffee table, sofa, etc.). Start in the areas of your home that are the most lived in and then work toward the smaller, less used areas.

Some other great tips to live by are:

- Put things "back" where they belong (don't wait until tomorrow).

- Put away one out-of-place item each time you leave a room and then gradually add to the list until it becomes a habit.

- Make the room a space to be proud of. Find or add something in each room that makes it unique and special to you (add a plant, a photograph, painting, special pillows, etc.).

WHAT DID YOU CHOOSE TO DO:

....
....
....
....

DESCRIBE HOW THIS IMPACTED YOU:

....
....

FURTHER ACTION:

....
....
....

Skill Builder 3 | Listen to Music to Relax and Enhance Your Environment

Buy and listen to a new music CD that helps you relax or enhances your environment.

WHAT DID YOU CHOOSE TO DO:

....
....
....
....
....

DESCRIBE HOW THIS IMPACTED YOU:

....
....
....

FURTHER ACTION:

....
....
....

Skill Builder 4 | Replace Your Light Bulbs with Fluorescent Light Bulbs

WHAT DID YOU CHOOSE TO DO:

....
....
....
....
....

DESCRIBE HOW THIS IMPACTED YOU:

....
....
....

FURTHER ACTION:

....
....
....

Obtain a scent (either in the form of a candle or essential oil) that is relaxing, stimulating, invigorating, etc. Be sure to get a natural scent that will not hurt you, your kids, pets, or the environment. For example, the wonderful smells of some candles can come from chemicals that are not health promoting.

WHAT DID YOU CHOOSE TO DO:

....
....
....
....

DESCRIBE HOW THIS IMPACTED YOU:

....
....
....

FURTHER ACTION:

....
....
....

Go somewhere that you don't typically go but that has natural beauty. Or maybe go canoeing or camping for the weekend. Soak in the scenery; enjoy the quiet and ambience. You will be blessed by the fresh air, sunlight, and beauty.

ENVIRONMENT

WHAT DID YOU CHOOSE TO DO:
....
....
....
....
....

DESCRIBE HOW THIS IMPACTED YOU:
....
....
....

FURTHER ACTION:
....
....
....
....

> *"When I admire the wonder of a sunset or the beauty of the moon, my soul expands in worship of the Creator."*
>
> **~ MAHATMA GANDHI**

Enjoy a refreshing hot and cold shower. Shower for three minutes in hot water, then thirty seconds in cold. This will probably feel cold the first round. Switch back to the hot for another three minutes. Then another thirty seconds of cold. By now the cold water should start feeling refreshing and stimulating. The reality is that the water is doing a wonderful job stimulating your circulation and immune system. You can continue for another round if you want. Always end with the thirty seconds of cold to close the pores. To benefit your immune system, don't get chilled.

This treatment is helpful and benefits your immune system if you do it every day. You can also do it for great results when you start feeling you are coming down with an illness, or are already sick. The hot and cold shower may feel like it "takes it out" of you, but in reality it is a powerful and natural way to help your body avoid illness and even recover from it.

ENVIRONMENT

WHAT DID YOU CHOOSE TO DO:

....

....

....

....

DESCRIBE HOW THIS IMPACTED YOU:

....

....

....

FURTHER ACTION:

....

....

....

"Music speaks what cannot be expressed,
soothes the mind and gives it rest,
heals the heart and makes it whole,
flows from heaven to the soul."
~ AUTHOR UNKNOWN

When you feel that you are coming down with an illness or have an injury that does not require immediate medical care, try some of the natural remedies and other immune-boosting tools listed below. Better yet, use nature to keep you from getting sick or help you recover quickly.

(You may choose to put a check mark on the lines provided if you choose to use several.)

___ Get into the sunlight and fresh air for a great boost to your body. Make sure to breathe deeply to get the full benefit of the fresh air.

___ Get light or moderate exercise in the fresh air and sunshine.

___ Do strength training exercises – research shows this stimulates the immune system.

___ Get extra rest or sleep.

___ Use stress-relieving techniques, and maybe talk about your stress with someone you trust, or take time to resolve the stressful situation. Remember, stress promotes sickness and compromises the immune system.

___ "Give it to the Lord" through prayer and meditation, or maybe spend time in Bible study to find solutions to your challenges. Pray for good health and God's healing. Always remember to pray for God's blessing on the simple, natural remedies He has given.

___ Use food to heal and boost your immune system. Take time to research what types of foods might be helpful, such as garlic. When you are getting sick, choose to eliminate food, such as sugar, from your diet that compromises your immune system.

___ Practice balance in all activities of life.

___ Use a natural herbal ointment to promote healing if you have a simple cut or abrasion. Also consider using fresh aloe vera gel when you have a minor burn.

___ Drink extra water to help flush out the body. And try some form of hydrotherapy such as a hot and cold shower.

___ Use steam with a natural remedy, for example eucalyptus oil, to help clean out your sinuses. Take time to research the benefits of other essential oils and consider trying them.

___ Focus your mind on positive things. Dwell on the good and beautiful. Be grateful and take time to express that gratitude; this is a positive influence on your immune system.

___ Appreciate the beauty of nature to benefit your mind, body, and soul.

___ Connect with animals to boost your immune system. Pet and/or hold your dog, cat, or other animal.

___ Connect with loved ones. Positive touch makes a difference. Also, getting a massage is a wonderful way to get healthy touch and increase circulation. Last, consider service to others. These connections will give your immune system, mind, and soul a powerful boost.

WHAT DID YOU CHOOSE TO DO:

....
....
....
....
....

DESCRIBE HOW THIS IMPACTED YOU:

....
....

FURTHER ACTION:

....
....
....

TIPS FOR SUCCESS

POWER TIPS: HOW TO IMPROVE YOUR ENVIRONMENT

Think about everything you do in light of how it impacts your environment and yourself. Ask – is this action or product healthy for me, my children, home, yard, community, and for my world?

Make your home an oasis by surrounding yourself with things that nurture your sight, hearing, smell, touch, and taste in a positive manner.

- **Sight** – Make the sights in and around your home appealing and peaceful. Organize your home and life so that it is free of clutter, which promotes renewed energy and fulfillment. Bring the blessings of nature into your home through plants, photos, paintings, and windows that showcase the beauty of nature.

- **Hearing** – Make the words spoken and sounds heard health promoting. May words of love be spoken in compassionate tones. May peace-promoting music and sounds surround you.

- **Smell** – Have flowers or other objects that release pleasant fragrances. Sometimes just burning a scented candle creates a positive atmosphere. However subtle, the impact can be beneficial.

- **Touch** – Appropriate, loving touch can increase your well-being.

Take in the beauty and healing power of nature. Through a window, on a walk with the love of your life, your children, friends, or the dog, enjoy nature during a meeting outdoors, or when sitting outside talking with friends. The soothing colors, fresh air, and sunshine of nature will make you feel better.

Always be aware of your environment. Is it too dark, hot, cold, noisy, etc? Even the small things can enhance or detract from your health and well-being. Know yourself. Take time to learn what things in the environment lift you up or depress you.

Reduce, reuse, and recycle. Remember, small changes make big impacts!

Choose to be energy efficient. Buy "green power," install fluorescent bulbs, adjust the thermostat, and when buying a new appliance, buy an energy-efficient one.

Buy with the environment and your health and well-being in mind. Buy organic. Buy recycled items that are recyclable or gently used, and buy local produce.

Enjoy the blessings of the natural world today.

- **Sunlight** – Enjoy a walk in the sunshine, or relax in the sun; open the drapes and let the sunshine in for a cleansing lift.

- **Fresh Air** – Get physical activity in the fresh air; go outside and take ten deep breaths while relaxing; open the windows where appropriate to circulate fresh air; increase productivity, schedule a walking brainstorming session or any other type of meeting outside.

- **Water** – Enjoy a relaxing bubble bath with scented candles, enjoy a refreshing hot and cold shower – then rest for a boost in your immune system. Visit a waterfall and enjoy its refreshing beauty.

- **Natural Remedies** – Try using simple environmental or healing activities when treating a common ailment before turning to a drug. Fresh air, sunshine, and water can all be healing forces in our lives.

- **Animals** – Take time to watch your fish, pet your cat, take your dog for a walk, or see wild animals at a zoo.

KNOW WHAT PRODUCTS ARE POISONOUS, AND KNOW WHERE THEY ARE

This information is taken directly from Poison Control Center information pamphlets

No list is ever complete. When in doubt, treat it as a poison!

Kitchen	Living Room	Bedroom
Automatic dishwasher products, cleaning agents, oven cleaner, drain cleaner, waxes and polishes, vanilla extracts, spray oils, liquor	Plants (dieffenbachia, philodendron, some types of ivy and fern), cleaning solutions for stereo and video, cigarettes and butts, liquor	Perfume, nail polish and remover, birth control pills, other medications, crafts and hobby supplies

Bathroom	Basement/Garage/Storage Room	Laundry Room
First-aid solutions and creams, toilet cleaners and drain openers, aftershaves, colognes, cosmetics, rubbing alcohol, hair products, cleaning and polishing agents	Weed killer, insecticides, charcoal lighter, gasoline and motor oil, antifreeze, windshield washer fluid, fertilizer, wood treatments, lye, mothballs, paints, lacquers and varnishes, turpentine and paint thinners	Bleach, detergents, fabric softeners, spot removers, cleaning agents, fabric dyes

NATURAL AIR CLEANERS – FRIENDLY CLEAN TOXIC EATERS[93]

Chemicals such as formaldehyde, benzene, and carbon monoxide are harmful. The good news is that plants can thrive on them while also removing them from the air. Plants that top the clean-air list include peace lily, bamboo palm, English ivy, mums, and gerbera daisies, all of which are both easy to find and easy to care for, so even if you don't have a green thumb, you can still have a green home or office.

Here is a great resource for improving air quality in your home or office:
How to Grow Fresh Air: 50 House Plants that Purify Your Home or Office by B. C. Wolverton

A number of plants appear helpful in removing specific gases or chemical smells, absorbing odors or indoor air pollution. They include: spider plant, aloe vera, Chinese evergreen, elephant ear philodendron, peace lily, mother-in-law's tongue, golden pothos, ficus, English ivy, bamboo palm, gerbera daisy, dieffenbachia, Janet Craig (corn plant), pot mums, mass cane, azaleas, and banana.

The following table identifies some toxic chemicals that plants can positively affect:

Toxic Chemicals	Source	Plant
Formaldehyde	Cleaning compounds, air fresheners, hair products, cosmetics, deodorants, some detergents, disinfectants, grocery bags, facial tissue, paper towels, crease-proof, wrinkle-proof, flame-retardant fabrics, carpet backing, cigarette smoke, natural gas, particle board, plywood, furnishings, adhesives	Spider plant, corn plant, pot mum, English ivy, gerbera daisy, golden pothos, azalea, ficus, aloe vera, philodendron, bamboo palm
Benzene	Detergents, pharmaceuticals, plastics, rubber, dyes, inks, paints, tobacco, smoke, synthetic fibers, cleaning solutions, deodorizers, degreasers, spot removers, furniture polish, aerosol, propellants, air fresheners, glue, fungicides	English ivy, Janet Craig, pot mum, gerbera daisy, peace lily, golden pothos
Trichlorethylene	Dry cleaning solvents, metal degreasers, inks, paints, lacquers, varnishes, adhesives	Gerbera daisy, pot mum, peace lily, English ivy, Warneckii dracaena
Toluene	Cleaning products, degreasers, deodorizers, glue, paint, petroleum products, plastics, solvent, polyethylene, carpets	Chinese evergreen
Fumes	Oil, gas, carbon monoxide	Spider plant, English ivy, dracaena

Please Note:
Indoor air pollution experts recommend one plant per every one hundred square feet. Effectiveness rating is 90%.

Although plants can be helpful in removing toxic chemicals from your home, the most effective means to improve and maintain healthy indoor air is to remove the source of contamination.

SMALL GROUP DISCUSSIONS

Directions: Review the discussion questions and choose one you would like to discuss first. Proceed through the rest of the questions as time allows.

1. Consider the following statement: "We are all stewards of this earth." Would you agree with this statement? What does it mean? How can we improve our stewardship? How can we better care for our planet?

   ....

   ....

2. At creation God blessed us with a beautiful environment that is healing, invigorating, and soothing. Look up the following texts/stories. What does the Bible teach us about how we are connected to creation? What can we learn from it (lessons from nature)? (See biblical references on next page.)

   A. Genesis 1:26–28   **B.** Job 12:7–8   **C.** Matthew 13:31–33   **D.** Psalm 92:12

   ....

   ....

3. Share and discuss your favorite ways to use your environment to de-stress and energize you. Be specific and list the how-tos within the group.

   ....

   ....

4. Share your favorite "green" tips:

   ....

   ....

5. Review the main points of the video. Was there anything that surprised you? Why? Were you inspired or convicted by anything that was said? Explain.

   ....

   ....

6. What are some things (from the video) that you may want to incorporate in your home/lifestyle routine?

   ....

   ....

Bible references for discussion point number 2 on previous page.

Bible verses teach us to care for and be responsible stewards of the earth.

A. Genesis 1:26–28

26-28 "God spoke: 'Let us make human beings in our image, make them reflecting our nature so they can be responsible for the fish in the sea, the birds in the air, the cattle, and, yes, Earth itself, and every animal that moves on the face of Earth.' God created human beings; He created them godlike, Reflecting God's nature. He created them male and female. God blessed them: 'Prosper! Reproduce! Fill Earth! Take charge! Be responsible for fish in the sea and birds in the air, for every living thing that moves on the face of Earth.'"

B. Job 12:7–8

7 "But now ask the beasts, and let them teach you; and the birds of the heavens, and let them tell you. 8 Or speak to the earth, and let it teach you; And let the fish of the sea declare to you."

C. Matthew 13:31–33

31 "He presented another parable to them, saying, 'The kingdom of heaven is like a mustard seed, which a man took and sowed in his field; 32 and this is smaller than all other seeds, but when it is full grown, it is larger than the garden plants and becomes a tree, so that the birds of the air come and nest in its branches.'"

D. Psalm 92:12

12 "The righteous man will flourish like the palm tree, He will grow like a cedar in Lebanon."

ADDITIONAL RESOURCES

Books:

The Healing Power of Pets, by Dr. Marty Becker

The Mozart Effect: Tapping the Power of Music to Heal the Body, Strengthen the Mind, and Unlock the Creative Spirit, by Don Campbell

Raising Baby Green: The Earth-Friendly Guide to Pregnancy, Childbirth, and Baby Care, by Alan Greene, Jeanette Pavini, and Theresa Foy DiGeronimo

Organic Baby: Simple Steps for Healthy Living, by Kimberly Rider

The Green Pharmacy: New Discoveries in Herbal Remedies for Common Diseases and Conditions From the World's Foremost Authority on Healing Herbs, by James A. Duke, Ph.D.

Books on gardening

Books on cleaning up the "clutter" in your life

Websites:

lowimpactliving.com
(Find great green products and local service providers, choose the best green projects for your life, learn more about global warming and environmental impacts, calculate your environmental impact and learn how to lower it)

kiwimagonline.com (Great resource for growing families the natural and organic way)

afhh.org
(This is the website of The Alliance for Healthy Homes. It is a national, nonprofit, public interest organization working to prevent and eliminate hazards in our homes that harm the health of children, families, and other residents)

healthyhome.com (Green building for life – products for building and supplying a green home)

homebasics.ca (Resources for your home and life)

realsimple.com (*Real Simple* magazine is great for a lot of topics on organizing, meals, cleaning, and life skills and offers some free online articles)

Other Resources:

Aromatherapy "kit"

Hydrotherapy "kit" – supplies used in hydrotherapy

CD of soothing/calming music

CD of nature sounds

Candles (scented and unscented)

Songs That Inspire a Healthy Environment:

The Basics of Life (4Him – Contemporary Christian Group)

Be Careful Little Hands (Children's Song)

For the Beauty of the Earth (Hymn)

We Are His Hands (Youth or Children's Song)

Somebody Bigger Than You and I (Gospel)

*"Music is a moral law.
It gives soul to the universe, wings to the mind,
flight to the imagination, and charm and
gaiety to life and to everything."*
~ PLATO

REFERENCES

1. Ryan, Terri Jo. "Reducing Workplace Clutter Might Just Lead to that Promotion." *Seattle Post-Intelligencer*. http://seattlepi.nwsource.com/business/236527_cleandesk15.html. Retrieved Feb. 14, 2008.

2. Zuckerman D, Zuckerman B. "Television's Impact on Children." *Pediatrics* February 1985 75 (2): 233.

3. Johnston W, Davey G. "The Psychological Impact of Negative TV News Bulletins: The Catastrophizing of Personal Worries." *British Journal of Psychology* 1997 88: 85–89.

4. Peper E as cited in Mander J. *Four Arguments for the Elimination of Television*. New York: Quill, 1977, 211.

5. Lumeng J, Rahnama S, et al. "Television Exposure and Overweight Risk in Preschoolers." *Archives of Pediatrics & Adolescent Medicine* 2006 160: 417–422.

6. Weber R, Ritterfeld U, Mathiak K. "Does Playing Violent Video Games Induce Aggression? Empirical Evidence of a Functional Magnetic Resonance Imaging Study." *Media Psychology* 2006 8: 39–60.

7. Jacobs K, Suess J. "Effects of Four Psychological Primary Colors on Anxiety State." *Perceptual and Motor Skills* 1975 41: 207–210.

8. Wexner B. "The Degree to Which Colors (Hues) Are Associated with Mood-Tones." *The Journal of Applied Psychology* 1954 38(6): 432–435.

9. Evans G, Bullinger M, et al. "Chronic Noise Exposure And Physiology Response: A Prospective Study of Children Living Under Environmental Stress." *American Psychological Society* January 1998 9(1): 75–77.

10. Evans G, Maxwell L. "Chronic Noise Exposure and Reading Deficits: The Mediating Effects of Language Acquisition." *Environment & Behavior* Sep 97 29(5): 638–656.

11. Evans G, Johnson D. "Stress and Open-Office Noise." *Journal of Applied Psychology* 2000 85(5): 779–783.

12. Van Kempen E, Kruize H, et al. "The Association Between Noise Exposure and Blood Pressure and Ischemic Heart Disease: A Meta-analysis." *JSTOR: Environmental Health Perspectives* Mar. 2002 110(3): 307–317.

13. Ravin K. "Smells Like Sales" *Los Angeles Times*, Aug. 20, 2007, in print edition F-1. Retrieved Jan. 30, 2009.

14. Lindstrom M. "Broad Sensory Branding." *Journal of Product & Brand Management* 2005 14(2): 84–87.

15. Hirsch A. "Effects of Ambient Odors on Slot Machine Usage in a Las Vegas Casino." *Psychology and Marketing* Oct.1995 12(7): 585–94.

16. Brumfield R, Goldney J, Gunning S. *Whiff! The Revolution of Scent Communication in the Information Age.* First Quimby Press, 2008, 33.

17. Rotton J, Barry T, et al. "The Air Pollution Experience and Physical Aggression." *Journal of Applied Social Psychology* 1979 9: 397–412.

REFERENCES

18. Redd W, Manne S, et al. "Fragrance Administration to Reduce Anxiety During MR Imaging." *Journal of Magnetic Resonance Imaging* July August 1994 4(4): 623–626.

19. NASA report Interior Landscape Plants for Indoor Air Pollution Abatement, September 15, 1989, by Dr. B.C. Wolverton, Anne Johnson, and Keith Bounds, National Aeronautics and Space Administration, John C. Stennis Space Center, Stennis Space Center, MS 39529-6000. http://ntrs.nasa.go/archive/nasa/casi.ntrs.nasa.gov.

20. Centers for Disease Control and Prevention and U.S. Department of Housing and Urban Development. Healthy Housing Reference Manual. Atlanta: US Department of Health and Human Services; 2006. Chpt. 5: Indoor Air Pollutants and Toxic Materials: 5-1. http://www.cdc.gov/nceh/publications/books/housing/2006_HHM_FINAL_chapter_05.pdf. Retrieved 4/10/09.

21. U.S. Environmental Protection Agency (U.S. EPA). "An Introduction to Indoor Air Quality." pg 1. http://www.epa.gov/iaq/voc.html. Retrieved 4/10/09.

22. U.S. Environmental Protection Agency (U.S. EPA). 1987. Unfinished Business: A Comparative Assessment of Environmental Problems. Overview Report. Washington DC: U.S. Environmental Protection Agency, 42.

23. Centers for Disease Control and Prevention and U.S. Department of Housing and Urban Development. Healthy Housing Reference Manual. Atlanta: US Department of Health and Human Services; 2006. Chpt. 5: Indoor Air Pollutants and Toxic Materials: 5-1. http://www.cdc.gov/nceh/publications/books/housing/2006_HHM_FINAL_chapter_05.pdf. Retrieved 4/10/09.

24. Grewen K, Girdler S, et al. "Effects of Partner Support on Resting Oxytocin, Cortisol, Norepinephrine, and Blood Pressure Before and After Warm Partner Contact." *Psychosomatic Medicine* 67: 531–538. (2005).

25. Halliday J. *Psychosocial Medicine: A Study of the Sick Society.* William Heinemann Medical Books Ltd. 1949, 93–94.

26. Lu C, Toepel K, et al. "Organic Diets Significantly Lower Children's Dietary Exposure to Organophosphorus Pesticides." *Environmental Health Perspectives* 2006 114: 260–263.

27. Kaplan R. "The Psychological Benefits of Nearby Nature." In D. Relf (Ed.) *The Role of Horticulture in Human Well Being and Social Development: A National Symposium*. Portland, OR: Timber Press, 1992, 128, 130.

28. Kaplan S. "The Restorative Environment: Nature and Human Experience." In D. Relf (Ed.) *The Role of Horticulture in Human Well Being and Social Development: A National Symposium*. Portland, OR: Timber Press, 1992, 134.

29. Ulrich R, Simons R, et al. "Stress Recovery During Exposure to Natural and Urban Environments." *Journal of Environmental Psychology* 1991 11: 201–230.

30. Leather P, Pygras M, Beale D, Lawrence C. "Windows in the Workplace: Sunlight, View, and Occupational Stress." *Environment and Behavior* 1998 30: 739–762.

REFERENCES

ENVIRONMENT

31. Boubekri M, Hulliv R, Boyer L. "Impact of Window Size and Sunlight Penetration of Office Workers' Mood and Satisfaction: A Novel Way of Assessing Sunlight." *Environment and Behavior* 1991 23: 474–493.

32. Heschong L. "Daylighting in Schools: Investigation into Relationship Between Daylighting and Human Performance." A Report to Pacific Gas and Electric Company, CA Board for Energy Efficiency. 1999.

33. "Effects of Outdoor Education Programs for Children in California." American Institutes for Research: Palo Alto, CA: 2005. http://www.air.org/news/documents/Outdoorschoolreport.pdf. Retrieved 2/1/09.

34. Lieberman G, Hoody L. "Closing the Achievement Gap: Using the Environment as an Integrating Context for Learning." State Education and Environment Roundtable 1998: 1–22.

35. Taylor A, Kuo F, et al. "Coping with ADD: The Surprising Connection to Green Play Settings." *Environment and Behavior* 2001 33(1): 54–77.

36. Ulrich R. "View Through a Window May Influence Recovery From Surgery." *Science* April 27, 1984 224: 420–422.

37. Moore E. "A Prison Environment's Effect on Health Care Service Demands." *Journal of Environmental Systems* 1981 11(2): 17–34.

38. Walch J, Rabin B, et al. "The Effect of Sunlight on Postoperative Analgesic Medication Use: A Prospective Study of Patients Undergoing Spinal Surgery." *Psychosomatic Medicine* 2005 67: 156–163.

39. Kuo F, Sullivan F, et al. "Nice to See You, How Trees Build a Neighborhood," condensed from "Fertile Ground for Community: Inner-City Neighborhood Common Spaces." *American Journal of Community Psychology* 1998 26(6): 823–851.

40. Kuo F, Sullivan W. "Environment and Crime in the Inner City: Does Vegetation Reduce Crime?" *Environment and Behavior* 2001 33(3): 343–367.

41. Kuo F, Sullivan W. "Aggression and Violence in the Inner City, Impacts of Environment via Mental Fatigue." *Environment and Behavior* 2001 33(4): 543–571.

42. Kuo F. "Coping with Poverty: Impacts of Environment and Attention in the Inner City." *Environment and Behavior* 2001 33(1): 5–34.

43. Kaplan R. "The Role of Nature in the Urban Context." In I. Altman & J. F. Wohlwill (Eds.), *Behavior and the Natural Environment*, New York: Plenum, 1983, 127–162.

44. King A, Castro C, et al. "Personal and Environmental Factors Associated with Physical Inactivity Among Different Racial-Ethnic Groups of US Middle-Aged and Older-Aged Women." *Health Psychology* 2000 19: 354–364.

45. Humpel N, Owen N, et al. "Environmental Factors Associated with Adults' Participation in Physical Activity: A Review." *American Journal of Preventive Medicine* 2002 22: 188–199.

46. Takano T, Nakamura K, et al. "Urban Residential Environments and Senior Citizens' Longevity in Megacity Areas: the Importance of Walkable Green Spaces." *Journal of Epidemiology and Community Health* 2002 56: 913–918.

47. Lambert G, Reid C, et al. "Effect of Sunlight and Season on Serotonin Turnover in the Brain." *The Lancet* Dec. 7, 2002 360: 1840–1842.

48. Kent L, Doerry U, et al. "Evidence that Variation at the Serotonin Transporter Gene Influences Susceptibility to Attention Deficit Hyperactivity Disorder (ADHD): Analysis and Pooled Analysis." *Molecular Psychiatry* 2002 7: 908–912.

49. Russo S, et al. "Irritability Rather Than Depression During Interferon Treatment is Linked to Increased Tryptophan Catabolism." *Psychosomatic Medicine* 2005 67: 773–777.

50. Baldwin D, Rudge S. "The Role of Serotonin in Depression and Anxiety." *International Clinical Psychopharmacology* Jan 1995 9 Suppl. 4: 41–5.

51. Coccaro E, et al. "Central Serotonin Activity and Aggression: Inverse Relationship with Prolactin Response to d-Fenfluramine but not CSF 5-HIAA Concentration, in Human Subjects." *American Journal of Psychiatry* 1997 154: 1430–1435.

52. Baldwin D, Rudge S "The Role of Serotonin in Depression and Anxiety." *International Clinical Psychopharmacology* Jan 1995 9 Suppl. 4: 41–5.

53. Warner J. "Seasonal Depression Tied to Serotonin." *WebMD Health News* Sept, 19 2007. http://www.webmd.com/mental-health/news/20070919/seasonal-depression-tied-to-serotonin. Retrieved 4/9/09.

54. Sommer C. "Serotonin in Pain and Analgesia." 2004 *Molecular Neurobiology* 30: 117–125.

55. Davis J, Alderson N, Welsh R. "Serotonin and Central Nervous System Fatigue: Nutritional Considerations." *American Journal of Clinical Nutrition* 2000 (suppl) 5732–85.

56. Grundy D. "5-HT System in the Gut: Roles in the Regulation of Visceral Sensitivity and Motor Functions." *European Review for Medical and Pharmacological Sciences* 2008 12 Suppl 1: 63–67.

57. Pigott T, Seay S. "A Review of the Efficacy of Selective Serotonin Reuptake Inhibitors in Obsessive-Compulsive Disorder." *Journal of Clinical Psychiatry* 1999 60(2): 101–106.

58. Juhl J. "Fibromyalgia and the Serotonin Pathway." *Alternative Medicine Review* 1998 3(5): 367–375.

59. Kling A, Rantapaa S, Stenlund H, Mjorndal T. "Decreased Density of Serotonin 5-HT2A Receptors in Rheumatoid Arthritis." *Annals of the Rheumatic Diseases* Jun 2006 65(6): 816–9.

60. Sharpe M, Hawton K, Clements A. "Increased Brain Serotonin Function in Men with Chronic Fatigue Syndrome." *BMJ* July 19, 1997 315: 164–165.

61. Bridge M, Weller A, Rayson M, Jones D. "Responses to Exercise in the Heat Related to Measures of Hypothalamic Serotonergic and Dopaminergic Function." *European Journal of Applied Physiology* 2003 89: 451–459.

62. Leibowitz S. "Hypothalamic Serotonin in Control of Eating Behavior, Meal Size, and Body Weight." *Biological Psychiatry* 44(9): 851–864.

63. Lidwell O, Lowbury E. "The Survival of Bacteria in Dust III: The Effect of Light on the Survival of Bacteria in Dust." *The Journal of Hygiene* 48(1): 28–37.

REFERENCES

64. Sigmundsdottir H, Pan J, et al. "DCs Metabolize Sunlight-Induced Vitamin D3 to 'Program' T Cell Attraction to the Epidermal Chemokine CCL27." *Nature Immunology* 2007 8: 285–293.

65. Munger K, Levin L, et al. "Serum 25-Hydroxyvitamin D Levels and Risk of Multiple Sclerosis." *Journal of the American Medical Association* 2006 296(23): 2832–2838.

66. Merlino L, et al. "Vitamin D Intake is Inversely Associated with Rheumatoid Arthritis: Results from the Iowa Women's Health Study." *Arthritis & Rheumatism* Jan. 2004 50(1): 72–7.

67. Hypponen E, Laara E, et al. "Intake of Vitamin D and Risk of Type 1 Diabetes: a Birth-Cohort Study." *The Lancet* 2001 358: 1500–3.

68. Holick M. "Vitamin D Deficiency." *New England Journal of Medicine* July 19, 2007 357(3): 266–277.

69. Fiori G, Facchini F, et al. "Relationships Between Blood Pressure, Anthropometric Characteristics and Blood Lipids in High- and Low-Altitude Populations from Central Asia." *Annals of Human Biology* 2000 27: 19–28.

70. Rostand S. "Ultraviolet Light May Contribute to Geographic and Racial Blood Pressure Differences." *Hypertension* 1997 30: 150–156.

71. Giovannucci E, Liu Y, Willett W. "Cancer Incidence and Mortality and Vitamin D in Black and White Male Health Professionals." Cancer Epidemiology Biomarkers & Prevention. Dec. 2006 15: 2467–2472.

72. Garland C, Comstock G, et al. "25-Hydroxy-Vitamin D and Colon Cancer: Eight-Year Prospective Study." *The Lancet* Nov 18, 1989 2(8673): 1176–8.

73. Berwick M. "Sun Exposure Mortality from Melanoma." *Journal of the National Cancer Institute* 2005 97: 195–9.

74. Ainsleigh H. "Beneficial Effects of Sun Exposure on Cancer Mortality." *Prevention Medicine* January 1993 22(1): 132–140.

75. Baldwin B. "Why is Fresh Air Fresh?" *The Journal of Health and Healing* 11(4): 26–27.

76. Duffee R, Koontz R. "Behavioral Effects of Ionized Air on Rats." *Psychophysiology* April 1965 1(4): 347–359.

77. Jordan J, Sokoloff B. "Air Ionization, Age and Maze Learning of Rats." *Journal of Gerontology* 1959 14: 344–348.

78. Reilly T, Stevenson I. "An Investigation of The Effects of Negative Air Ions on Responses to Submaximal Exercise at Different Times of The Day." *Journal of Human Ergology*. (Tokyo) June 1993 22(1): 1–9.

79. Mitchell B, King D. "Effect of Negative Ionization on Airborne Transmission of Newcastle Disease Virus." *Avian Diseases* October 1994 38(4): 752–732.

80. Giannini A, Jones B, et al. "Reversibility of Serotonin Irritation Syndrome with Atmospheric Anions." *Journal of Clinical Psychiatry* March 1986 47(3): 141–143.

81. Gabbay J, Bergerson O, et al. "Effect of Ionization on Microbial Air Pollution in the Dental Clinic." *Environmental Research* June 1990 52(1): 99–106.

REFERENCES

82. Linder J, Herren D, et al. "Effect of Ozone on Physical Performance Capacity." *Soz Praventivmed* 1987 32(4–5): 251–252.

83. Neher J, Keonig J. "Health Effects of Outdoor Pollution." *American Family Physician* May 1, 1994 49(6): 1397–1404, 1407–1408.

84. Bieger W, Penz M, et al. "Immunology of the Hardening Reaction Following Hydrotherapy." *Physikalische Medizin Rehabilitationsmedizin Kurortmedizin* (Germany), 1988. [DR. W.P. Bieger, Medizinisch-Immunologische Laboratorien, Mittererstrasse 3,80336 munchen, Germany].

85. Chan J, Knutsen S, et al. "Water, Other Fluids, and Fatal Coronary Heart Disease: The Adventist Health Study." *American Journal of Epidemiology* 2002 155(9): 827–33.

86. Becket R, Coombs T. "Charcoal Cloth and Malodorous Wounds." *The Lancet* September 13, 1980 316(8194): 594.

87. Mayo Clinic Staff, "Aloe (Aloe vera)". Natural Standard® Patient Monograph, Copyright © 2009 (www.naturalstandard.com). http://www.mayoclinic.com/health/aloe-vera/NS_patient-Aloe. Retrieved 4/13/09.

88. Lissoni P, Giani L, et al. "Biotherapy with The Pineal Immunomodulating Hormone Melatonin Versus Melatonin Plus Aloe Vera in Untreatable Advanced Solid Neoplasms." *Nature Immunology* 1998 16(1): 27–33.

89. Vinson J, Kharrat H, et al. "Effect of Aloe Vera Preparations on the Human Bioavailability of Vitamins C and E." *Phytomedicine* 2005 12(10): 760–765.

90. Reynolds T, Dweck A. "Aloe Vera Leaf Gel: A Review Update." *Journal of Ethnopharmacology* Dec. 1999 68(1–3): 3–37.

91. Danhof I, McAnally B, et al. "Stabilized Aloe Vera: Effect on Human Skin Cells." *Drug and Cosmetic Industry* August 1983 52–54, 105–106.

92. http://www.epa.gov/osw/conserve/rrr/reduce.htm (HTML). Retrieved Feb. 1, 2009.

93. Woods J. *Indoor Air Pollution...the Silent Killer!* Sunset Printing (1999).

NOTES

NOTES

ACTIVITY

....

unlock your reservoir of vitality

creation® HEALTH

CONTENTS

MAKE IT WORK

Further Explanation of the DVD Topics

> *"No one can avoid aging, but aging productively is something else."*
>
> ~ KATHARINE GRAHAM

THE BIG PICTURE

Activity includes both mental and physical movement and development. The mind and the body are intimately connected. A fit mind promotes a fit body, and a fit body promotes a fit mind. In other words, you will get the best performance from your mind when you regularly exercise your body, and you will get more from your body when you regularly exercise your mind. It's *that* simple.

Planned positive mental activity allows one to embrace and enjoy chances to learn; it helps keep one open-minded and accepting of others, as opposed to being closed and judgmental; it helps one show respect and curiosity for other ideas without feeling a need to conform; and it provides confidence when confronted with unfamiliar situations, facts, and figures.[1]

Big Heads

Scientists have made an amazing discovery: the adult brain can grow in response to regular demands placed on it. This was once thought impossible. The exercise of the brain is much like the exercise of the body. It helps keep us mentally fit and increases our mental ability.

In fact, mental activity *can change the physical structure of our brain*. One study used structural magnetic resonance imaging (MRI) to measure hippocampal volume (an area of the brain involved in memory) of London taxi drivers. The results showed that persons with intensive spatial training (e.g. taxi drivers) had significantly more hippocampal gray matter than usual. In other words, this area of the brain, which is involved in memory, was enlarged in the taxi drivers who used this part of their brain extensively and daily.[2] This has also been proven in other species, in particular with birds and their ability to return to sites where they had found or stored food.[3] So, just as the heart, muscles, and cardiorespiratory system respond to physical activity that increases their efficiency, power, and size, the brain can, too.

The fact is – if we fail to use brain cells, they die! A twenty-eight year study of four thousand people in the state of Washington revealed the principle: "Use it or lose it!"[4]

Strength Training the Gray Matter

Indeed, it is important to regularly exercise our brain. It is also important to be careful regarding *how* we exercise it, too. When choosing activities for your brain, be careful to avoid those that require activity with no real meaningful application or usefulness. Activities that increase brain fitness will include information and/or exercises that improve your performance in other meaningful endeavors.

Some examples might include things such as reading a book that interests you or challenges you and has substantive, edifying information. Books such as the classics or the Bible are excellent choices. Other activities that exercise your brain include memorizing poems or Bible verses, doing jigsaw puzzles, learning a new language, increasing your vocabulary, and practicing a task with your nondominant hand.

> *"The quality of life is determined by its activities."*
> ~ ARISTOTLE

Brain Food

In order to sustain regular, effective mental activity, you must give your brain its needed fuel. Breakfast is especially important because your body has had a fast during the night. In 1995, the Pediatrics Department at the University of California at Davis hosted a group of psychologists, neuroscientists, nutritionists, and physiologists who reviewed the scientific research on breakfast. The researchers concluded that the "eating of breakfast is important in learning, memory, and physical well-being in both children and adults."[5] In an even more recent review, University of Florida researchers reviewed forty-seven studies examining the association of breakfast consumption with the parameters of good health in children. Investigators noted that children who reported eating a consistent breakfast tended to have better nutrition, were less likely to be overweight, and tended to show improved cognitive function related to memory, test grades, and school attendance.[6] A good breakfast is important for everyone.

The next question is, what kind of breakfast is best? The answer is foods with a low glycemic index. The glycemic index is a measure of how quickly carbohydrates are absorbed into our body and converted into blood sugar. Scientists measure how fast and high 100 grams of plain sugar or 100 grams of plain white bread raise the blood sugar in the body. These foods are used as a standard and represent 100%. Other foods are then compared to the standard and given a percentage rating. Broccoli or spinach would have a low glycemic index rating, but soda, french fries, or ice cream would have

higher ratings. In general we can say that the lower the glycemic index, the better a food is for our bodies and brains. That is, the energy comes into our blood slowly, over time, rather than rushing in like a tidal wave. That's much easier for our bodies to handle and healthier, too.

While you can find lists of foods with their glycemic index, there is a basic principle that makes it easier to make good choices. **"The closer we get our food to the way God made it, the better."** Whole foods tend to be higher in fiber and lower in sugar. Even if they taste sweet they don't raise the blood sugar as fast as foods that have been processed and refined.

Let's get back to the breakfast experience…even though bowls of oatmeal and sugary cereals have a similar number of carbohydrates, they have different glycemic index measures. The sugary cereal absorbs into your body quickly, peaking sugar levels, then drops dramatically about two hours later. This releases hormones that negatively affect your mood, concentration, memory, and promote weight gain.

Oatmeal and other whole-grain cereals, however, are absorbed slowly, giving only a slow rise in blood sugar that provides a longer, steady fuel release that lasts until lunchtime. Terrill Bravender, professor of pediatrics at Duke University, explains that foods that are low on the scale, such as whole grains, are preferable when it comes to sustained brain power.[7] In a scientific study done in 2006 looking at students who ate sweetened oatmeal compared with those who ate high-sugar cereal, the oatmeal eaters performed 20% better in school.[8] It's important to note that both cereals had the same sugar content. But the oatmeal had more fiber and protein, giving it a lower glycemic index.

Today, more than ever, options like instant oatmeal and 100% whole-grain bagels provide a quick and convenient breakfast. So choose a "healthier brain" for yourself by simply beginning the day with a healthy breakfast, preferably one with a low glycemic index.

Air Heads

In order for your brain to function at its optimal level, it needs a tremendous amount of oxygen.[9] Doing physical activity helps the brain function better in part by increasing blood flow, enabling the delivery of its requisite oxygen. A research study showed that elderly people who are in good physical condition scored higher on fluid intelligent tests, experienced faster response times,[10] improved mental performance and short term memory,[11] and had an overall improvement of cognitive functioning.[12] Another study showed that school-age children who participate daily in physical activity actually did better on language, reading, and a basic battery of tests.[13] Countless studies demonstrate the close relationship between physical fitness and mental health. When you exercise your body you are not just helping your heart, lungs, and so forth, you are helping your brain also.

Exercise for Life

Physical activity promotes cardiorespiratory endurance, muscular strength, endurance, and muscular flexibility, as well as good body composition. The benefits of regular physical activity include improved quality of life and greater longevity. In their recommendations on physical activity, the Centers for Disease Control and Prevention and the American College of Sports Medicine state that the benefits of physical activity include a number of factors that lowered the risk of coronary heart disease: improved blood lipid profiles, better resting blood pressure in border-line hypertensives, improved body composition, better glucose tolerance and insulin sensitivity, better bone density, immune function, and psychological function.[14]

Physical activity is also protective. Epidemiologic studies show that low levels of activity and fitness are associated with markedly increased all-cause mortality rates. It is estimated that of 250,000 deaths per year in the United States, approximately 12% of the total are attributed to a lack of regular physical activity.[15]

Dr. Paffenbarger conducted a large study of sixteen thousand Harvard alumni.[16] His research showed that for every hour spent exercising, subjects could add four or more hours to their life. The additional hours of life are especially appealing because it's not just the added hours that you experience but also a higher quality of life. Physical activity is certainly a good investment, at least when it comes to time and health.

In the *Journal of the American Medical Association*, exercise was shown to be protective against coronary heart disease and cancer.[17] Physical activity was also shown to be a stronger predictor of mortality rate than high blood pressure, smoking, and high cholesterol. The researchers also found that physically fit people with any combination of smoking, elevated blood pressure, or elevated cholesterol levels had lower death rates overall than low-fit people with none of these problems. In other words, this research indicated that if a person smokes and has high blood pressure but is physically active, his or her chances of dying prematurely are lower than someone who does not smoke and does not have high blood pressure but is inactive. This demonstrates the powerful protective effect of physical activity and its ability to promote health and well-being.

An expert panel – after reviewing physiological, epidemiological, and clinical evidence – formulated a recommendation for physical activity. The expert panel included the American College of Sports Medicine and the American Heart Association. They have given us the following physical activity guidelines: To promote and maintain health, all healthy adults aged eighteen to sixty-five years need *moderate-intensity aerobic physical activity* for a minimum of thirty minutes five days each week OR *vigorous-intensity aerobic activity* for a minimum of twenty minutes three days each week. Also, combinations of moderate and vigorous intensity activity can be performed to meet this recommendation. Moderate-intensity aerobic activity, which is generally equivalent to a

brisk walk, will accelerate the heart rate. Exercise can be *accumulated* toward the thirty-minute minimum as long as the exercise lasts at least ten minutes. It is also recommended that *eight to ten exercises* be performed on two or more nonconsecutive days each week *using the major muscle groups*. To maximize strength development, a resistance (weight) should be used that allows eight to twelve repetitions of each exercise. People who wish to further improve their personal fitness, reduce their risk for chronic diseases and disabilities, or prevent unhealthy weight gain will likely *benefit by exceeding the minimum recommended amount* of physical activity. Moderate or vigorous-intensity activities should be performed in addition to light-intensity activities frequently performed throughout the day.[18]

> *"Commit to be fit."*
> ~ AUTHOR UNKNOWN

Moderation

First, let's look at the significance of the word *moderate*. One of the most exciting discoveries is that scientific evidence clearly demonstrates that regular, *moderate-intensity* physical activity provides substantial health benefits. We don't all need to be marathon runners! Adults can expect many health benefits from moderate-intensity activity that expends approximately two hundred calories per day. For most healthy adults a moderate level of exercise would be the equivalent of a brisk walk at 3 to 4 mph. That is about fifteen to twenty minutes per mile. To meet the standard of expending approximately two hundred calories, one would walk at that speed for about two miles.[19] Other exercises could work as well.

Moderation in exercise is an appealing concept, as it does not require vigorous exercise. An Aerobics Center Longitudinal Study reinforced this point by demonstrating that changing activity patterns from *"no exercise"* to *"moderate and regular exercise"* provides a greater improvement in health than the *change from "moderate" to "high exercise."*[20] It is good news that *any regular exercise* will be beneficial!

A simple way to gauge whether or not an individual is getting benefits from exercise is to utilize the talk/sing test. This is done by paying attention to breathing patterns during exercise. A good measure of appropriate exercise level is the sensation of being a *little* winded while carrying on a conversation. It should not be to the point of gasping for breath or necessitate stopping or postponing conversation. This would indicate a level of exercise too high to allow your heart, lungs, and muscles to sustain the effort, and would fall short of maximum benefit. But if a person can sing a song, then there would be benefit to "stepping up the pace." For maximum benefit, a person need only be mildly winded; that's the level of exercise where the most health benefits are acquired.

In the Finnish Twin Cohort Study, participants were divided into quintiles (five groups) based on exercise intensity. In this study the researchers found that the higher the intensity of regular physical activity, the lower the mortality rate.[22]

Continuous aerobic activity is an important component to an exercise program that is focused on the development and maintenance of fitness. However, another way to gain additional benefit is to use interval training techniques. Interval training is a type of physical activity that consists of timed intervals of different intensities done in the same activity session. It involves periods of high-intensity activity alternated with those of lower intensity or even rest. The intervals can be done at a lower moderate intensity pace. Interval training offers great benefits and can help make physical activity more interesting, enjoyable, and efficient.

Researchers report that interval training is a time-efficient way to get good results. One study examined the changes in exercise capacity and molecular and cellular adaptations in skeletal muscle after low volume sprint-interval training and high volume endurance training. The participants performed six training sessions over fourteen days. Two different exercise patterns were compared: one session consisted of either four to six repetitions of thirty seconds of "all out" cycling with four-minute recovery and the other of 90-120 minutes of continuous cycling. The training time commitment over two weeks was *approximately* 2.5 hours for the sprint-interval training group and approximately 10.5 hours for the endurance training group. The researchers found that both types of training induced similar improvements in muscle oxidative capacity, muscle buffering capacity, and exercise performance.[23] Other studies found improvements in performance and VO_2 max through incorporating intervals.[24-29]

It is important to take care when doing intense physical activity such as intervals. Be sure to increase your intensity gradually, pay close attention to how you are feeling, and do not overdo it. This will help you avoid injury. Many athletes incorporate interval training into their physical activity to gain a competitive edge. Remember, in order to gain benefits from interval training it does not have to be an "all out" effort. The great news is everyone can get impressive benefits from incorporating intervals into their regular physical activity.

Go for Vigorous Physical Activity

Moderate aerobic physical activity definitely has many substantial health benefits. Vigorous, intense physical activity can provide added benefits. After an individual has become used to regular moderate exercise for several weeks, the intensity may be increased for a more vigorous workout. Those over age forty who have a heart condition or other serious health problems should get permission from a physician before increasing the intensity to vigorous.

Vigorous, intense activity is exemplified by jogging and causes rapid breathing and a substantial increase in heart rate.[21] When doing intense physical activity a person feels winded.

A Healthy Mix of Rest and Motion

There is yet another type of training that uses intervals of activity and rest. It is called intermittent training, or simply IT. This is a noncontinuous technique of physical activity that incorporates moderate aerobic or anaerobic intervals of physical activity with active rest periods. An example of this would be spacing regular walking between intervals of running or jogging. This type of activity incorporates rest into the exercise routine! The activity and rest periods may be as short as thirty seconds or as long as six minutes. Intermittent training offers many benefits. Researchers have found that this technique of physical activity affords equivalent aerobic benefits to continuous aerobic exercise with the added benefits of greater weight and body fat loss.[30-31] Investigators measured the effects of continuous and IT training on aerobic capacity, body composition, and blood lactate response in sedentary college-aged females.[32] After an eight-week training program, both the continuous training and IT groups had significant reductions in body weight and fat percentage, increased time to fatigue, and increased aerobic capacity. However, the IT group had significantly lower blood lactate responses for each stage of their max exercise test. No improvement in the lactate response was seen in the continuous training group. Additional research supporting this finding found that the after-exercise increase in calorie burn was greater with intermittent aerobic exercise than with continuous aerobic exercise.[33] This increase in post-exercise metabolism enhances weight loss.

Intermittent training is appealing because it offers rest as a part of the exercise. You get exercise credit for the resting time, too. It is a great way for someone to begin exercise who has been inactive. It is not as intimidating. The fact that IT brings faster improvements in fitness and faster weight loss makes it the best choice for many people. Additional benefits include a positive influence on attitude toward physical activity along with requiring less time and effort, thus building confidence. All of this makes IT training very appealing!

The importance of the rest is quite significant. This is well illustrated with the benefits that are gained by marathon, long, and ultradistance runners who take a period of rest in the form of a walk after every mile or so of running, even during a race. Jeff Galloway, an Olympic athlete and a running teacher and author of *Galloway's Book on Running* and *Marathon: You Can Do It!* has reported significant improvement using walking breaks throughout his marathon training and in marathons.[34]

THE WALKING BREAK

Marathon: You Can Do It!, by Jeff Galloway, states that the walking break:

- Allows people who can run only two miles to go three or four and feel fine

- Helps beginners or heavy runners to increase their endurance to 5K, 10K, or even as far as the marathon in as little as six months

- Reduces the likelihood of injury and overtraining

- Restores resiliency to the main running muscles before they fatigue – it's like getting a muscle strength booster shot every break

- Speeds up post-marathon recovery

- Helps runners of all ages to improve ten to forty minutes in their marathon when compared to running continuously[34]

Many marathon veterans whose goal is to run faster have improved their times by ten, twenty, thirty, even forty minutes by taking walking breaks early and often in the race. You might wonder how walking breaks, or resting, work to improve their times? By using muscle groups in varying ways – from the beginning – the leg muscles keep their bounce and conserve resources. IT also impacts a marathoner psychologically. Knowing a rest is coming soon is motivating when exercising near physical limits; this sets the mind free to run, swim, or bike faster and harder. IT all adds up to better performance.

The power of rest is illustrated in ultra long distance running. Tom Osler first tested the method of walking for himself in races lasting as long as two days. He wrote about it in his *Serious Runner's Handbook*. "Anyone can double the length of his or her current longest nonstop run by inserting brief walking breaks early and often," states Osler. "Brief" means walking for about one or two minutes. "Often" means doing it every mile or two. "Early" means starting to walk after the first mile or two.[35]

Joe Henderson, an editor for *Runner's World* for twenty-five years who has written more than a dozen books, countless articles, and has run

more than seven hundred races, put Tom Osler's advice to the test on a one-hundred-mile run. His longest previous nonstop run – actually a race – had been only thirty-two miles. Henderson shares this in his book, *Better Runs: 25 Years' Worth of Lessons for Running Faster and Farther.* "I failed the test in one way, by dropping out at 70 miles, but succeeded in other ways: more than doubling my longest nonstop distance; averaging only a half-minute per mile slower than usual marathon pace for the running portion; and suffering fewer after effects than if it had been a marathon. I've since inserted planned walking into most of my marathons, and it has worked every time. The running distance gained more than makes up for the walking time lost."

So, you may ask, how much should I rest or walk? Galloway recommends that beginners take jogging breaks in their walks, which means they might take one-minute jogs for about every five minutes of walking. As beginners get in better shape, they may reduce the walking segments gradually to one minute of jogging and then four minutes of walking. Then to one minute of jogging and three minutes of walking, and progress until it is one minute of each. "Fitness runners" will take a two-minute walk break after two to three minutes of jogging. Average runners will take one to two-minute walk breaks after about three to eight minutes of running.

Accumulation

Evidence suggests that the amount of activity you complete is more important than the specific manner in which the activity is performed. When this is understood, the principle of *accumulation* becomes very appealing. Short sessions of physical activity might fit better into a busy schedule than a single long session. Accumulating thirty minutes of activity in short sessions brings substantial benefits. Activities may include walking upstairs instead of taking an elevator, walking instead of driving short distances, or pedaling a stationary cycle while watching TV. Gardening, housework, raking leaves, or even playing actively with children can also contribute to a thirty-minute-per-day total if performed at an intensity equivalent to brisk walking.

One option is breaking daily exercise into two fifteen-minute sessions – walk one mile briskly in the morning, then mow the lawn for fifteen minutes in the evening. One could alternately choose three ten-minute sessions – walk ten minutes to work, walk another ten minutes during your lunch break, and then ride your stationary bike for another ten minutes in the evening.

Researchers evaluated two groups on the increase in their fitness level using two different regimens. One was thirty minutes of continuous activity; the other was three ten-minute exercise sessions. They found that the multiple shorter sessions of exercise produced similar and significant improvement in fitness levels when compared with the continuous exercise.[36] In another similar study, researcher Ebisu studied the effects of running on fitness and blood lipids. He found similar results in fitness level improvement but found that the high-density lipoprotein – the healthy cholesterol – increased more in the group who spread their exercise over three times per day.[37]

The Arnold Schwarzenegger Factor

Some have called strength training the best anti-ager that we have. Why such a strong statement? Miriam E. Nelson's research created news worldwide when the results were published in the prestigious *Journal of the American Medical Association*. After a year of strength training twice a week, women's bodies were fifteen to twenty years more youthful. Without the use of drugs, they regained bone density, which helps prevent osteoporosis. They became stronger – in most cases even stronger than when they were young. Their flexibility and balance improved. Without changing what they ate, they were leaner and trimmer. What's more, the women in this study were so energized that they become 27% more active.[38-39] The anti-aging benefits were found in men also. A study revealed that persons unable to walk at a normal pace experienced physical limitation in other areas as well, such as doing heavy housework (washing the car, raking leaves, mowing the lawn, or cleaning up the garage), lifting something ten pounds, walking a half mile, walking up a flight of stairs, dressing, eating, and bathing. The study concluded that in order to remain independent as you get older, it is vital to maintain good muscle strength.[40]

The book *Biomarkers: The 10 Determinants of Aging You Can Control,* vividly illustrates how strength training is a fountain of youth. The ten determinants that you can control are your muscle mass, strength, basal metabolic rate, body fat percentage, aerobic capacity, blood-sugar tolerance, cholesterol/HDL ratio, blood pressure, bone density, and your body's ability to regulate its internal temperature. Every one of these determinants is directly and significantly affected by strength training.[41]

The most obvious determinants affected are muscle mass and strength, the immediate results of this important component of physical activity. We create good muscle mass by resistance exercise that stimulates the muscle to grow. The loss of muscle mass can create a domino effect. Imagine if you lined up ten dominos in a row, and each represented one determinant of aging that you could control. The first domino would be muscle mass, and once you knocked it over (had a loss of muscle mass) each of the other dominos would be knocked over (that is, they would be affected negatively). A positive way to look at this is that by maintaining or increasing your muscle mass, you help keep all of the other nine determinants of aging at good levels.

These are some of the benefits that a well-planned strength program will provide (and the great news is, you don't have to look like Arnold Schwarzenegger or work as hard as he did to get these benefits):

- Increased muscular strength, endurance, and tone.

- Increased ligament and tendon strength, which reduces arthritic pain.

- Increased bone density, the opposite of osteoporosis.

- Better posture.

- Easier acquisition of sport skills.

- Greater joint stability.

- Higher resting metabolic rate – which means one burns more calories, therefore promoting weight loss and maintenance. Each pound of muscle tissue gained increases the resting metabolism by thirty-five calories a day.

- Less risk of injury and falls.

- Aid in childbearing.

- Reduced chronic lower back pain.

- Improved cholesterol levels.[42]

More Activity Gives You More Benefits

The recommendations we have been reviewing are the minimum recommendations for physical activity. If you wish to further improve your personal fitness, reduce your risk for chronic diseases and disabilities, or prevent unhealthy weight gain, you will likely benefit by *exceeding* the minimum recommended amount of physical activity.[43]

In the past few years several large-scale prospective observational studies, involving tens of thousands of people, have clearly documented lower levels of risk of cardio-vascular disease and premature mortality with greater amounts of physical activity. These studies included both men and women and ethnically diverse populations. These include well known and often quoted studies such as the College Alumni Health study, the Health Professionals' Follow-up Study, the Nurses' Health Study, the Women's Initiative, and the Women's Health Study.[44-52]

In Summary...

Activity is a powerful way to grow, feel great, keep healthy, and thrive! Take time today to grow your brain by doing positive activity and eating healthy food. Then participate in regular physical activity to provide the nourishment and oxygen your body needs. Your participation in regular physical activity will give you great rewards, such as a healthier life full of energy and vitality. You can gain the best results from your physical activity by incorporating moderate and vigorous activity with interval and intermittent physical activity. And don't forget how rest and the accumulation of activity can benefit you, too. Also, regularly including strength training helps keep your "dominos" and you standing and moving strong. Last of all, remember that choosing to go above the minimum recommendations will richly repay you. Physical activity definitely helps you be fit for life! Choose today to get your healthy mix of rest and motion.

ACTIVITY

> *"Focus on the journey, not the destination.*
> *Joy is found not in finishing an activity but in doing it."*
> ~ GREG ANDERSON

REINFORCE THE MESSAGE

SKILL BUILDERS

Choose the Skill Builders below that you would like to experience in your own life, then write a response on how they impacted you. Last, write further actions, if any, that you would like to take as a result of doing the Skill Builders.

Skill Builder 1 | **Plan Your Exercise**

Plan your exercise for two weeks, taking the opportunity to insert a variety into your activity. Your plan might include a variety of activities, from swimming or participating in an appropriate sport, to working out at the gym or doing yard work. Try to include some exercise that you can do with another person, such as walking in a park or at the local mall, cycling, or cleaning out the garage. Check the long-term weather report and try to match the activities to the weather forecast. If you plan a two-week schedule, you can keep it enjoyable and be more likely to continue your exercise program.

DESCRIBE HOW THIS IMPACTED YOU:

....

....

....

FURTHER ACTION:

....

....

....

ACTIVITY

An important tool when it comes to developing your brain is the application of reasoning. We can't always have all the information we would want about a particular situation or decision. Therefore we must rely more heavily on exercising our reasoning abilities to make good choices. We can use what we do know about the situation and apply the principles that we live by, the rules we have to keep, the laws we are bound by, and good old common sense in order to make good choices. We can use deductive or inductive reasoning to develop various rationales that in turn can help to guide our decision making. Just as we need to always increase our knowledge base, we also need to constantly improve our reasoning abilities. Meet regularly with a group of friends and engage in stimulating and constructive debate/discussions/conversations. Practice reasoning with yourself about various issues throughout the day.

> *"Come now, let us reason together..."*
> **~ ISAIAH 1:18**

Look for applicable principles in the Bible. The book of Proverbs is full of lessons and parables helpful for daily challenges. The more we practice these critical thinking skills, the better we will become at making good choices, even when we have relatively little information available.

Within the next week, meet with one or more people for at least thirty minutes to discuss current events or areas of interest.

ACTIVITY

DESCRIBE HOW THIS IMPACTED YOU:

....

....

....

....

FURTHER ACTION:

....

....

....

....

> *"A body in motion tends to stay in motion and a body at rest tends to stay at rest."*
>
> ~ SIR ISAAC NEWTON

Skill Builder 3 | **Personal Training Session**

Meet with a local personal trainer and develop a personal fitness plan.

DESCRIBE HOW THIS IMPACTED YOU:

....

....

....

....

FURTHER ACTION:

....

....

....

....

Skill Builder 4 | **New Physical Activity or Skill**

Attend a fitness class that you have never gone to before AND/OR try a new form of physical activity you have never done before.

DESCRIBE HOW THIS IMPACTED YOU:

....

....

....

FURTHER ACTION:

....

....

....

....

Exercise in a different environment than you typically do, i.e., go to a park, a new walkway, or a new trail in the woods. As you engage in physical activity, soak in the sights and sounds around you. Experience how this can energize and put new life into your physical activity.

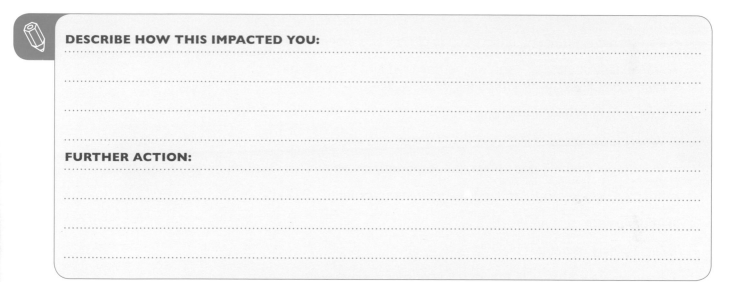

"Come near to God and He will come near to you…"

~ JAMES 4:8

DESCRIBE HOW THIS IMPACTED YOU:

....

....

....

....

FURTHER ACTION:

....

....

....

....

ACTIVITY

TIPS FOR SUCCESS

POWER TIPS: IMPROVE YOUR PHYSICAL HEALTH

Consider these practical suggestions for improving your physical health.

How to Start Getting Active and Maintain Regular Physical Activity:

- Choose activities you enjoy

- Ease into it – gradually increase intensity and duration

- Be sure to set short-term goals all along the way – this will prevent you from being overwhelmed by larger, long-term goals

- Celebrate your success in reaching your goals

- Schedule a regular time for exercise, just like an important appointment

- Plan a different exercise each day; schedule for two weeks in advance

- Remember intermittent, short periods of activity are beneficial

- Plan it early in the day – you will be less tired and there will be fewer complications, interruptions, or conflicts

- Exercise with a friend or group

- Variety is the spice of life – mix it up for renewed energy

- Use proper clothing and equipment, especially shoes

- Keep an exercise log – you will see your improvement

- Add music

- Drink plenty of water

- Energize your body with the food it needs for optimal performance

Get Moving Activities:

- Play with your kids/grandkids, kick a soccer ball, play catch, play tag or basketball, etc.

- Wash your car

- Take the stairs instead of the elevator

- Walk – around your house, down the street, around your neighborhood, etc.

- Tend to your garden and do some yard work

- Ride your stationary bike or walk on the treadmill while you watch TV

- Find a parking spot farthest from the entrance

- Put some extra energy and joy into mowing the lawn or vacuuming the carpet

- Keep moving while you wait

Get started and make great progress with the following physical activity recommendations:

CARDIORESPIRATORY RECOMMENDATIONS:

(aerobic physical activity – endurance)[53]

Be FITTE

Frequency – *five days a week*

Intensity – *a combination of moderate and intense activity*

> *MODERATE (i.e., brisk walking at 3-4 mph, 15-20 minutes per mile)*
>
> *For most healthy adults, you should feel a little winded*
>
> *or*
>
> *INTENSE*
> *Exemplified by jogging, and should cause rapid breathing and a substantial increase in heart rate*

Time – *thirty minutes or more a day*

> *(can be intermittent exercise of ten minutes or more in order to accumulate the thirty minutes)*

Type – *walk, cycle, swim, run, aerobics, etc.*

Enjoyment – *do physical activities you enjoy and try new ones*

Strength Training

"Resistance training should be progressive in nature, individualized, and provide a stimulus to all the major muscle groups."[54]

Frequency: a minimum of two days per week

Mode: eight to ten dynamic strength training exercises involving the body's major muscle groups

Resistance: enough weight resistance to perform eight to twelve repetitions to near fatigue (ten to fifteen repetitions with less weight for older and more frail individuals)

Sets: A minimum of one set of repetitions

Flexibility

"Flexibility exercises should be incorporated into the overall fitness program sufficient to develop and maintain range of motion."[55]

Frequency: two to three days per week (four to seven days a week for increased range of motion)

Mode: appropriate static or dynamic (slow ballistic or PNF) techniques

Intensity: stretch to a point of mild discomfort

Repetitions: four repetitions per muscle group holding each stretched position for ten to thirty seconds

Warm-up, Cooldown, Stretch for Success

Warm-up and cooldown are a pertinent part of any physical activity program. They are sometimes not done or understood. Both typically take three to five minutes and are well worth the time. They are many times completed by participating in the same activity that will be done during the physical activity session, but at a slower, gentler pace. If one wants, he or she can do a warm-up and cooldown doing something unrelated, such as when doing a lower body strength-training session, one might warm up or cool down by walking. The principle is that the same body parts to be worked during the session should be used for the warm-up or cooldown, too.[56]

Warm-up takes place at the beginning of an exercise session, and it prepares the body for movement.

The benefits of warming up include:

1. Getting blood to the muscles with all of its nutrients and oxygen.

2. Warm-up literally "warms up" the muscle, therefore decreasing the chance of injury.

3. It also permits gradual changes, which in turn results in increased performance.

4. Helps prevent premature fatigue by avoiding premature onset of blood lactate accumulation.

5. It also provides an important increased emphasis on physical activity.

6. Last, it improves coronary blood flow in the early part of exercise. This lessens the potential for myocardial ischemia.

> *"Movement is a medicine for creating change in a person's physical, emotional, and mental states."*
>
> ~ CAROL WELCH

Cooldown is done at the end of an exercise session, and it helps bring the body back down to a resting state.

The benefits of cooling down include:

1. Slowly decreasing heart rate and bringing the body back to a normal state.

2. Helping to work out the by-products that can cause muscle soreness.

3. Reducing the tendency for immediate post-exercise muscle spasm or cramping.

4. Preventing the blood from pooling in the extremities, and blood pressure from rapidly dropping, thereby reducing the likelihood of light-headedness and fainting.

Stretching is also important to any physical activity session. Warm-up should always be done before stretching. This increases the safety and effectiveness of the stretching session. The very best time to stretch is after you have done your full exercise session because your body is fully warmed up and you are the most flexible and least likely to injure yourself. The only exception to this is if you are going to do intense exercise that will stretch your joints to the limit, such as sprinting. In this situation it is best to have a good, long warm-up and then stretch before the activity. Stretching is important because it can increase your performance not only in the activity that you are doing but also in daily life. For example, inflexible hamstrings make it difficult for you to pick up things. Stretching also decreases the likelihood of you injuring yourself during your exercise session and in daily living. Last, stretching after physical activity decreases muscle soreness and can also decrease tension.

SMALL GROUP DISCUSSIONS

Directions: Review the discussion questions and choose one you would like to discuss first. Proceed through the rest of the questions as time allows.

1. What are some enjoyable ways you can get daily exercise? Are there any groups you could join or sports you could get involved in that could enable you to get the exercise you need?

   ....

   ....

2. We are all so busy. How can we learn to make the time to exercise? How can we better understand just how important exercise is for our overall health? That is, how can we learn to give it the priority it really deserves in our life?

   ....

   ....

3. What are ways that we can stimulate our minds other than by watching TV?

   ....

   ....

4. What kind of hobbies can we get involved in that could help give us the mental and/or physical activity that is so important for us?

   ....

   ....

5. What are some of the excuses we conveniently use to avoid exercise?

   ....

   ....

6. If we are struggling with certain health issues, why is it important to consult with our physicians first before we start an exercise program?

   ....

   ....

7. In the group, talk about books you have read and can recommend to each other that could provide great mental exercises for the mind.

   ....

   ....

ADDITIONAL RESOURCES

Books:

Healing the Broken Brain, by Elden M. Chambers, Ph.D.

Strong Women Stay Young, by Miriam E. Nelson, Ph.D.

Websites:

health-fitness-tips.com (Tips on exercise and health)

kidshealth.org (Children, Teen, Parent health tips)

nlm.nih.gov/medlineplus/exerciseandphysicalfitness.html
(Nice overview site about exercise and activity)

Other Resources:

Set of dumbbells for strength training

Stretch tubing for strength training

Appointment(s) with a personal trainer

Exercise ball

Exercise mat

Arm and wrist blood pressure monitors, pedometer, and heart rate monitor

Songs That Promote Spiritual and Physical Activity:

Every Move I Make (Praise and Worship Song)

The Hammer Holds (Bebo Norman)

Tough (Morgan Craig)

Let It Begin with Me (Message of Mercy)

As I Went Down to the River to Pray (Allison Krauss; *O Brother, Where Art Thou*)

I Surrender All

REFERENCES

1. Hoeger W, Turner L, et al. *Wellness: Guidelines for a Healthy Lifestyle*. Belmont, CA: Wadsworth/Thomson Learning, 2002, 8–9.

2. Maguire E, Gadian D, et al. "Navigation-Related Structural Change in the Hippocampi of Taxi Drivers." *Proceedings of the National Academy of Sciences of the United States of America* April 11, 2000 97(8): 4398–4403.

3. Sherry D, Vaccarino A, et al. "The Hippocampal Complex of Food Storing Birds." *Brain, Behavior and Evolution* 1989 34: 308–317.

4. Chalmers E. *Healing the Broken Brain.* Remnant Publications, July 1999, 10.

5. Matthews R. "Importance of Breakfast to Cognitive Performance and Health." *Perspectives in Applied Nutrition* 1996 3(3): 204–212.

6. Rampersaud G, Pereira M, et al. "Breakfast Habits, Nutritional Status, Body Weight, and Academic Performance in Children and Adolescents." *Journal of the American Dietetic Association* 2005 105: 743–760.

7. Aubrey A. "A Better Breakfast Can Boost a Child's Brainpower." NPR Script aired on Aug. 31, 2006. www.npr.org/templates/story/story.php?storyId=5738848. Retrieved Aug. 31, 2006.

8. Mahoney C, Taylor H, et al. "Effect of Breakfast Composition on Cognitive Processes in Elementary School Children." *Physiology and Behavior* 2005 85(5): 635–45.

9. Magistretti P, Pellerin L, Martin J. *Neuropsychopharmacology: The Fourth Generation of Progress (Chapter: Brain Energy Metabolism: An Integrated Cellular Perspective)*. New York: Raven Press, 1995.

10. Glenn B, Puglisi J. "Exercise, Fitness, and Aging: Psychological Perspectives" in *Mind-Body Maturity* by Louis Diamant. Taylor & Francis, 1991, 145–149.

11. Davey C. "Physical Exertion and Mental Performance." *Ergonomics* 1973 16: 595–599.

12. Molley D, Beerschoten D, et al. "Acute Effects of Exercise on Neuropsychological Function in Elderly Subjects." *Journal of the American Geriatrics Society* 1988 36(29): 29–33.

13. Davey C. "Physical Exertion and Mental Performance." *Ergonomics* 1973 16: 595–599.

14. Pate R, Pratt M, et al. "Physical Activity and Public Health." *Journal of the American Medical Association* February 1, 1995 273(5): 403.

15. Pate R, Pratt M, et al. "Physical Activity and Public Health. A Recommendation From the Centers for Disease Control and Prevention and the American College of Sports Medicine." *Journal of the American Medical Association* Feb 1, 1995 273(5): 402–407.

16. Paffenbarger R, Hyde R, et al. "Physical Activity, All-Cause Mortality, and Longevity of College Alumni." *New England Journal of Medicine* March 6, 1986 314(10): 605–13.

ACTIVITY

REFERENCES

17. Blair S, Kampert J, et.al. "Influences of Cardiorespiratory Fitness and Other Precursors on CVD and All-Cause Mortality in Men and Women." *Journal of the American Medical Association* July 17, 1996 276(3): 205.

18. Haskell W, Lee I, et al. "Physical Activity and Public Health: Updated Recommendation for Adults from the American College of Sports Medicine and the American Heart Association." *Medicine and Science in Sports and Exercise* 2007 39(8): 1423–1434.

19. Ibid.

20. Blair S, Kampert J, et al. "Influences of Cardiorespiratory Fitness and Other Precursors on Cardiorespiratory Disease and All-Cause Mortality in Men and Women." *Journal of the American Medical Association* July 17, 1996 276: 205–210.

21. Haskell W, Lee I, et al. "Physical Activity and Public Health: Updated Recommendation for Adults from the American College of Sports Medicine and the American Heart Association." *Medicine and Science in Sports and Exercise* 2007 39(8): 1423–1434.

22. Kujala U, Kaprio J, et al. "Relationship of Leisure-Time Physical Activity and Mortality: The Finnish Twin Cohort." *Journal of the American Medical Association* Feb. 11, 1998 279(6): 440–444.

23. Gibala M, Little J, et al. "Short-Term Sprint Interval Versus Traditional Endurance Training; Similar Initial Adaptations in Human Skeletal Muscle and Exercise Performance." *Journal of Physiology* 2006 557(3): 901–911.

24. Acevedo E, Goldfarb A. "Increased Training Intensity Effects on Plasma Lactate, Ventilatory Threshold, and Endurance." *Medicine and Science in Sports and Exercise* 1989 21: 563–568.

25. Gaskill S, Serfass R, et al. "Responses to Training in Cross-Country Skiers." *Medicine and Science in Sports and Exercise* 1999 31: 1211–1217.

26. Lindsay F, Hawley J, et al. "Improved Athletic Performance in Highly Trained Cyclists After Interval Training." *Medicine and Science in Sports and Exercise* 1996 28: 1427–1434.

27. MacDougall J, Hicks A, et al. "Muscle Performance and Enzymatic Adaptations to Sprint Interval Training." *Journal of Applied Physiology* 84: 2138–2142.

28. Stepto N, Hawley J, et al. "Effects of Different Interval-Training Programs on Cycling Time-Trial Performance." *Medicine and Science in Sports and Exercise* 1999 31: 735–741.

29. Tabata I, Nishimura K, et al. "Effects of Moderate-Intensity Endurance and High-Intensity Intermittent Training on Anaerobic Capacity and VO2max." *Medicine and Science in Sports and Exercise* 1997 28: 1327–1330.

30. Meyer K, Samek L, et al. "Interval Training in Patients with Severe Chronic Heart Failure: Analysis and Recommendations for Exercise Procedures." *Medicine and Science in Sports and Exercise* 1997 29(3): 377–381.

REFERENCES

31. Mayer H, DeRose D, et al. "A Comparison Between Intermittent Versus Continuous Aerobic Training on Cardiorespiratory & Body Composition Responses in Sedentary Adults." *Medicine & Science in Sports & Exercise* 2000 32(5): S218.

32. Roberts S. "Intermittent Aerobic Training. Part 2 Tech Brief" *American Fitness*. May-June 2002. http://findarticles.com/p/articles/mi_m0675/is_3_20/ai_86230660/.

33. Brockman L, Berg K, Latin R. "Oxygen Uptake During Recovery from Intense Intermittent Running and Prolonged Walking." *Journal of Sports Medicine and Physical Fitness* 1993 33(4): 330–336.

34. Galloway J. *Marathon: You can do it!* Bolinas, CA: Shelter Publications, Inc., 2001, 13–15.

35. Henderson J. *Better Runs: 25 Years' Worth of Lessons for Running Faster and Farther.* Champaign, IL: Kinetics, 1996, 19.

36. DeBusk R, Stenestrand U, et al. "Training Effects of Long Versus Short Bouts of Exercise in Healthy Subjects." *American Journal of Cardiology* 1990 65: 1010–1013.

37. Pate R, Pratt M, et al. "Physical Activity and Public Health. A Recommendation from the Centers for Disease Control and Prevention and the American College of Sports Medicine." *Journal of the American Medical Association* Feb 1, 1995 273(5): 402–407.

38. Nelson M, Fiantarone M, et al. "Effects of High-Intensity Strength Training on Multiple Risk Factors for Osteoporotic Fractures." *Journal of the American Medical Association* 1994 272(24): 1909–1914.

39. Nelson M. *Strong Women Stay Young*. New York: Bantam Books, 1997. Inside flap of jacket cover.

40. Rantanen T, Guralnik J, et al. "Midlife Hand Grip Strength as a Predictor of Old Age Disability." *Journal of the American Medical Association* Feb. 10, 1999 281(6): 558–60.

41. Evans W, Rosenberg I. *Biomarkers: The 10 Determinants of Aging You Can Control.* New York: Simon & Schuster, May 15, 1991.

42. Pollock, Gaesser G, et al. "The Recommended Quantity and Quality of Exercise for Developing and Maintaining Cardiorespiratory and Muscular Fitness, and Flexibility in Healthy Adults." *Medicine & Science in Sport & Exercise* 1998 30(6): 975–991.

43. Haskell W, Lee I, et al. "Physical Activity and Public Health: Updated Recommendation for Adults from the American College of Sports Medicine and the American Heart Association." *Medicine & Science in Sport & Exercise* 2007 39(8): 1423–1434.

44. Kesaniemi Y, Danforth E, et al. "Dose-Response Issues Concerning Physical Activity and Health: An Evidence-Based Symposium." *Medicine & Science in Sport & Exercise* 2001 33(6 Suppl): S531–S538.

45. Lee I, Skerrett P. "Physical Activity and All-Cause Mortality: What is the Dose-Response Relation?" *Medicine & Science in Sport & Exercise* 2001 33(6 Suppl): S459–S471.

REFERENCES

46. Lee I, Rexrode K, et al. "Physical Activity and Coronary Heart Disease in Women: Is 'No Pain, No Gain' Passé?" *Journal of the American Medical Association* 2001 285: 1447–1454.

47. Manson J, Greenland P, et al. "Walking Compared with Vigorous Exercise for the Prevention of Cardiovascular Events in Women." *New England Journal of Medicine* 2002 347: 716–725.

48. McGuire M, Wing R, et al. "Long-Term Maintenance of Weight Loss: Do People Who Lose Weight Through Various Weight Loss Methods Use Different Behaviors to Maintain Their Weight?" *International Journal of Obesity and Related Metabolic Disorders* 1998 22: 572–577.

49. Paffenbarger R. Jr, Hyde R, et al. "The Association of Changes in Physical-Activity Level and Other Lifestyle Characteristics with Mortality Among Men." *New England Journal of Medicine* 1993 328: 538–545.

50. Rockhill B, Willett W, et al. "Physical Activity and Mortality: A Prospective Study Among Women." *American Journal of Public Health* 2001 91: 578–583.

51. Tanasescu M, Leitzmann M, et al. "Exercise Type and Intensity in Relation to Coronary Heart Disease in Men." *Journal of the American Medical Association* 2002 288: 1994–2000.

52. Yu S, Yarnell J, et al. "What Level of Physical Activity Protects Against Premature Cardiovascular Death? The Caerphilly study." *Heart* 2003 89: 502–506.

53. Haskell W, Lee I, et al. "Physical Activity and Public Health. Updated Recommendation for Adults from the American College of Sports Medicine and the American Heart Association." *Circulation* 2007 116: 1081–1093.

54. Pollock, Gaesser G, et al. "The Recommended Quantity and Quality of Exercise for Developing and Maintaining Cardiorespiratory and Muscular Fitness, and Flexibility in Healthy Adults." *Medicine & Science in Sport & Exercise* 1998 30(6): 975–991.

55. Ibid.

56. Cotton RT, Ekeroth CJ. Assoc. Ed., *Personal Trainer Manual*, 2nd Edition. American Council on Exercise 1996, 210–212.

NOTES

NOTES

> "Humor is by far the most significant activity of the human brain."
> ~ FRANCIS CHARLES PUBLIUS

ACTIVITY

TRUST

···

enrich every facet of your life

c·r·e·a·t·i·o·n®
HEALTH

CONTENTS

MAKE IT WORK

Further Explanation of the DVD Topics

THE BIG PICTURE

A loving, all-powerful, all-knowing Creator God is the focus of this seminar. When we come to Him just as we are, He works to transform us and to re-create us into His image. If we realize that God loves us despite our flaws, and that His will can lead to our joy and fulfillment, then we can begin to trust Him. And, it is only when trusting Him that we receive the power to be transformed by His love and grace. A trusting relationship with the Creator empowers every aspect of our lives and enables us to achieve the fullness of CREATION Health.

> *"We're never so vulnerable than when we trust someone — but paradoxically, if we cannot trust, neither can we find love or joy."*
> **~ WALTER ANDERSON**

Getting Grounded

The Bible promises that "The righteous shall flourish like the palm tree; he shall grow like a cedar in Lebanon," Psalm 92:12.[1] Imagine the mighty cedars of Lebanon, their roots often reaching deep into the ground, anchoring the trees to solid rock. When we anchor ourselves in our Rock, He will give us His permanence, wisdom, and strength.

God gives us everything we need in order to grow and flourish. Through an intimate and trusting connection to Him, and because of His blessing, we will produce fruit: the fruit of good and wise choices; the fruit of rest that is restorative; the fruit of seeking an environment that is invigorating and refreshing; the fruit of continual growth through mental and physical activity; the fruit of being able to continually grow in our trust in God; the fruit of meaningful interpersonal relationships; the fruit of seeing life from a positive outlook (even when challenges are all around); and, finally, the fruit of a bountiful diet, as originally given in the nutrition of Eden.

TRUST

A Believing People

In challenging times, Americans have shown a remarkable commitment to faith and spirituality. According to the CRRUCS/Gallup Spiritual State of the Union Study, 97% of Americans consider themselves religious or spiritual, and 75% believe that America's overall well-being is highly dependent upon the spiritual health of the nation. The same study also found that 60% of Americans believe spirituality is involved in every aspect of their lives, and 70% have more meaning and purpose because of their faith. Only 13% claim no religious tradition at all.[2]

Even though a majority realize their need for God, many still limit His transformational power in their lives, often failing to see how critically important a relationship with Him is in their life. Often missed is the importance of what a relationship with Him can mean, not only to spiritual health but to every other area of health as well. A trusting relationship with Him is the foundation for true success and abundance in all aspects of CREATION Health.

"Trust is both an emotional and logical act. Emotionally, it is where you expose your vulnerabilities to people, but believing they will not take advantage of your openness."

~ AUTHOR UNKNOWN

The Power of God's Love

A trusting relationship with our Creator begins with the realization that He loves us unconditionally and desires to prosper us. He says to us, "For I know the plans I have for you," declares the Lord, "plans to prosper you and not to harm you, plans to give you hope and a future," Jeremiah 29:11.[3] God's love is the key that unlocks human potential. His love transforms our lives. It empowers us to rise above our challenges, and this love helps to heal our wounds. A loving relationship with God also enables us to place our trust in Him and to place our lives in His care.

God is the source of all love. And His love is a powerful, life-promoting force. Researchers have found that emotions powerfully impact our health, either positively or negatively. Experts have singled out love as foremost among the human emotions capable of promoting and maintaining health and achieving healing."[4] "It seems something deep inside our cells responds positively when we feel love. Love appears capable of sparking healthy biological reactions in much the same way as good food and fitness."[5]

Dr. Bernie Siegel, a Yale physician and the author of the best-selling book *Love, Medicine and Miracles*, affirms the power of love. "Unconditional love is the most powerful stimulant of the immune system. The truth is love heals."[6] This gift of love from God is a wonderful promoter of well-being and has amazing healing effects, not only when it is shared between God and man, but also in relationships with others. One study found that recipients of love can reduce the risk of coronary artery disease, hypertension, cancer,[7] and alcoholism.[8] Another reports that feeling loved is the strongest predictor of an individual's sense of positive self-esteem.[9] Other benefits of being loved include increased levels of immunoglobulin A (a marker of immune function) and smoother, more regular heart rhythms.[10-11] On the other hand, another study found that a lack of love shown to parents by their children was associated with higher levels of psychological distress.[12] Loss of love was among the most common reasons given for suicide or suicidal behavior.[13]

The results of these studies add an important perspective to our understanding of how belief in God affects our well-being. How we believe in God is also important. We receive the most benefits when we place our trust in God's unconditional love for us. Jesus said, "Love the Lord your God with all your heart and with all your soul and with all your mind," and "Love your neighbor as yourself," Matthew 22:37, 39.[14]

It is important to realize that all love originally comes from God. Love flows from God to us, which in turn enables us to love Him back. This relationship then frees us to have pure, God-given love for ourselves. Only when we have pure love for God and for ourselves can we truly love our neighbors. This amazing flow of love promotes life and healing.

When we accept God's unconditional love for us and wholly trust in His power to transform our lives, we are energized to take better care of ourselves in order to reflect His character to a needy world. Love will motivate us to make healthy choices, to rest in His peace, to surround ourselves with a healing, health-promoting environment, to be active in mind and body, to trust fully in Him, to serve others, to have a positive outlook colored by love's grace, and to eat for strength, vigor, and health. We will be motivated to take care of ourselves so that we might fulfill His mission of service.

TRUST

Healing Love

The American Heritage Dictionary defines "trust" as "firm reliance on the integrity, ability, or character of a person or thing; confident belief; faith."[15] These expectations have a powerful effect on our well-being, more so than many of us understand. This fact is illustrated by a report in the prestigious *Journal of the American Medical Association* in 1994. It reviewed pain medications over the previous twenty-five-plus years. The conclusion was stated like this: "The quality of interaction or trust between the patient and the physician can be extremely influential in patient outcomes, and in some (perhaps many) cases, patient and provider expectations and interactions may be more important than the specific treatments."[16]

Another way this was vividly illustrated was through research that asked participants the following question: "Is your health excellent, good, fair, or poor?" This is called a self-rating of health, or subjective health questioning. It shows the person's belief about their health. Subjective health is considered by researchers to be a reliable indicator of one's overall state of health and one of the best predictors of mental health, the level of functional disability, the rate of physician use, and even of longevity.[17] It is said that "self-ratings of health are the easiest and most reliable way to summarize the complex issue of health status."[18]

This self-rating may also be used in assessing one's faith. In this setting it is identified as "subjective religiousness." It is simply a self-rating of one's belief about his/her personal religiosity.

Subjective religiosity is considered a marker for the strength of one's faith. Research using this tool has produced good evidence of faith's overall health benefits. Researchers state that "the more religious faith people had, the greater their life satisfaction. Amazingly, not only was this a strong determinant of well-being – it was a stronger determinant than age and even health."[19]

Other studies have found that religious people have a more positive outlook, a higher level of emotional balance, greater life satisfaction, and more happiness than those who don't have faith.[20] When we believe in something, when we have faith, when we trust God, our health is impacted positively.

Our relationships with others can have similar effects to religiosity. Healthy, trusting relationships give a sense of love and belonging that is so essential to the enjoyment of life. We often try to meet or exceed the expectations of our close friends and family because we value this sense of belonging.

There is more than just a psychological reason for this effect. Chemical reactions in our bodies are associated with psychological feelings. When we see a person with whom we have a trusting relationship, oxytocin is released within the brain as part of the recognition process. Research suggests that oxytocin is responsible for the feelings of well-being associated with interacting with close friends. This feeling of well-being also apparently inhibits the stress hormone cortisol.[21]

"Do not let your hearts be troubled. Trust in God; trust also in me."

~ JOHN 14:1

The Power of Trust in God

It is easy to see how trusting relationships can create a sense of security. Interestingly enough, this feeling, and other benefits, exist even within relationships where there is little opportunity for reciprocity. While we often experience limitations in human relationships, God has promised to meet all our needs no matter how big or small.[25]

No wonder, then, that one study found that belief in God reflected an overall increase in life satisfaction, as well as a greater satisfaction with one's community, job, and even marriage.[26] Another interesting study conducted at UCLA revealed that people who were most likely to perceive God as a remedy, as a being or force that releases them from or resolves problems of living, reported the highest levels of marital satisfaction and satisfaction with personal health.[27] These research studies support the biblical truth that a positive, loving view of God is a powerful healing force in our lives. Doing things that enhance our trust in God, such as attending church, praying, studying the Bible, and praising God all make our life better.

Our view of God is indeed important. It is easy to understand scientific observations that belief in a loving God contributes to positive outcomes while a perspective that emphasizes obedience to a punitive God contributes to negative outcomes.[28] This research illustrates that the way we view God matters to our health. A positive view of God and the practice of a religious life, including forgiveness, promotes better health.

In our world we are surrounded by challenges. Sometimes they are small, and sometimes they are big and can seem totally overwhelming. No matter what we face today or tomorrow, experiencing the transformational power of a loving, trusting God can have a profound and positive effect on us. God has expressed His desire to be by our side through every challenge.[29] When we hurt, He hurts with us. He longs for us to trust Him with our challenges, to look up to Him and cling to His strong hand. He longs for us to rest in His loving arms. He will give us strength, courage, and peace.

The Power of Forgiveness

Forgiveness has an important role to play in trusting relationships as well. Forgiveness has long been considered to be one of the foundational principles of spiritual well-being. Research now suggests that its healing effects extend beyond the spiritual realm. "The practice of forgiveness has been shown to reduce anger, hurt, depression and stress and leads to greater feelings of hope, peace, compassion and self-confidence."[22] Dr. Dick Tibbits, in his book *Forgive to Live*, writes about the healing that forgiveness brings to inmates and how this changes their outlook for the future.

Researchers found that when subjects were encouraged to think forgiving thoughts, the stress response was diminished.[23] Another study found that forgiveness is directly related to fewer problems with substance abuse.[24]

Science has shown the powerful, positive impact of exercising forgiveness. This supports the biblical instruction to forgive those who have hurt us. While it is not easy to do, the effort can pay off in improved relationships and physical health. If you would like further help with this process, go to forgivetolive.net.

Faith and Emotional Health

Studies looking at the role of faith in the process of coping with stress, loss, or death have found it to be an important variable. One study found that faith was rated as the single most effective coping strategy in dealing with loss; another study found 78% of the respondents reporting that religion was involved in helping them cope with a significant negative life event.[30]

Religion has been identified as an important coping resource for many health challenges. Positive impacts have been noted, including reducing depressive symptoms, increasing satisfaction with life, reducing the length of hospital stay, and reducing the risk of alcohol abuse.[31] More than eighty studies published over the last one hundred years showed that religious/spiritual factors were generally linked with lower rates of depression.[32]

Researchers have found that spiritual resources contribute to a patient's ability to deal with the physical and emotional stresses of surgery or chronic or serious medical illness as well. One particular study revealed that, after controlling for severity of fracture, elderly women who underwent surgery for hip fractures had the best surgical outcome when they indicated that God was a strong source of strength and comfort and that they attended religious services frequently. These women were less depressed and walked farther when discharged from the hospital than those who lacked a strong religious commitment.[33]

> *"Thy word is a lamp unto my feet and a light unto my path."*
>
> ~ PSALM 119:105

The research seems clear: religious beliefs and faith clearly bring both emotional and physical benefits. This shouldn't be at all surprising, should it? It is God's will and desire for us to have an abundant life that is filled with health, peace, purpose, and meaning.

When you face emotional challenges, talk to God. Go to His Word and seek His face. Continue trusting Him. Although we cannot know the future, we can know that God is on our side and only has our best in mind.[34-35] He longs for us to trust Him and enjoy an intimate relation with Him. Look up to God, focus on Him, and allow His love and mercy to calm your soul. By focusing on Him and His transformational love, you will be lifted above your challenges. Knowing Him brings healing. In John 10:10, Christ says, "I have come that they may have life, and that they may have it more abundantly."[36] He longs to give us the life He designed for us at Creation.

TRUST

The Bible

God has richly blessed us through the Bible, for it vividly introduces His loving character and will for us. God's Word is full of wisdom about how to face every challenge with confidence and peace. Take time to search the Scriptures daily in order to find what God has to say to you personally. You will be richly blessed.

Studying the Bible helps us to develop our trust in God through several means. First, Bible study helps us to know God – that is, to know His trustworthy character. We read the stories of how God made promises and always kept them. This knowledge strengthens our confidence in Him.

Reading the Bible helps us to develop a relationship with Him, too. When we get to know God intimately, we trust Him more and more, and our relationship with Him grows.

A common practice of those who study the Bible is to memorize its inspiring words. The act of memorization challenges the brain, which, as we learned in our previous study on Activity, is important in keeping our minds healthy and active. The memorized passages are also a source of encouragement as we make them our own to recall during times of need.

In the Bible, God has given us insights into living happy and satisfying lives. Because God is all knowing, good, and loving, the things that He tells us to do reflect the best choices for us to make. God's commandments or rules are not arbitrary. Each one expresses a cause-effect relationship. If we choose to ignore one we will live with the negative consequences. This truth is reflected in the Bible book of Isaiah. God is speaking to His people. If you listen carefully, you can almost hear the tears in His voice as He contemplates the blessings His people have ignored: "Thus says the LORD, your Redeemer, The Holy One of Israel: 'I am the LORD your God, Who teaches you to profit, Who leads you by the way you should go. Oh, that you had heeded My commandments! Then your peace would have been like a river, And your righteousness like the waves of the sea,'" Isaiah 48:17–18.[37] If we trust that He knows what is best for us, we will want to follow His leading. Sometimes we

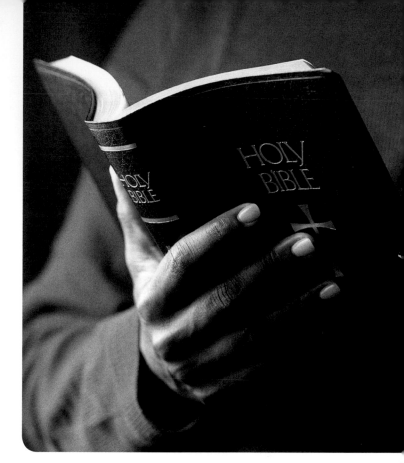

cannot clearly see the cause-effect relationship until after we have made the "right" decision. But if we know the true character of the One who tells us the "way we should go," we will TRUST Him enough to CHOOSE to obey the principles He has revealed to us.

When Cognitive Dissonance Strikes

Research has shown that if we don't practice what we preach, it can lead to increased anxiety, depression, guilt, and stress in general.[38] Merriam-Webster's dictionary defines "cognitive dissonance" as psychological conflict resulting from incongruous beliefs and attitudes held simultaneously, or simply "not practicing what we preach." When talking about God's law and our obedience we might experience cognitive dissonance between our beliefs and our behaviors.[39] If we claim to be Christians, but we are not living the way we believe is right, then we will experience cognitive dissonance until we take the effort to re-harmonize our actions. When we do this, the dissonance goes away and our relationship with God is strengthened, and so is our health.

"Remember, there are no mistakes, only lessons. Love yourself, trust your choices, and everything is possible."

~ CHERIE CARTER-SCOTT

TRUST

The Power of Prayer

Frequent prayer, whether public or private, is associated with better health and emotional well-being and lower levels of psychological distress.[40] Researchers have found this to be true, irrespective of ethnic group or religious denominational affiliation. Prayer is a powerful promoter of well-being. It connects us with the Almighty. Prayer is our time to talk with God as a friend. We can share with Him our joys, challenges, and requests, but prayer is much more than making requests of God. Being in communication with Him has a powerful influence on our lives.[41] Prayer is a powerful means of confiding in God. He loves us unconditionally and wants to help us with every challenge, big or small.

Another way prayer benefits us is through our expressions of gratitude to God. The benefits of gratitude are many. This topic is covered in the lesson on Outlook.

Devotional Activities

Personal and daily devotional time with God is a powerful promoter of well-being. Time spent in honest communication with God (worship) has a healing effect.[42] Just as we receive benefits from the qualities of a good friend when we spend time with them, so it is with God. Prayer, Bible study, and time spent in meditation and worship are channels of direct communion with God, through which we are richly blessed. The benefits are not only physical but also emotional.

The Power of Fellowship

Attending religious services or church is one of the most common ways that people seek to enhance their relationship with God. This has also demonstrated a positive effect on health and well-being. One study found that attending religious services can increase the life span by an average of seven years for Caucasians and potentially fourteen years for African-Americans.[43] An additional study of over 100,000 people done at Johns Hopkins University found that attending religious services on a weekly basis reduced the risk of death the following year by almost 50%.[44] Another group of researchers found that adults who reported weekly attendance were more likely to improve health behaviors and maintain good ones than those who did not attend church. The researchers also noted that attending religious services was associated with significantly lower smoking rates, higher levels of physical activity, less depression, more personal relationships, and longer, healthier, marriages.[45]

When we worship, pray, and study our Bibles with others in a community of trust, we gain tremendous social support. Many times people don't have friends outside of church. Families are scattered all over the world, people move often, and homes are broken, and so this connection with others is especially important. Fellowship has a profound positive impact on our well-being (a topic covered thoroughly in the lesson on Interpersonal Relationships).

Now What?

The science is in, and it's pretty clear: religious belief, trust in God, and religious activity can have a very positive and powerful impact on our health. Why not seek to learn more about God, about His Word, about His promises and will for your life?[46]

REINFORCE THE MESSAGE

SKILL BUILDERS

Choose the Skill Builders below that you would like to experience in your own life, then write a response on how they impacted you. Last, write further actions, if any, that you would like to take as a result of doing the Skill Builders.

Skill Builder 1 | **Pray Each Morning**

Pray each morning before talking to anyone, and each night before bedtime.

DESCRIBE HOW THIS IMPACTED YOU:

....
....
....

FURTHER ACTION:

....
....
....
....

Skill Builder 2 | **Read a Daily Devotional**

Purchase an inspirational devotional and read it daily.

DESCRIBE HOW THIS IMPACTED YOU:

....
....
....

FURTHER ACTION:

....
....
....
....

Skill Builder 3 | Ask God for Help

Ask God for help in any area of life that you cannot control; trust Him to help you, and look for and read relevant Bible promises.

DESCRIBE HOW THIS IMPACTED YOU:

....

....

....

....

FURTHER ACTION:

....

....

....

....

Skill Builder 4 | Keep a Personal Prayer Journal

Keep a personal prayer journal in which you write down your prayer requests, and then write the answers you receive to these specific prayer requests.

DESCRIBE HOW THIS IMPACTED YOU:

....

....

....

....

FURTHER ACTION:

....

....

....

....

Skill Builder 5 | **Join a Bible Study Group**

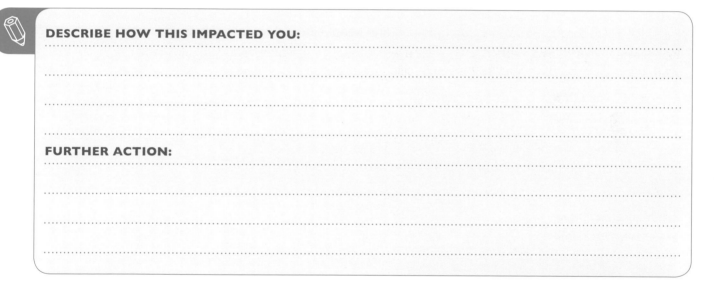

DESCRIBE HOW THIS IMPACTED YOU:

....

....

....

FURTHER ACTION:

....

....

....

....

Skill Builder 6 | **Read the New Testament Gospels for Encouragement**

DESCRIBE HOW THIS IMPACTED YOU:

....

....

....

....

FURTHER ACTION:

....

....

....

....

*"Taste and see
that the Lord is good."*

~ PSALM 34:8

Skill Builder 7 | **Memorize a Bible Promise Each Week**

Choose a Bible promise each week to memorize and apply to your life.

 DESCRIBE HOW THIS IMPACTED YOU:

....

....

....

....

FURTHER ACTION:

....

....

....

....

Skill Builder 8 | **Read the Bible from Beginning to End**

Read the Bible through from beginning to end and keep a journal on the insights you gain for personal growth as you go.

 DESCRIBE HOW THIS IMPACTED YOU:

....

....

....

....

FURTHER ACTION:

....

....

....

....

*"Commit your way to the LORD,
trust also in Him."*

~ PSALM 37:5

DESCRIBE HOW THIS IMPACTED YOU:

....

....

....

....

FURTHER ACTION:

....

....

....

....

"Behold, God is my salvation, I will trust and not be afraid;
For the Lord God is my strength and song,
And He has become my salvation."

~ ISAIAH 12:2

TRUST

TIPS FOR SUCCESS

POWER TIPS: STRENGTHEN YOUR FAITH AND TRUST

Consider these suggestions for improving your faith and trust in God.

Get connected with a church family.

Spend time outdoors asking God to speak to you and teach you lessons from nature.

Read the Bible with a prayerful spirit.

1. Read through the Bible passages.

2. Ask God to help you understand the Scripture passage as you read.

3. Underline anything that you like and/or have questions about within the passage.

4. Pray at the end of the study, asking God to help you to apply what you have learned to your spiritual walk.

Make a pros/cons list about trusting a person.

Look up – because above all the challenges of life, there is a God whom you can trust.

Enjoy the benefits of following God's will.

Have a vision and purpose in life. Seek to understand God's will and purpose for you.

Take a day of Sabbath rest and enjoy connecting with God and serving others.

Use the Bible as a guidebook for life. Search the Scripture for solutions and ways of handling all of life's situations.[47]

Receive God's love, love God, and love one another.

Sing praises to God. This will help your attitude to be positive.

Meditate on the amazing qualities of God.

Challenge your brain by memorizing Scripture passages and anything that is meaningful to you.

Give and receive forgiveness.

TRUST

TRUST

CREATION HEALTH

146

SMALL GROUP DISCUSSIONS

Directions: Review the discussion questions and choose one you would like to discuss first. Proceed through the rest of the questions as time allows.

1. In a group, discuss your favorite Bible texts, what they mean to you, and how they have helped you deal with some of the struggles you have faced.

....

....

2. Talk about what your faith means to you and how it has impacted your life.

....

....

3. This section talked about the healing power of forgiveness. Dwell on the promises of forgiveness that God has given us. How can we learn from receiving His forgiveness to forgive those who have hurt us?

....

....

4. Talk about how at times we might have been disappointed with God. That is, we prayed for something to happen, or to not happen, and our prayers were not answered. How do we learn to trust God despite outcomes like this? How can we know that He still loves us and cares about us even when we don't get the things we have prayed for? Why is it important to not lose faith when prayers are not answered as we would like?

....

....

> *"If we can surround ourselves with people we trust, then we can create a safe present and an even better future."*
>
> ~ **AUTHOR UNKNOWN**

THE SERENITY PRAYER

Rev. Karl Paul Reinhold Niebuhr (1892–1971)

GOD, grant me the serenity
to accept the things
I cannot change,

Courage to change the
things I can, and the
wisdom to know the difference.

Living one day at a time;
Enjoying one moment at a time;
Accepting hardship as the
pathway to peace.

Taking, as He did, this
sinful world as it is,
not as I would have it.

Trusting that He will make
all things right if I
surrender to His Will;

That I may be reasonably happy
in this life, and supremely
happy with Him forever in
the next.

Amen

ADDITIONAL RESOURCES

Books:

The Bible (Bible study helps)

Steps to Christ, by Ellen G. White

Secrets of the Vine, by Bruce Wilkinson (topic: spiritual growth)

Heaven's Lifestyle Today, by William Dysinger, M.D.

God, Faith, and Health, by Jeff Levin, PH.D.

Desire of Ages, by Ellen G. White

Forgive to Live, by Dick Tibbits

The Radical Prayer, by Dr. Derek Morris

God Encounters, by Lynell LaMountain, Shayna Bailey, Allan Martin

Websites:

coping.org/growth/trust.htm (Website gives excellent information on building trust. What is trust? Why do people have trouble developing trust in others? What are some beliefs of people who have problems trusting? What behavioral traits do people need in order to develop trust? What steps can be taken to improve trust building?)

goodcharacter.com/ISOC/Trustworthiness.html (Website specifically for teens, though others could benefit too. Has a self-test, and many other resources)

edis.ifas.ufl.edu/FY748 (Gives tips for developing trust in groups)

bibleschools.com (Free Bible studies and more)

Bibleuniverse.com (Free Bible studies and much more)

HopeTV.org (Stories, church services, music, and Bible studies)

3abn.org (TV, radio, Internet stories, and Bible studies)

awr.org (testimonials, stories, radio feeds live from all over the world)

Songs That Inspire and Build Trust:

Trust and Obey (Hymn)

Leaning on the Everlasting Arms (Hymn)

Lord I Believe in You (Christian Contemporary)

Somebody Bigger Than You and I (Gospel)

Take My Life (Third Day)

You Raise Me Up (Selah and Josh Groban)

The Gentle Healer (Michael Card)

Yes, I Believe (Point of Grace)

Where There Is Faith (4Him)

God Is With You (Message of Mercy)

Confessions (Jennifer LaMountain)

REFERENCES

1. Psalm 92:12, KJV.

2. "Center for Research on Religion and Urban Civil Society." *CRRUCS/Gallup Spiritual State of the Union*: Center for Research on Religion and Urban Civil Society, University of Pennsylvania 2003.

3. Jeremiah 19:11, NIV.

4. Siegel B. *Love, Medicine and Miracles: Lessons Learned about Self-Healing from a Surgeon's Experience with Exceptional Patients*. New York: Harper Perennial, 1986, 181.

5. Padus E. *The Complete Guide to Your Emotions and Your Health: New Dimensions in Mind/Body Healing*. Emmaus, PA: Rodale Press, 1986, 648.

6. Siegel B. *Love, Medicine and Miracles: Lessons Learned about Self-Healing from a Surgeon's Experience with Exceptional Patients*. New York: Harper Perennial, 1986, 181.

7. Thomas C. "Precursors of Premature Disease and Death: The Predictive Potential of Habits and Family Attitudes." *Annals of Internal Medicine* 85: 653–658.

8. Russek L, Schwartz G, et al. "Feelings of Parental Caring Predict Health Status in Midlife: A 35-Year Follow-up of the Harvard Mastery of Stress Study." *Journal of Behavioral Medicine* Feb. 1997 20(1): 1–13.

9. Walsh A, Walsh P. "Love, Self-Esteem, and Multiple Sclerosis." *Social Science and Medicine* 1989 29: 793–798.

10. McClelland D, Kirshnit C. "The Effect of Motivational Arousal Through Films on Salivary Immunoglobulin A." *Psychology and Health 2* 1988: 31–52.

11. Levine J. "A Prolegomenon to Epidemiology of Love: Theory, Measurement, and Health Outcomes." *Journal of Social Psychology* Spring 2000 19(1): 117–27.

12. Marinoni A, Degrate A, et al. "Psychological Distress and Its Correlates in Secondary School Students in Pavia, Italy." *European Journal of Epidemiology* 1997 13(7): 779–786.

13. Hattori T, Taketani K, et al. "Suicide and Suicide Attempts in General Hospital Psychiatry: Clinical and Statistical Study." *Psychiatry and Clinical Neurosciences* 1995 49: 43–48.

14. Matthew 22:37, 39, NIV.

15. William M, ed. *American Heritage Dictionary.* Boston: Houghton Mifflin Company, 1976.

16. Turner J, Deyo R, Loeser J, et al. "The Importance of Placebo Effects in Pain Treatment and Research." *Journal of the American Medical Association* May 25, 1994 271(20): 1609–1614.

17. George L, Landerman R. "Health and Subjective Well-Being: A Replicated Secondary Data Analysis." *International Journal of Aging and Human Development* 1984 19: 133–156.

18. Levin J. *God, Faith, and Health: Exploring the Spirituality-Healing Connection*. New York: John Wiley & Sons, Inc., 2001, 128.

19. Levin J, Chatters L, et al. "Religious Effects on Health Status and Life Satisfaction Among Black Americans." *Journal of Gerontology: Social Sciences* 1995 50B: S154–S163.

REFERENCES

20. Levin J, Ellison C, "Modeling Religious Effects on Health and Psychological Well-Being: A Replicated Secondary Data Analysis of Seven Study Samples." Unpublished research quoted in Levin J. *God, Faith, and Health: Exploring the Spirituality-Healing Connection*, New York: John Wiley & Sons, Inc., 2001, 131.

21. Kreutz G, Bongard S, et al. "Effects of Choir Singing or Listening on Secretory Immunoglobulin A, Cortisol, and Emotional State." *Journal of Behavioral Medicine* 2004 27(6): 623–635.

22. Luskin F. *Forgive for Good: A Proven Prescription for Health and Happiness*, New York: HarperCollins Publishers, Inc., 2002.

23. Witvliet C, Ludwig T, et al. "Granting Forgiveness or Harboring Grudges: Implications for Emotion, Physiology, and Health." *Psychological Science* 2001 12(2): 117–123.

24. Webb J. "Spiritual Factors and Adjustment in Medical Rehabilitation: Understanding Forgiveness as a Means of Coping." *Journal of Applied Rehabilitation Counseling* 2003 34(3): 16–24.

25. Philippians 4:19.

26. Willits FK, Crider, Donald W. et al. "Religion and Well-Being: Men and Women in the Middle Years." *Journal of Health and Social Behavior* 1988 29: 281–294.

27. Pollner M. "Divine Relations, Social Relations, and Well-Being." *Journal of Health and Social Behavior* 1989 30: 92–104.

28. Pargament K, Koenig H, et. al. "Religious Struggle as a Predictor of Mortality Among Medically Ill Elderly Patients: A Two-Year Longitudinal Study." *Archives of Internal Medicine* 2001 161: 1881–1885.

29. Hebrews 13:5.

30. Pargament K, Ensing DS, et al. "God Help Me: I. Religious Coping Efforts as Predictors of the Outcomes to Significant Life Events." *American Journal of Community Psychology* 1990 18: 793–824.

31. Beatz M, Larson D, et al. "Canadian Psychiatric Impatient Religious Commitment: An Association with Mental Health." *Canadian Journal of Psychiatry* 2002 47(2): 159–165.

32. McCullough M, Larson D. "Religion and Depression: A Review of the Literature." *Twin Research* 1999 2: 126–136.

33. Pressman P, Lyons J, et al. "Religious Belief, Depression, and Ambulation Status in Elderly Women with Broken Hips." *American Journal of Psychiatry* 1990 147(6): 758–760.

34. Jeremiah 29:11.

35. Romans 8:28.

36. John 10:10, KJV.

REFERENCES

37. Isaiah 48:17–18, NKJV.

38. Stone J, Fernandez N. "To Practice What We Preach: The Use of Hypocrisy and Cognitive Dissonance to Motivate Behavior Change." *Social and Personality Psychology Compass 2/2* 2008: 1024–1051.

39. Merriam-Webster's Online dictionary. http://www.merriam-webster.com/dictionary/ Cognitive%20dissonance/. Retrieved 1/19/09.

40. Levin J. *God, Faith, And Health*. Canada: John Wiley & Sons, Inc. 2001, 77.

41. Levin J, Taylor R. "Panel Analyses of Religious Involvement and Well-Being in African Americans: Contemporaneous vs. Longitudinal Effects." *Journal for the Scientific Study of Religion* 1998 37: 695–709.

42. Larson DB, Larson SS. "Religious Commitment and Health: Valuing the Relationship." *Second Opinion: Health, Faith, and Ethics 1991 17(1):* 26–40.

43. Musick M. "Religion and Subjective Health Among Black and White Elders." *Journal of Health and Social Behavior* 1996 37: 221–237.

44. Hummer RA, et al. "Religious Involvement and U.S. Adult Mortality." *Demography* May 1999 36(2): 273–85.

45. Comstock G, et al. "Education and Mortality in Washington County, Maryland." *Journal of Health and Social Behavior* 1977 18: 54–61.

46. Psalm 34:8, NIV.

47. Psalm 119:105, KJV.

TRUST

NOTES

INTERPERSONAL

RELATIONSHIPS

create a full and happy life

creation®
HEALTH

CONTENTS

MAKE IT WORK

Further Explanation of the DVD Topics

THE BIG PICTURE

What do we mean by "social connection" or "social connectedness"? In the broadest sense, it means interacting with other people, such as friends or relatives. These connections will not be the same in every respect for any two people, although ideally these connections should generate a similar sense of openness, generosity, and goodwill. Although they take work, good relationships are one of our greatest blessings.

Is there anyone who really cares for you, or feels close to you, or loves you, or wants to help you? Is there someone you can confide in? If so, then according to some studies, you may have three to five times lower risk of premature death and disease from all causes than those who don't have these kinds of relationships.[1]

Perhaps the best known example of the link between social connectedness and health has been seen in Dr. Dean Ornish's intervention for reversing heart disease. When most people think of this program, they tend to think of low-fat diets, exercise, and meditation. But if you ask Dr. Ornish about the most important part of his program, his answer might surprise you, because he identifies it as interpersonal relationships.[2]

Dr. Dean Ornish, in his book *Love and Survival: The Scientific Basis for the Healing Power of Intimacy,* writes that "I'm not aware of any other factor in medicine – not diet, not smoking, not exercise, not stress, not genetics, not drugs, not surgery – that has a greater impact on our

> "The mandate to 'Love your neighbor as you love yourself' is not just a moral mandate. It is a physiological mandate. Caring is biological. One thing you get from caring for others is you are not lonely; and the more connected you are to life, the healthier you are."
>
> ~ DR. JAMES LYNCH,

quality of life, incidence of illness, and the premature death from all causes than does love and intimacy."[3] Jeff Levin, epidemiologist, puts it this way, "…experts have singled out love as foremost among the human emotions capable of promoting and maintaining health and achieving healing." *The Complete Guide to Your Emotions and Your Health*, published by *Prevention* magazine, says: "It seems something deep inside our cells responds positively when we feel love. Love appears capable of sparking healthy biological reactions in much the same way as good food and fitness."[4] Dr. Bernie Siegel, Yale physician and author of the best-selling book, *Love, Medicine and Miracles*, affirms the power of love: "Unconditional love is the most powerful stimulant of the immune system. The truth is love heals."[5] Dr. Siegel works with cancer patients to help them experience the blessings of love and other positive emotions. Throughout this seminar on Interpersonal Relationships, we will look at some of this compelling and many times overlooked research.

INTERPERSONAL

The Roseto Effect

Social support is probably one of the least focused on areas of health, and yet it has one of the most powerful influences. It can come in the form of a spouse, a close-knit family, a network of friends, a church, or other group affiliations. Even a connection to animals can have a powerful, positive effect on one's well-being.

The link between social support and health is very strong. "So many studies have supported this powerful link that it has been given a name – the Roseto effect."[6] The name comes from a study that spanned fifty years in the little town of Roseto, Pennsylvania. Researchers discovered that the incidence of coronary heart disease in Roseto at the beginning of the period was about half that of the two neighboring towns, despite the same risk factors in all three locations.

What was the difference? Researchers discovered that Roseto was settled by a tightly knit group of religious immigrants from Southern Italy. During the first thirty years of the study, they were characterized by a high level of social connectedness: extensive intermarriage, strong family ties, and a supportive, nurturing community. The researchers hypothesized that this high level of social connectedness might buffer residents from heart disease and early death. This was shown to be true when, in the 1960s and 1970s, the cohesiveness of the community began to weaken and the heart disease rates in Roseto climbed to the same levels as those in the other two communities.[7]

Drs. Syme and Berkman have co-authored what many consider to be the definitive study on social support and the risk of death. The Alameda County Study is one of the most quoted studies in the field of health. "Statistically, under the topic of social support, this is one of the strongest areas under study," says Dr. Syme, professor of epidemiology at the University of California at Berkeley and one of the leading experts on relationships.[8]

This study, which dealt with more than seven thousand people followed for forty years, showed:

- People classified as lonely and isolated had three times higher mortality rates.

- People with many social contacts had the lowest mortality rates.

- The amount of social support was the best predictor of good health.

In this study, the association between social and community ties and premature death was found to be independent of the more powerful predictors of health and longevity: age, gender, race, socioeconomic status, self-reported physical health status and health practices, i.e., smoking, alcoholic beverage consumption, overeating, physical activity, and utilization of preventive health services. Those who lacked social ties had an increased risk of dying from coronary heart disease, stroke, cancer, respiratory diseases, gastrointestinal diseases, and all other causes of death.

Many other large-scale studies have replicated and confirmed the results from the Alameda research. Each gives additional valuable information regarding the effects of social connectedness on the quality and length of our lives. The data gathered in these studies includes all different types of populations (tens of thousands of participants) and many different countries.

"Those who bring sunshine to the lives of others cannot keep it from themselves."
~ **ELEANOR ROOSEVELT**

"Friendly" Immune Boosters

More friends can mean fewer illnesses. An interesting study illustrates how connecting with other people can boost our immune system. Volunteers were given nasal drops containing rhinovirus – the virus that causes the common cold. Almost all of the people exposed to the rhinovirus were infected by it, but those with more friends were less likely to develop signs and symptoms of a cold.[9]

Another study involving elderly people showed increased immune function in terms of both natural killer cells and antibodies after weekly visitations by friends or relatives.[10] Lack of connection has been found to reduce suppressor T-cells and is associated with recurrence of some illnesses.[11] Researchers at Ohio State University College of Medicine found that women who perceived their marriages as satisfying and supportive had better immune defenses (higher % T-cells, and more helper lymphocytes) as well as less depression and loneliness.[12]

On the other hand, negative social interactions can weaken the important functions of the immune system. The immune system is less effective when one is in conflict with a spouse or companion, even when one is otherwise happy.[13]

> *"As iron sharpens iron,*
> *so a friend sharpens a friend."*
> **~ PROVERBS 27:17**
> **NEW LIVING TRANSLATION**

Group Therapy

In a landmark study published in the prestigious medical journal *The Lancet*, Dr. David Spiegel of Stanford University and his colleagues found that women with breast cancer who participate in psychosocial support groups live significantly longer than those who do not. In this study, Dr. Spiegel intended to disprove the idea that psychosocial interventions could prolong the life of women with breast cancer, but he found, instead, that the women who had the weekly support group lived an average of twice as long as those who didn't.[14]

In a study done at UCLA, a group of malignant melanoma cancer patients participated in a six week, ninety-minute weekly support group; another group did not participate. The sessions included education, stress management techniques, ways of enhancing coping skills, and social support. Six years later the people in the support group had a 70% reduction in death rate, and almost half as many recurrences of the cancer.[15]

Another study on heart disease included 2,320 men who had survived a heart attack. Even after researchers statistically controlled for genetics, exercise, diet, weight, smoking, alcohol, and so on, the men who were socially isolated and had high stress revealed more than four times the risk of dying sooner than those who had a stronger social network. The psychosocial factors had a much stronger relationship to mortality than did the drug being tested in this research, even though these factors are often ignored by physicians prescribing such drugs.[16]

Touchy Feely

Touch is one of the most basic expressions of social connectedness.[17] Hundreds of studies over the past forty years have helped us better understand the powerful effects of physical touch.

In one study in which tactile/kinesthetic stimulation was given to preterm babies, researchers found that touch was very powerful. The touching or stimulation consisted of body stroking and passive movements of the limbs for three fifteen-minute periods per day for ten days. The touched-and-moved babies averaged a 47% greater weight gain per day. They were also more active and alert during sleep/wake behavior observations. Finally, those babies who had human touch and movement had a hospital stay six days shorter than those who weren't touched in the same manner, which yielded a cost savings of approximately $3,000 per baby![18]

Interestingly enough, observations made by researchers decades ago as they watched groups of monkeys provided additional information on the power of touch. University of Wisconsin researchers Harry and Margaret Harlow compared monkeys who were raised together in cages with monkeys whose only social contact came through seeing, hearing, and smelling other monkeys. The Harlows found that the monkeys who did not have touch or actual body contact with other monkeys grew up with a variety of emotional abnormalities. As these monkeys grew older, early self-aggression turned into aggression against other monkeys. Perhaps most striking was the example of how mothers behaved with their young. Mothers who grew up without touch showed less warmth and affection toward their offspring; some were actually physically abusive to their babies.[19]

Many years ago a now famous research study was done at an orphanage. The researchers wondered why at that particular orphanage the children were living, while at the other ones children seemed more likely to die. They found that the assistant at the orphanage where the children weren't dying simply hugged and held the children![20]

Touch is very important to our health, and it doesn't have to be dramatic or uncomfortable to make a difference. An unusual study was conducted in a university library. As they left the library, students were stopped and asked how satisfied they were with the service they had received. What the students didn't know was that the study wasn't about the library – it was about *touch*. The library clerk had received specific instructions that half the people checking out were to have their hands touched as they got their cards back. They were touched just lightly, almost imperceptibly. But, however casual and meaningless this contact may have seemed, the researchers found that the students who had been touched had much higher opinions of the library service than those who were not touched.[21]

Animal Therapy

In contrast to life's destructive stressors, domestic animals offer an unconditional love that can soothe and heal the mind and body. This unconditional love may be considered a glimpse of how God loves us. In a well-demonstrated study, it was found that the positive effect a dog companion can have on lowering blood pressure reactivity was greater than the effect a good friend could have.[22] Why? The friend was often perceived as judgmental, in contrast to the dog, which (obviously) wasn't.

Another study found that one year after being hospitalized with chest pains or a heart attack, only 6% of the pet owners died, compared to 28% of the patients who did not own pets.[23] This finding was independent of disease severity, exercise, or other known factors. Another study found that, among those receiving Medicare benefits, those with pets made fewer visits to their physicians than those without pets.[24]

Pets even help those in prison. In one of the most successful programs of its kind, social worker David Lee of Lima State Hospital for the Criminally Insane, in Ohio, introduced small animals – fish, parakeets, and so on – to prisoners as "mascots." Among the prisoners were many who had committed violent crimes. Allowing them to care for the animals almost completely stopped the fighting and suicide attempts.[25]

INTERPERSONAL

Domestic animals offer an unconditional love that can soothe and heal the mind and body.

No Age Limits

The impact of social connection is powerful at all ages. In a review of 144 studies, Drs. Hoffman and Hatch at Columbia University concluded that intimate social support from a partner or family member is associated with improved fetal growth, regardless of a woman's level of acute stressors.[26] Two studies conducted in Guatemala City found that the presence of a supportive companion during labor and delivery reduced the need for cesarean section and other interventions. It is common in this city to go through labor alone, a situation that provides the perfect opportunity to investigate the effects of a supportive companion during labor and delivery. One group in the study went through labor alone, while the other group had – from admission to the hospital to delivery – constant support by a friendly companion known as a "doula," whom the pregnant woman had never met. "The duration of labor in the group of women left alone was 19.3 hours, compared to only 8.7 hours for the women with the doula." Also the mothers with doulas were more likely to smile, stroke, and talk to their baby than those in the control group.[27]

Children and Adolescents

A qualitative synthesis of over one hundred resiliency-related studies revealed that resilient children tend to have all of the following factors, which are related to social connection: good social skills and support from mentors or peers; a close connection to family; and a caring relationship with a caregiver. Aside from these, resilient children have positive self-esteem, a good sense of the future, and clear expectations and achievement in school.[28]

The scientific evidence of how connectedness protects also shows up in the growing body of research on adolescents. In 1997, a massive capstone study was launched, collecting data from ninety thousand teens and eighteen thousand of their parents across the United States. The one word that encapsulates all this research is *connectedness*. In short, kids who feel connected to family, church, school, and community are far less likely to participate in risky behaviors than those who don't have tight connections.[29]

Adults

In the research on adults, one of the most interesting and powerful examples of how loving relationships may affect susceptibility to disease in general is found in the Harvard Mastery of Stress Study. Researchers combined ratings from two measures of parental caring, and the number of positive descriptions given when asked, "What kind of person is your mother and your father?" They found 95% of subjects who used few positive words about their parents and who also rated their parents low in parental caring had diseases diagnosed in midlife, in contrast to only 29% of subjects who used many positive words and who rated their parents high in parental caring.[30]

In a related study, researchers at Johns Hopkins Medical School tested and followed 1,337 male medical students. They were looking at whether or not the quality of human relationships might be a factor in the development of cancer. Researchers used a questionnaire called the "Closeness to Parents Scale" to assess the quality of the students' relationships with their parents. At the time of this questionnaire, as in the Harvard study described above, all of these students were healthy.[31]

Medical students who subsequently developed cancer were more likely than their healthy classmates to have described a lack of closeness with their parents when tested up to forty-five years earlier. They found the predictive value of this test did not diminish over time and was not explained by other known risk factors, such as smoking, drinking, or radiation exposure. The studied learned that the best predictor of who would get cancer decades later was the closeness of the father-son relationship earlier in life.[32]

Many studies have shown that married individuals live longer, with lower mortality for almost every major cause of death, than those who are single, separated, widowed, or divorced.[33] One study asked a simple question. "Does your wife show you her love?" Those who answered yes to this question showed a reduced risk of angina pectoris, even in the presence of high risk factors.[34] While other psychosocial factors, such as anxiety and family problems, consistently affect the incidence of angina, spousal support in the form of perceived love seems to significantly diminish the risk of angina, even more so than other serious risk factors.

Old Age

Last, in the longest continuous study in the world on aging, Dr. George Vaillant and colleagues found that a warm relationship with our spouse is an excellent predictor of aging well.[35] The fact that social connection is an excellent predictor of healthy aging has been well supported in many other studies. In one study, a team of researchers found that over 2,800 Dutch citizens, ages fifty-five to eighty-five, were positively affected by loving relationships. Specifically, they found that those who perceived themselves as being surrounded by a loving, supportive circle of friends decreased their death rate by approximately half when compared with those who did not feel the close social support.[36] Another study found that older individuals who perceived their social support as impaired were 340% more likely to die prematurely from all causes.[37]

The Endurance of the Glow

One study showed that what older adults contributed to their social network had more to do with their health than what they *received* from it. In other words, the more they gave, the more they received.[38] Another important research study found that 95% of those who had regular personal contact with the individuals whom they helped were blessed with a feel-good sensation which became known as the "helper's high."[39] Nationwide surveys indicate that close to 90% of committed volunteers say they are healthier or as healthy as others their age.[40]

Another study's participants commented on "the endurance of the glow," or the helper's high. Amazingly, of those who commented, most say that the glow kept returning when they remembered helping. Volunteering is a blessing that "keeps on giving" back to the giver.[41]

INTERPERSONAL

REINFORCE THE MESSAGE

SKILL BUILDERS

Choose the Skill Builders below that you would like to experience in your own life, then write a response on how they impacted you. Last, write further actions, if any, that you would like to take as a result of doing the Skill Builders.

 Skill Builder I | **Social Circles Exercise**

1. In the innermost circle write the names of people who are your most important and direct supporters.

2. In the next circle write the names of friends and relatives who are not as significant but who still provide support.

3. In the third circle write the names of people you have a relationship with, don't really get support from, but feel you could if you really needed it.

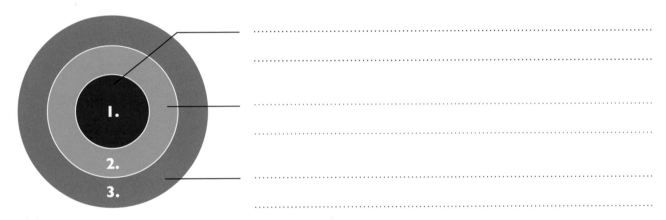

NOTE: Most of the time when people do this exercise, gender differences show up. Women tend to have more support than men. Much research suggests that social support is a key factor in prolonging a person's life. This may partly explain why women, with their larger social support networks, tend to live longer than men. If you currently have a good support system, then you can focus on strengthening and expanding it; if you don't, then what you have learned should help you get started improving one step at a time.

 DESCRIBE HOW THIS IMPACTED YOU:

FURTHER ACTION:

Our connection through touch is indeed healing to mind, body, and soul. It can take many forms and it can have profound effects on our whole being. Try these simple ways to add more touch to your life:

- **Connect to your children** with a hug, kiss, or a gentle squeeze of the arm.

- **Shake hands and smile** when greeting someone.

- **Hold a friend's hand** while you take time to talk with them.

- **Get a massage** or a manicure.

- **Volunteer** at an animal shelter or petting zoo, or pet or hold a dog, cat, or bird.

> *"The first handshake in life is the greatest of all; the clasp of an infant fist around the parent's finger."*
> ~ **MARK BELTAIRE**

DESCRIBE HOW THIS IMPACTED YOU:

....

....

....

....

FURTHER ACTION:

....

....

....

....

INTERPERSONAL

We all have heard the adage, if you want to make friends, be friendly. But most of us tend to underestimate the significance of this truth. If we want to have strong, healthy friendships that sustain us through the good times as well as the bad, we must be the kind of person that we want our friends to be. In other words, the adage above is just a variation of the Golden Rule: treat others the way you want them to treat you. Being a friend means being positive and supportive to those we associate with.

Consider the following: Shelly Gable, professor of psychology at UCLA, demonstrated through her research that how people talk about the good things that happen to them is more predictive of strong relationships than how people handle the bad things. People whom we care about often tell us about a triumph, victory, and many other smaller things that happen to them on a daily basis. How we respond to them can either build up the relationship or undermine it.[42] We can bond with others through open, positive, supportive communication. These bonds will strengthen when we affirm others more by focusing on their positive traits and the positive events in their lives, and by verbally and physically expressing support for them in a sincere, authentic way.

Over the next week practice the following: be on the lookout for and try to elicit good news from your friends and family. When they share good news with you, make an effort to respond with genuine support and enthusiasm. Let them know that you are truly happy for them and want to celebrate with them. Write down your interactions on the lines below. After you write each one down, look at it and think of how you could have done it better. Practice being supportive in this way by doing it three or four times this week.

Sunday

GOOD NEWS:
....
....

YOUR RESPONSE:
....
....

NEXT TIME YOU WILL:
....
....

Monday

GOOD NEWS:
....

YOUR RESPONSE:
....

NEXT TIME YOU WILL:
....
....

Tuesday

GOOD NEWS:

....

....

YOUR RESPONSE:

....

....

NEXT TIME YOU WILL:

....

....

*Golden Rule: treat others the way
you want them to treat you.*

Wednesday

GOOD NEWS:

....

....

YOUR RESPONSE:

....

....

NEXT TIME YOU WILL:

....

....

INTERPERSONAL

Thursday

GOOD NEWS:

....

....

YOUR RESPONSE:

....

....

NEXT TIME YOU WILL:

....

....

Friday

GOOD NEWS:

....

YOUR RESPONSE:

....

NEXT TIME YOU WILL:

....

....

Saturday

GOOD NEWS:

....

....

YOUR RESPONSE:

....

NEXT TIME YOU WILL:

....

....

> *"The heartfelt counsel of a friend is as sweet as perfume and incense."*
> ~ PROVERBS 27:9

Week in Review

DESCRIBE HOW THIS IMPACTED YOU:

....

....

....

....

FURTHER ACTION:

....

....

....

....

Skill Builder 4 | Time Well Spent

A. **Connect with "an old friend"** or someone you have not been in contact with recently.

B. **Spend time** with someone who is special to you.

C. **Be there for another person.** In our fast-paced society, time is precious. Loving someone often means setting aside time to spend with them. We may let them know we love them by telling them so, but if we don't back up those words with actions, the words may have little meaning to them. This week, set aside three or four ten-minute blocks of time and let someone know you want to talk with them during those times. During these blocks of time turn off your cell phone, TV, radio, etc. and don't answer your house phone either. Use this time strictly to interact with the person. At the end of the week, spend a few minutes thinking about how this exercise changed your relationship.

DESCRIBE HOW THIS IMPACTED YOU:

FURTHER ACTION:

INTERPERSONAL

Skill Builder 5 | Forgive One Another

When we forgive others, we give healing not only to the other person but to ourselves, too. Think about someone who has wronged you that you still have negative feelings toward. If you can think of more than one person, repeat this exercise as many times as needed, but be sure to do so at a comfortable pace because forgiving can be hard work. Ask God to help you forgive this person and continue to pray about them and yourself until you are able to truly let go of all animosity and forgive them. If possible, let them know that you have forgiven them. Enjoy the freedom that truly forgiving someone brings to your life!

DESCRIBE HOW THIS IMPACTED YOU:

....
....
....
....

FURTHER ACTION:

....
....
....
....

> *"Forgiveness is not an occasional act, it is a permanent attitude."*
> ~ MARTIN LUTHER KING JR.

INTERPERSONAL

Get involved by serving others. You might be wondering what is the best way to get started. Allan Luks and Peggy Payne, in their book *The Healing Power of Doing Good: The Health and Spiritual Benefits of Helping Others,* give guidelines that have emerged from Allan Luks's research that demonstrate how to maximize the health-enhancing effects of service.

HOW TO ENHANCE YOUR SERVICE EXPERIENCE

1. Have personal contact with the person you help (especially a stranger), or at least a strong emotional connection, such as using a phone on a telephone hotline.

2. Set a goal of two hours of service per week.

3. Volunteer at something you are already equipped to do, or will be trained in.

4. Choose an opportunity that is especially relevant to your personal interests.

"Often people say, 'Oh, I tried giving time at that place, but volunteering just isn't right for me.'" The truth of the matter is a particular experience may not have been right, but it's important to persist in finding what works for you. It is interesting to note that altruism's pleasure does not appear to arise from donating money, no matter how important the cause, nor does it arise from volunteering without close personal contact.

> *"Genuine concern for others is a lifestyle more than a technique."*
>
> **~ JOHN MAXWELL**

INTERPERSONAL

DESCRIBE HOW THIS IMPACTED YOU:

....
....
....

FURTHER ACTION:

....
....
....
....

VOLUNTEER SERVICES CONTACT LIST

Adventist Disaster Relief Agency (A.D.R.A.)
adra.org

American Red Cross
redcross.org

The Association of Junior Leagues International Inc.
90 William Street, Suite 200, New York, NY 10038
Phone: (212) 951-8300
Fax: (212) 481-7196
E-mail: info@ajli.org
Website: ajli.org

Boys & Girls Clubs of America
National Headquarters
1230 W. Peachtree Street, NW, Atlanta, GA 30309
Phone: (404) 487-5700
E-mail: info@bgca.org
Website: bgca.org

Gray Panthers
733 15th Street, NW, Suite 437, Washington, DC 20005
Phone: (800) 280-5362 or (202) 737-6637
Fax: (202) 737-1160
E-mail: info@graypanthers.org

Kiwanis International
3636 Woodview Trace, Indianapolis, IN 46268-3196
Phone: (317) 875-8755
Fax: (317) 879-0204
Website: kiwanis.org

National AIDS Network
Phone: (202) 293-2437

National Association of Town Watch
P.O. Box 303, Wynnewood, PA 19096
Phone: 1(800) NITE-OUT
E-mail: info@natw.org
Website: natw.org

National Coalition for the Homeless
2201 P St NW, Washington, DC 20037
Phone: (202) 462-4822
Fax: (202) 462-4823
E-mail: info@nationalhomeless.org
Website: nationalhomeless.org

National Community Action Foundation
810 First Street, Suite 530
Washington, DC 20002
Phone: (202) 842-2092
Fax: (202) 842-2095
Website: ncaf.org

Older Women's League
1750 New York Ave. NW, Suite 350
Washington, DC 20006
Phone: (202) 783-6686 or (800) 825-3695
Fax: (202) 628-0458
E-mail: owlinfo@owl-national.org
Website: owl-national.org

Oxfam America
26 West Street, Boston, MA 02111
Phone: (800) 77-OXFAM or (800) 776-9326
Website: oxfamamerica.org

Rotary International
One Rotary Center
1560 Sherman Ave., Evanston, IL 60201, USA
Website: rotary.org

United States Jaycees
PO Box 7, Tulsa, OK 74102-000
Phone: (800) JAYCEES or (918) 584-2481
Fax: (918) 584-4422
E-mail: DirectorCommunications@usjaycees.org
Website: usjaycees.org

Volunteers in Technical Assistance
1600 Wilson Boulevard, Suite 1030
Arlington, Virginia 22209
Phone: (703) 276-1800
Fax: (703) 243-1865
E-mail: info@enterpriseworks.org
Website: enterpriseworks.org

GUIDELINES FOR MODELING GOOD LISTENING SKILLS

Source: focusas.com/ListeningSkills.html   Used with Permission

- **Be interested and attentive.** Children can tell whether they have a parent's interest and attention by the way the parent replies or does not reply. Forget about the telephone and other distractions. Maintain eye contact to show that you are really listening.

- **Encourage talking.** Some children need an invitation to start talking. Children are more likely to share their ideas and feelings when others think them important.

- **Listen patiently.** People think faster than they speak. Children often take longer than adults to find the right words. Listen as though you have plenty of time.

- **Hear children out.** Avoid cutting children off before they have finished speaking. It is easy to form an opinion or reject children's views before they finish what they have to say. It may be difficult to listen respectfully and not correct misconceptions, but respect their right to have and express their opinions.

- **Listen to nonverbal messages.** Many messages children send are communicated nonverbally by their tone of voice, their facial expressions, their energy level, their posture, or changes in their behavior patterns. You can often tell more from the way a child says something than from what is said. When a child is obviously upset, be sure to take the time to give them the attention they need.

> "When I ask you to listen to me and you start giving advice,
> you have not done what I asked.
>
> When I ask you to listen to me and you begin to tell me that I
> shouldn't feel that way, you are trampling on my feelings.
>
> When I ask you to listen to me and you have to do something to solve
> my problem, you have failed me, strange as that may seem.
>
> So, please listen and just hear me.
> And, if you want to talk, wait a minute for your turn;
> and I'll listen to you."
>
> ~ AUTHOR UNKNOWN

INTERPERSONAL

ADDITIONAL RESOURCES

Books:

Forgive to Live, by Dr. Dick Tibbits

Forgive To Live Devotional: 56 Spiritual Insights on Forgiveness That Could Save Your Life by Dr. Dick Tibbits

Forgive To Live Workbook, by Dr. Dick Tibbits

Forgive To Live Spiritual Workbook, by Dr. Dick Tibbits

The Five Love Languages, by Gary Chapman

Websites:

ForgiveToLive.net

familyfun.go.com
(Ideas to bring families together, activities)

managementhelp.org/intrpsnl/intrpsnl.htm
(Good resource link for books and ideas relating to trust and interpersonal relationships)

marriagebuilders.com
(Great resources for building a happy, healthy marriage)

deltasociety.org
(A nonprofit organization that has the mission of "Improving human health through service and therapy animals." This site is loaded with information on the power of pets to positively impact our well-being. Includes research on this topic, interesting stories, and other resources)

Other Resources:

Massage – healthy touch

Animals – great for companionship and increasing social interactions

Songs That Encourage Positive Relationship Building:

What a Friend We Have in Jesus (Hymn)

Shall We Gather at the River (Gospel)

People Need the Lord (Steve Green)

Let It Begin with Me (Message of Mercy)

Cat's in the Cradle (Harry Chapin)

You've Got a Friend (James Taylor)

REFERENCES

1. Kaplan R, Kronick R. "Marital Status and Longevity in the United States Population." *Journal of Epidemiology and Community Health* 2006 60: 760–65.

2. Robison J, Carrier K. *The Spirit and Science of Holistic Health: More Than Broccoli, Jogging, and Bottled Water …More Than Yoga, Herbs, and Meditation*. Indiana: Author House, 2004, 106–107.

3. Ornish D. *Love and Survival: The Scientific Basis for the Healing Power of Intimacy*. New York: HarperCollins, 1998, 2–3.

4. Padus E. *The Complete Guide to Your Emotions and Your Health: New Dimensions in Mind/Body Healing*. Emmaus, PA: Rodale Press, 1986, 648.

5. Siegel B. *Love, Medicine and Miracles: Lessons Learned About Self-Healing from a Surgeon's Experience with Exceptional Patients*. New York: Harper Perennial, 1986, 181.

6. Egolf E, Lasker J, et al. "The Roseto Effect: A Fifty-Year Comparison of Mortality Rates." *American Journal of Public Health* 82(8): 1089–1092.

7. Wolf S, Bruhn J. *The Power of Clan: The Influence of Human Relationships on Heart Disease*. New Brunswick, NJ: Transaction, 1993.

8. Berkman L, Syme S. "Social Networks, Host Resistance, and Mortality: A Nine-Year Follow-Up Study of Alameda County Residents." *American Journal of Epidemiology* 109 (1979): 186–204.

9. Cohen S, Doyle W, et al. "Social Ties and Susceptibility to the Common Cold." *Journal of the American Medical Association* 1997 277: 1940–44.

10. Kiecolt-Glaser JK. "Psychosocial Enhancement of Immunocompetence in a Geriatric Population." *Health Psychology* 1985 4(1): 25–41.

11. Kiecolt-Glaser J, Glaser R, et al. "Marital Stress: Immunologic, Neuroendocrine, and Autonomic Correlates." *Annals of The New York Academy of Sciences* 840: 656–663.

12. Kiecolt-Glaser J, et.al. "Marital Quality, Marital Disruption, and Immune Function." *Psychosomatic Medicine* 1987 49: 13.

13. Kiecolt-Glaser J, et al. "Negative Behavior During Marital Conflict is Associated with Immunological Down-Regulation." *Psychosomatic Medicine* 1993 55(5): 395–409.

14. Spiegel D, Kraemer H, et al. "Effect of Psychosocial Treatment on Survival of Patients with Metastatic Breast Cancer." *The Lancet* 1989 2: 888–91.

15. Fawzy I. "Malignant Melanoma: Effects of an Early Structured Psychiatric Intervention, Coping, and Affective State of Recurrence and Survival Six Years Later." *Archives of General Psychiatry* 1993 50: 681-89.

16. Ruberman W, Winblatt, et al. "Psychosocial Influences on Mortality After Myocardial Infarction." *New England Journal of Medicine* 1984 311(9): 552–59.

REFERENCES

17. Hafen B, Karren K, et al. *Mind/Body Health: The Effects of Attitudes, Emotions, and Relationships.* Boston: Allyn & Bacon, 1996, 285.

18. Field T, Schanberg S, et al. "Tactile/Kinesthetic Stimulation Effects on Pre-Term Neonates." *Pediatrics* 1986 77(5): 654–58.

19. McKinney Wm. T. "Primate Social Isolation: Psychiatric Implications." *Archives of General Psychiatry* 1974 31: 422–426.

20. Spitz, R. "Hospitalism. An Inquiry in to the Genesis of Psychiatric Conditions in Early Childhood." *The Psychoanalytic Study of the Child* (1945). Found in *"The First Year of Life. A Psychoanalytic Study of Normal and Deviant Development of Object Relations."* New York: International Universities Press Inc., 1965, 277–278.

21. Barnhouse T. "A Study on the Effects of Touch and Impression Formation." Department of Psychology. Missouri Western University 2008 (last edited). http://clearinghouse.missouriwestern.edu/manuscripts/41.php date of retrieval 3/24/09.

22. Allen K, Blascovich J, et al. "Presence of Human Friends and Pet Dogs as Moderators of Autonomic Responses to Stress in Women." *Journal of Personality and Social Psychology*, 1991 61(4): 582–589.

23. Friedmann E, Honori A, et al. "Animal Companions and One-Year Survival of Patients After Discharge From a Coronary Care Unit." *Public Health Reports* 1980 95: 307–12.

24. Seigel J. "Stressful Life Events and Use of Physician Services Among the Elderly: The Moderating Role of Pet Ownership." *Journal of Personality and Social Psychology* 1990 58(6): 461–65.

25. Hafen B, Karren K, et al. *Mind/Body Health: The Effects of Attitudes, Emotions, and Relationships*. Boston: Allyn & Bacon, 1996, 313.

26. Hoffman S, Hatch M. "Stress, Social Support and Pregnancy Outcome: A Reassessment Based on Recent Research." *Pediatric & Perinatal Epidemiology* 1996 10(4): 380–405.

27. Sosa R, Kennel J, et al. "The Effective of a Supportive Companion on Perinatal Problems, Length of Labor and Mother-Infant Interactions." *New England Journal of Medicine* 1980 303: 597–600.

28. Klaus M, Kennell J, et al. "Effects of Social Support During Paturation on Maternal and Infant Morbidity." *British Medical Journal* Sept. 1996 293: 585.

29. Benard B. "Fostering Resiliency in Kids: Protective Factors in the Family, School, and Community." Portland, OR: Western Center for Drug-Free Schools and Communities, August 1991.

30. Russek L, Schwartz G. "Feelings of Parental Caring Predict Health Status in Midlife: A 35-Year Follow-Up of the Harvard Mastery of Stress Study." *Journal of Behavioral Medicine* 1997 20: 1–13.

31. Lynch J. *The Broken Heart: Medical Consequences of Loneliness*. Baltimore: Bancroft Press, 1998.

REFERENCES

32. Graves P, Thomas C, Mead L. "Familial and Psychological Predictors of Cancer." *Cancer Detection and Prevention* 1991 15(1): 59–64.

33. Ortmeyer C. "Variations in Mortality, Morbidity, and Health Care by Marital Status." In L. L. Erhardt and J. E. Beln, eds., *Mortality and Morbidity in the United States*. Cambridge: Harvard University Press, 1974, 159–184.

34. Medalia J, Goldbourt, U. "Angina Pectoris Among 10,000 Men. II. Psychosocial and Other Risk Factors as Evidenced by Multivariate Analysis of the Five-Year Incidence Study." *American Journal of Medicine* 1976 60(6): 910–921.

35. Vaillant G, Mukamal K. "Successful Aging." *American Journal of Psychiatry* June 2001 158(6): 839–847.

36. Penninx B, van Tilburg T, et al. "Effects of Social Support and Personal Coping Resources on Mortality in Older Age: The Longitudinal Aging Study Amsterdam." *American Journal of Epidemiology* 1997 146(6): 510–19.

37. Blazer D. "Social Support and Mortality in an Elderly Community Population." *American Journal of Epidemiology* 1982 115(5): 684–694.

38. Luks A. "How Alive is the Helping Connection?" *Spirituality and Health Magazine* May–June 2003.

39. Luks A. "Helper's High," *Psychology Today* October 1988 22(10): 39, 42.

40. Ibid.

41. Ibid.

42. Gable S, Gonzaga G, Strachman A. "Will You Be There for Me When Things Go Right? Supportive Responses to Positive Event Disclosures." *Journal of Personality and Social Psychology* 2006 91(5): 904–917.

43. Used with permission, © 2000, Wellsource, Inc, www.wellsource.com.

INTERPERSONAL

NOTES

NOTES

OUTLOOK

the key to a life of abundance

CONTENTS

MAKE IT WORK

Further Explanation of the DVD Topics

THE BIG PICTURE

What is Outlook? Outlook refers to how we approach the world and our lives. In other words, it is our general attitude. Outlook affects how we perceive the world, what we think of ourselves, of the people around us, our job, our home, our friends – everything. Our outlook impacts everything we think about and do. Some people tend to be optimistic, a definite asset; others tend to be pessimistic, which can lead to difficulties. In this section, we will focus on how to have a more positive and optimistic attitude toward life.

From Sports to Life Insurance

In *Learned Optimism*, Dr. Martin Seligman reported on an attributional style questionnaire he developed that ranks individuals on an optimism-pessimism scale. He did a longitudinal study on schoolchildren (a longitudinal study is a study that is done over a pre-specified period of time). What this study found was that those who scored the highest for optimism stayed non-depressed or, if they did get depressed, they recovered rapidly. In contrast, the pessimists were most likely to get and stay depressed.

Seligman also found through his research that high scores for optimism are predictive of excellence in many areas of life – from sports performance to life insurance sales performance. This finding saved Metropolitan Life millions of dollars in personnel selection. He also found that college freshman who rose to the challenges of their first year and who did better than expected

> *"We don't see things as they are; we see things as we are."*
>
> ~ **OLD JEWISH PROVERB**

were optimists when they entered college. Those who did much worse than expected (the expectations in both groups were based on measures such as GPA, SAT, and other achievement tests) entered their freshman year as pessimists.

Dr. Seligman summarizes his many studies on optimism and pessimism by stating, "Over and above their talent-test scores, we repeatedly find that pessimists drop below their potential and optimists exceed it. I have come to think that the notion of potential, without the notion of optimism, has very little meaning."[1]

Overall, optimists tend to have feelings of control over their lives. Seligman states in his book that "becoming an optimist consists not of learning to be more selfish and self-assertive, or presenting yourself to others in overbearing ways, but simply of learning a set of skills about how to talk to yourself when you suffer a personal defeat."[2] As you learn to be more optimistic, you will be learning to speak to yourself about your setbacks from a more encouraging viewpoint.

Depressing Statistics

Focusing on the negative instead of being optimistic can lead to depression. Depression has a powerful impact on society. About two hundred million people worldwide are depressed. It affects over nineteen million Americans and costs over $70 billion in treatment, disability, and lost productivity each year.

One study included 817 patients assessed for depression the day prior to coronary artery bypass surgery, and then again six months later. It included follow-up for up to twelve years. Researchers found that the patients with moderate to severe depression prior to their surgery or six months after surgery had more than a twofold higher risk of dying earlier than non-depressed patients. Those who were depressed before surgery, but were able to get rid of the depression, were at no greater risk of dying early than those who were never depressed.[3]

Dr. Seligman wrote about the value of cognitive therapy in helping depression. The idea is to help people be more optimistic. It also prevents relapses into depression because the people acquire a skill that they can use again and again without relying on drugs or doctors. "Drugs relieve depression, but only temporarily; unlike cognitive therapy, drugs fail to change the underlying pessimism which is the root of the problem."[4]

EXPLANATORY STYLES

PESSIMISTIC EXPLANATORY STYLE

People who generally tend to blame themselves for negative events believe that such events will continue indefinitely. They let these events affect many aspects of their lives, and they display what is called a pessimistic explanatory style.

OPTIMISTIC EXPLANATORY STYLE

Conversely, people who generally tend to blame others for negative events believe that such events will end soon, and do not let these events affect too many aspects of their lives. They display what is called an optimistic explanatory style.

Attitude Adjustment

Even more good news is that optimism can be learned and that it has a wonderful impact on every aspect of your life.

1. **Optimism will help you realize you have more CHOICES.** It will help you think of and act on good, healthy choices. When you are optimistic, you understand that your choices really make a difference.

2. **Optimism will help you REST easier;** a positive view of your future will allow you to relax today and help you sleep well at night.

3. **Optimism will help you seek an ENVIRONMENT** that is healing and restorative. When you are optimistic, you will believe that you can make changes in your space by cleaning a closet, getting organized, and keeping it that way.

4. **Optimism will help you believe** that you have what it takes to be mentally and physically **ACTIVE** on a regular basis. When you do have setbacks or "road blocks," your optimistic outlook will help you get back on track.

5. **Optimism will help you TRUST.** Optimism will help you trust in God and believe that He has your best interest in mind. Optimism will help you trust others, too; it will assist in building relationships, having peace of mind, and lowering your stress.

6. **Optimism will help you have a positive, cheery outlook,** and this will improve your **INTERPERSONAL RELATIONSHIPS** because others will be drawn to you. When we have a positive outlook, we will look for the positive in others and will encourage them. We will also "stick with" others through challenging times because we believe in them and that it all will work out for the good.

7. **Optimism will help you think positively** about your **NUTRITION** choices. If you have had challenges with diet in the past, if you feel like you have "never" been able to eat the way you want, then having an optimistic outlook will help you succeed. It will help you realize that you do have the power to influence your health by choosing the best possible food for your body.

What You See Is What You Get

Hope and positive belief are bridges from your thoughts to your success. What do you see in the following string of letters? **OPPORTUNITYISNOWHERE**. Do you see that "opportunity is now here?" or do you see that "opportunity is nowhere?" What you choose to focus on is important. Your belief or perception will profoundly impact your reality.

This fact has been well illustrated scientifically. Researchers at Rutgers University and Yale Medical School asked more than 2,800 men and women aged sixty-five and older the following question, "Is your health excellent, good, fair, or poor?" Those people who perceived their health as "poor" were as many as six times more likely to die earlier than those who perceived their health to be "excellent."[5] This is considered by many to be the best study of the impact of people's opinions on their health. The results of this study are consistent with the results of five other large studies involving a total of more than 23,000 people, ranging in age from nineteen to ninety-four years old.

"The question, how is your health, is a way of asking what our health means to us – what it represents or symbolizes in our thoughts and imagination – and is an example of the vital interplay between meaning and matter."[6]

The Placebo Effect

Beliefs and perceptions can indeed be the bridge to success. Your mind is very powerful. Perhaps the best-known example of the power of the mind to create physical changes in the body is found in what science terms "the placebo effect." A placebo is defined as "a treatment or aspect of a treatment that does not have a specific action on a patient's symptom or disease; an inactive substance, a procedure with no therapeutic value."

Placebos are often considered to be useless substances or procedures. Yet across a broad range of medical conditions and treatments, the placebo effect accounts for 25%–35% of the beneficial effect. When the procedure or drug is brand new, the placebo effect explains up to 70%–80% of the beneficial effect.[7] What a powerful effect our OUTLOOK has on our health and well-being.

In 1994, the *Journal of the American Medical Association* printed a review of pain medication research over the previous twenty-five-plus years. Its telling and thought-provoking conclusion states: "The quality of interaction between the patient and the physician can be extremely influential in patient outcomes, and, in some (perhaps many) cases, patient and provider expectations and interactions may be more important than the specific treatments."[8]

Garbage In, Garbage Out

It makes sense that if our thoughts and beliefs can affect us in such powerfully positive ways, they can also affect us in negative ways. This fact provides strong encouragement to choose positive thoughts and beliefs.[9-12]

"HOPE" is the thing with feathers –
That perches in the soul –
And sings the tune
without the words –
And never stops – at all –"

~ EMILY DICKINSON
NO. 254 (C. 1861)

As we have seen, what we believe about our health impacts our health. The following passage makes the connections between thoughts and health, but it also takes it a step further and shows us how thoughts even affect our destiny.

- Watch your thoughts; they become your words.

- Watch your words; they become your actions.

- Watch your actions; they become your habits.

- Watch your habits; they become your character.

- Watch your character; it becomes your destiny.[13]

Because our thoughts shape who we are, it is vitally important that we are careful with what enters our minds. It is important for us to think about what we are feeding our minds through TV, movies, music, radio, and the Internet.

The Biology of Hope

Being hopeful in the face of challenges is a powerful way to turn positive thinking into action. Norman Cousins is known for what he called "the biology of hope." He relates an experience of physician William Buchholz reported in the *Western Journal of Medicine*. As Buchholz was eating breakfast one morning, he overheard two oncologists discussing papers they were going to present that day at the national meeting of the American Society of Clinical Oncology.

One of the physicians complained bitterly, "You know, Bob, I just don't understand it. We use the same drugs, the same dosage, the same schedule, and the same entry criteria. Y et, I got a 22% response rate, and you got a 74% response rate. That is unheard of for metastatic lung cancer. How do you do it?"

The other responded, "We're both using Etoposide, Platinol, Oncovin, and Hydroxyurea. You call yours EPOH. I tell my patients I'm giving them HOPE. Sure, I tell them this is experimental, and we go over the long list of side effects together. But I emphasize that we have a chance. As dismal as the statistics are for non-small cell, there are always a few percent who do really well."[14]

Researcher Toshihiko Marta and colleagues found that an optimistic explanatory style was associated with a 50% decrease in the risk of mortality or early death.[15] They found that optimists had a decrease in bodily pain and role limitations due to emotional and physical problems. In the same study, these optimists also enjoyed an increase in physical function and vitality, general health perception, and social functioning and mental health.[16] Hope, or the lack thereof, has been shown to impact other diseases (such as Parkinson's) as well.[17-18]

The Vision Thing

Vision is connected to our perception. The video "Celebrate What's Right With The World" teaches what a powerful force having a vision full of possibilities can be. In this video, Dewitt Jones states the following: "For 20 years I worked for National Geographic photographing stories all over the globe, creating extraordinary visions. I learned a great deal from these visions; about society, about geography, about people. But the vision that most changed my life was not photographic. It was an attitude, a perspective that exists at the core of the National Geographic. A vision so simple, yet so profound. A vision I'd like to share with you: Celebrate What's Right with the World. When I was growing up I used to hold that maxim: I won't believe it until I see it, yet the more I shot for the National Geographic the more I realized that I had it backwards. That the way it really works is, I won't see it, till I believe it. That's the way life works. Well I believed it, I believed the vision of the National Geographic and the more I did the more I'd see it in everything."[19]

A good vision means that you have meaning and purpose in your life. It means you have a positive outlook. In fact, a person's positive outlook helps their vision become a reality, for it becomes fuel for living out that vision.

A vision is a dream in action. Optimists have a dream. They hold onto it when passing through life's dark valleys. They will live and die for their vision. This important truth is well illustrated by Victor Frankl, a psychiatrist from Vienna who survived the Auschwitz concentration camp. Frankl found that survivors had something to live for – a golden thread of hope.

An optimistic person identifies something to live for and then takes positive action in achieving that dream. This makes life worth living. "It is a peculiarity of man," wrote Frankl, "that he can only live by looking to the future… And this is his salvation in the most difficult moments of his existence."[20]

Eugene Lang, a successful self-made millionaire, had graduated from P.S. 121 Elementary School in Harlem and was invited back as the commencement speaker for the 1981 graduating sixth-grade class. As he spoke, he looked at the fifty-two students gathered there and sensed he wasn't getting his message – the fact that they had a future – through to them. He laid aside his notes and gave an unplanned talk that changed their lives forever. He reminded them of Martin Luther King's "I Have a Dream" speech. He told them that everyone must have a dream if his or her life is to go anywhere. He emphasized the value of education and of going to college but then realized that most of them couldn't afford it.

"Don't think for a minute," he said, "that you can't go to college, because you can."

He then promised to pay the college tuition for every student who would go on and graduate from high school. For the first time, many of the students sensed hope and started developing a vision for their life. One student said, "I had something to look forward to, something waiting for me. It was a golden feeling."[21] Although Mr. Lang sat down that day to a cheering audience, he knew that money alone wasn't the answer. He created a support structure of teachers, parents, and community that worked together with the students in order to help them manifest a vision for their lives.

Past history had predicted that of the fifty-two sixth graders in that class, only 25% would graduate from high school. And of that 25%, almost none would go to college. But, thanks to Mr. Lang and the support of others, forty-eight of the fifty-two sixth graders graduated from high school, and forty attended college.[22]

In *The Future Focused Role Image*, Benjamin Singer reports that, in his research, IQ and family background were not key indicators of successful students. The characteristics that all successful students shared was a profound and positive vision of their future.[23]

The Gratitude Attitude

Another important part of your outlook is the expression of gratitude for whatever you have. Regularly express gratitude. Thanksgiving is a primary ingredient of optimism and a positive outlook.

Right now, start making a mental list of what you're grateful for. It can be people or things or whatever. Just start listing them in your head. By doing this, you're counting your blessings. It's as simple as that! Every day, we're either counting or discounting our blessings.

Research has shown that people who regularly listed what they were thankful for experienced higher levels of optimism, alertness, enthusiasm, determination, attentiveness, and energy than those who didn't. Those who expressed gratitude more often helped others, exercised regularly, made progress toward personal goals, enjoyed satisfying sleep, and felt connected.[24]

Grateful people enjoy higher levels of positive emotions, life satisfaction, and vitality than do pessimists. They experience less depression and stress, too. Researchers learned that grateful people do not deny or ignore the negative aspects of life; they just rise above them. Optimistic and grateful people are also more empathetic and are considered more helpful and generous by the people in their social networks.[25]

In short, your attitude and outlook can make a big difference in the quality of your mental and physical health. You can't always change your circumstances, but you can change your attitude toward them, and sometimes that makes all the difference in the world.

KEY FACTORS FOR CREATING YOUR VISION

1. Identify your core values that will never change.

2. Determine who you want to be.

3. Set challenging but achievable goals – both short and long term.

4. Write down your vision for the future and place it where you will see it often. Create a vibrant, engaging, and specific description of what it will be like when you achieve your goal.

5. Articulate your vision often. Pray about it, talk about it, and rework it as needed, keeping in mind that certain aspects of it should never change while other aspects must change as circumstances demand. Always remain true to your core values and beliefs.

OUTLOOK

REINFORCE THE MESSAGE

SKILL BUILDERS

Choose the Skill Builders below that you would like to experience in your own life, then write a response on how they impacted you. Last, write further actions, if any, that you would like to take as a result of doing the Skill Builders

 Skill Builder 1 | **What's So Great About My Life?**

Why write down positive events? Many times the good things in our lives slip by without our notice. This Skill Builder will help you to practice looking at the good in life. It will also help you attain the benefits of optimistic thinking. Dr. Seligman stated in his book *Learned Optimism* that "over and above their talent test scores, we repeatedly find that pessimists drop below their 'potential' and optimists exceed it. I have come to think that the notion of potential, without the notion of optimism, has very little meaning."[26]

EVERYDAY EXAMPLES

ONE GOOD THING THAT HAPPENED TO ME TODAY:
My child brought me a bouquet of wildflowers from our yard.
My explanation for why this good thing happened:

OPTION #1: *She has such a tender heart, she knows I love flowers, and always thinks of me when she sees them.*

OPTION #2: *She knows that I am desperately missing her grandma, my mother, who passed away three weeks ago, so she picked them to cheer me up.*

ONE GOOD THING THAT HAPPENED TO ME TODAY:
My wife made my favorite meal for supper this evening.
My explanation for why this good thing happened:

OPTION #1: *Today is our anniversary.*

OPTION #2: *My wife is thoughtful; she knows that the stress at work is getting to me and that I would enjoy having this special dinner.*

OPTION #3: *I requested this meal because we haven't had it in a while.*

ONE GOOD THING THAT HAPPENED TO ME TODAY:
I got the new job I had interviewed for two weeks ago!
My explanation for why this good thing happened:

OPTION #1: *God blessed me and opened a door of opportunity!*

OPTION #2: *I knew the right people that helped me get this job.*

OPTION #3: *My resume included just what they were looking for.*

Why you should write down the good things that happen in your life:

It is very common for us to analyze why things go wrong in our lives. Many times we even overanalyze those events. This is the pattern of someone with a pessimistic explanatory style, and much of the time it leads to depression. On the other hand, we often tend to underanalyze what went well – we take those events for granted. The analysis of good events is beneficial because it helps put us in touch with the pleasures, successes, positive events, and blessings that are in all of our lives. It helps us to focus on the good, on the "silver lining." It helps us celebrate what is right with the world! It helps us develop an optimistic explanatory style. The more we practice using this positive explanatory style, the more optimistic we will become in our way of thinking and behaving.

Every evening for the next week, write down one unique thing that went well for you and then write down why you think this good event happened. The things you list can be ordinary and small in importance or they may be grand and very important.

Sunday

GOOD THING THAT HAPPENED:

....

....

....

YOUR EXPLANATION OF WHY:

....

....

....

Monday

GOOD THING THAT HAPPENED:

....

....

....

YOUR EXPLANATION OF WHY:

....

....

....

OUTLOOK

Tuesday

GOOD THING THAT HAPPENED:

....

....

YOUR EXPLANATION OF WHY:

....

....

....

Wednesday

GOOD THING THAT HAPPENED:

....

....

YOUR EXPLANATION OF WHY:

....

....

....

> *"It is not how much we have, but how much we enjoy, that makes happiness."*
> ~ CHARLES SPURGEON

Thursday

GOOD THING THAT HAPPENED:

....

....

YOUR EXPLANATION OF WHY:

....

....

....

OUTLOOK

Friday

GOOD THING THAT HAPPENED:

....

....

....

YOUR EXPLANATION OF WHY:

....

....

....

Saturday

GOOD THING THAT HAPPENED:

....

....

....

YOUR EXPLANATION OF WHY:

....

....

....

Week in Review

DESCRIBE HOW THIS IMPACTED YOU:

....

....

....

....

FURTHER ACTION:

....

....

....

....

Each day this week, purposefully express your gratitude to others through words of thanks, a written thank-you note, a letter thanking someone for their positive impact on your life (be sure to list specifics), or an e-mail thanking someone for something they have done. Express your gratitude to someone in your life at least once each day, and write down what you were thankful for at the end of each day.

Sunday

WHAT ARE YOU THANKFUL FOR:
....
....

TO WHOM & DATE:
....
RESPONSE, IF ANY:
....
....

Monday

WHAT ARE YOU THANKFUL FOR:
....
....

TO WHOM & DATE:
....
RESPONSE, IF ANY:
....
....

Tuesday

WHAT ARE YOU THANKFUL FOR:

....

....

TO WHOM & DATE:

RESPONSE, IF ANY:

....

....

Wednesday

WHAT ARE YOU THANKFUL FOR:

....

....

TO WHOM & DATE:

RESPONSE, IF ANY:

....

....

Thursday

WHAT ARE YOU THANKFUL FOR:

....

....

TO WHOM & DATE:

RESPONSE, IF ANY:

....

....

"Being happy doesn't mean everything is perfect.
It means you have decided to look beyond the imperfections."
~ **UNKNOWN AUTHOR**

OUTLOOK

Friday

WHAT ARE YOU THANKFUL FOR:

....

....

TO WHOM & DATE:

....

RESPONSE, IF ANY:

....

....

Saturday

WHAT ARE YOU THANKFUL FOR:

....

....

TO WHOM & DATE:

....

RESPONSE, IF ANY:

....

....

Week in Review

DESCRIBE HOW THIS IMPACTED YOU:

....

....

....

FURTHER ACTION:

....

....

....

TIPS FOR SUCCESS

POWER TIPS: IMPROVE YOUR OUTLOOK ON LIFE

Six ways to start enjoying a positive outlook now:

1. **Hope and believe in the best.**
   We can choose to find the good in every situation.

2. **Choose to focus on the positive and not the negative things.**
   An optimist sees an opportunity in every calamity.

   A pessimist sees a calamity in every opportunity.

3. **Express gratitude. Thanksgiving is a pillar of optimism.**
   Optimists count their blessings.

   Pessimists count their burdens.

4. **Color your world with optimism.**
   Be optimistic about your choices.
   If your choices have not gotten you what you want, then choose differently. Be diligent in finding a better way!

   Be optimistic about your life. Optimism about the future gives us peace of mind in the present. This peace helps us rest well and sleep soundly.

   Be optimistic about your environment.
   You can always make improvements to your environment.

   Be optimistic about your activity.
   Optimism can give you the power and discipline to stay physically and mentally active.

   Be optimistic about your trust in God and others. Being optimistic about your relationship with God will foster its growth. Trusting in others will also build bridges of unity.

   Be optimistic about your interpersonal relationships. See the best in others; be the friend you want to have, and believe that "things will work out." Remember that optimism is a learned behavior. It is a habit of thought. We can learn how to be less pessimistic and more optimistic.

   Be optimistic about your diet.
   Optimism empowers you to eat healthfully. If you have been challenged by an imbalance in this area, being optimistic can help you have the success that you may have never thought possible.

5. **Live your vision.**
   Optimists have purpose in life; they are headed somewhere and are getting there, too. A vision is a dream in action. Your vision gives your dreams wings to fly!

6. **Dare to dream. Be bold.**
   Optimists dare something worthy. They take calculated risks, and they keep taking them until they succeed. Optimists don't quit no matter what comes their way in life.

THE OPTIMIST CREED

By Christian D. Larson   *Public Domain*

Promise Yourself:

- **To be** so strong that nothing can disturb your peace of mind.

- **To talk** health, happiness, and prosperity to every person you meet.

- **To make** all your friends feel that there is something worthwhile in them.

- **To look** at the sunny side of everything and make your optimism come true.

- **To think** only the best, to work only for the best, and to expect only the best.

- **To be** just as enthusiastic about the success of others as you are about your own.

- **To forget** the mistakes of the past and press on to the greater achievements of the future.

- **To wear** a cheerful expression at all times and give a smile to every living creature you meet.

- **To give** so much time to improving yourself that you have no time to criticize others.

- **To be** too large for worry, too noble for anger, too strong for fear, and too happy to permit the presence of trouble.

- **To think** well of yourself and to proclaim this fact to the world, not in loud word, but in great deeds.

- **To live** in the faith that the whole world is on your side, so long as you are true to the best that is in you.

ATTITUDE BY CHARLES SWINDOLL

"The longer I live, the more I realize the impact of attitude on life.

Attitude, to me, is more important than facts. It is more important than the past, than education, than money, than circumstances, than failures, than successes, than what other people think or say or do. It is more important than appearance, giftedness or skill. It will make or break a company... a church... a home.

The remarkable thing is we have a choice every day regarding the attitude we will embrace for that day. We cannot change our past... we cannot change the fact that people will act in a certain way. We cannot change the inevitable. The only thing we can do is play on the one thing we have, and that is our attitude... I am convinced that life is 10% what happens to me and 90% how I react to it.

And so it is with you... we are in charge of our attitudes."

OUTLOOK

DREAM

By Paulo Coelho   *Used with Permission*

You are in a store. You try on a garment that fits you perfectly. You try on another, but it's too large, it itches a bit, the sleeves drag on the floor. Both garments sell for the same price. Which do you buy?

It isn't a trick question: You should buy the one that fits better, of course. This logic can also apply to the way we decide to live our lives. We know intuitively that there's a life we long to have, a dream we've harbored – sometimes since childhood. But too often we decide to follow a path that is not really our own, one that others have set for us. We forget that whichever way we go, the price is the same: In both cases, we will pass through difficult and happy moments, hours of solitude, and many complex situations. But when we are living a dream, the difficulties we encounter make sense.

You may have heard the parable of the three men laboring in a field of rocks. Each is asked what he's doing. The first man says, "Can't you see? I'm breaking rocks!" The second man replies, "Can't you see? I'm earning my salary!" The third man answers, his eyes gleaming with enthusiasm, "Can't you see? I'm building a cathedral!" This lovely story, which my mother first told me when I was a child, illustrates both the necessity of hard work in realizing a dream as well as the need to keep vision in your mind's eye – even when others don't see or understand it.

The money we receive in return for eight hours of work each day can be spent in any number of ways; the only thing we cannot buy is extra time. So during the minutes we have, I believe it is better to live a dream rather than to simply dream it. The dream is the start of something greater, something that impels us to make daring decisions. And it's true that the person who pursues a dream takes many risks. But the person who does not dream runs risks that are even greater.[27]

Dream:
"A visionary creation
of the imagination."

~ WEBSTER'S THIRD
NEW INTERNATIONAL DICTIONARY

OUTLOOK

SMALL GROUP DISCUSSIONS

Directions: Review the discussion questions and choose one you would like to discuss first. Proceed through the rest of the questions as time allows.

1. In your group, ask each person to talk about their blessings. Ask them to talk only of the positive things in their lives and the things that they have to be thankful for.

   ....
   ....

2. What have been your own experiences with how your mental attitude impacts your physical health? Have you seen the importance of a positive outlook for optimum health?

   ....
   ....

3. Do you know someone who seems optimistic and positive, even amid some dreadful circumstances? If so, what is the key to that attitude? More so, how can you learn to apply that to your life?

   ....
   ....

4. What role can and should faith play in helping us have a positive outlook? What Bible texts do you find especially reassuring when it comes to helping you feel positive about things?

   ....
   ....

5. What practical steps can you take and what changes can you make in your lifestyle that could contribute toward a more positive outlook on life?

   ....
   ....

"Perpetual optimism is a force multiplier."

~ **COLIN POWELL**

ADDITIONAL RESOURCES

Books:

Learned Optimism: How to Change Your Mind and Your Life, by Martin Seligman

The Optimistic Child: Proven Program to Safeguard Children from Depression & Build Lifelong Resilience, by Martin E. Seligman

Man's Search for Meaning, by Victor Frankl

An Attitude of Gratitude, by Keith Harrell

The Purpose Driven Life, by Rick Warren

Websites:

wikihow.com/Be-Positive

plr.org (Positive Life Radio)

Songs to Inspire and Improve Outlook:

It Is Well with My Soul (Hymn)

This Is My Father's World (Hymn)

Be Thou My Vision (Celtic Melody)

For the Beauty of the Earth (Thanksgiving Hymn)

You Raise Me Up (Selah and Josh Groban)

Endless Hope (Message of Mercy)

Lookin' Forward (Message of Mercy)

Anyway (Martina McBride)

Yes, I Believe (Point of Grace)

Singin' in the Rain (The Ruppes)

OUTLOOK

REFERENCES

1. Seligman M. *Learned Optimism: How to Change Your Mind and Your Life*. New York: Pocket Books, 1998, 154, 207.

2. Ibid.

3. Blumenthal J, et. al. "Depression as a Risk Factor for Mortality After Coronary Artery Bypass Surgery." *The Lancet* August 23, 2003 362(9384): 604–609.

4. Seligman M. *Learned Optimism: How to Change Your Mind and Your Life.* New York: Pocket Books, 1998, 81.

5. Idler E, Stanislav K. "Health Perceptions and Survival: Do Global Evaluations of Health and Status Really Matter? *Journal of Gerontology* 1991 46(2): S55–65.

6. Dossey L. *Meaning & Medicine: Lessons from a Doctor's Tales of Breakthrough and Healing*, New York: Bantam Books, 1991, 16.

7. Robison J, Carrier K. "*The Spirit and Science of Holistic Health.*" Bloomington, IN: AuthorHouse, 2004, 91.

8. Turner J, Deyo R, et al. "The Importance of Placebo Effects in Pain Treatment and Research." *Journal of the American Medical Association* May 25, 1994 271(20): 1609–1614.

9. Eaker E, Pinsky, J. et al. "Myocardial Infarction and Coronary Death Among Women: Psychosocial Predictors for a Twenty-Year Follow-Up of Women in the Framingham Study." *American Journal of Epidemiology* 1992 135: 854–64.

10. Luparello T, Lyons H, et al. "Influences of Suggestion on Airway Reactivity in Asthmatic Subjects." *Psychosomatic Medicine* 1968 30: 819–25.

11. Blakeslee D. "Placebos Prove So Powerful Even Experts Are Surprised: New Studies Explore the Brain's Triumph over Reality." *New York Times* October 13, 1998.

12. Fielding J. "An Interim Report of a Perspective, Randomized, Control Study of Adjuvant Chemotherapy in Operable Gastric Cancer: British Stomach Cancer Group." *World Journal of Surgery* 1983 7: 390–99.

13. Kinkade T. *My Father's World.* San Jose, CA: Thomas Kinkade, Media Arts Group, Inc., 2000.

14. Cousins N. *Head First, The Biology of Hope*. New York: E. P. Dutton,1989, 99.

15. Maruta T, Colligan R, et al. "Optimists vs Pessimists: Survival Rate Among Patients Over a 30-Year Period." *Mayo Clinic Proceedings* Feb 2000 75(2): 140–143.

16. Maruta T, Colligan R, et al. "Optimism-Pessimism Assessed in the 1960s and Self-Reported Health Status 30 Years Later." *Mayo Clinic Proceedings* 2002 77: 748–753.

17. Fowler S. "Hope and a Health-Promoting Lifestyle in Persons with Parkinson's Disease." *Journal of Neuroscientific Nursing* April 1997 29(2): 111–116.

18. Everson S, Goldberg D, et al. "Hopelessness and Risk of Mortality and Incidence of Myocardial Infarction and Cancer." *Psychosomatic Medicine* March–April 1996 58(2): 113–21.

OUTLOOK

REFERENCES

19. "Celebrate What's Right With The World with Dewitt Jones." Video. Saint Paul, MN: Star Thrower Distribution, 2001.

20. Frankl VE. *Man's Search for Meaning*. Boston, MA: Beacon Press Publishing Company, 1963, 115–116, 126.

21. Geist W. "One Man's Gift: College for 52 in Harlem." *New York Times* (1857–Current file); 19 Oct. 1985; ProQuest Historical Newspapers. *New York Times* (1851–2001).

22. *The Power of Vision with Joel Barker Training Manual*, St. Paul, MN: Charthouse International Learning Corporation, Distributed by Star Thrower Distribution, 1993, 116.

23. Singer B. "Future Focused Role Image," in *Learning for Tomorrow: The Role of the Future of Education*, edited by Tofler A. New York: Vintage Books, 1974, 19–32.

24. Emmons RA, McCullough ME. "Counting Blessings Versus Burdens: An Experimental Investigation of Gratitude and Subjective Well-Being in Daily Life." *Journal of Personality and Social Psychology* 2003 84(2): 377–389.

25. McCullough M, Emmons R, Tsang J. "The Grateful Disposition: A Conceptual and Empirical Topography." *Journal of Personality and Social Psychology* 2002 82(1): 112–127.

26. Seligman M. *Learned Optimism: How to Change Your Mind and Your Life*. New York: Pocket Books, 1998, 154.

27. Coelho P. "Dream" *Self* 1995: 194. This essay was translated from Coelho's native Portuguese by Alan R. Clark, Ph.D. Reprinted with permission.

NOTES

NOTES

NUTRITION

your source for growth, regeneration, and delight

creation®
HEALTH

CONTENTS

MAKE IT WORK

Further Explanation of the DVD Topics

THE BIG PICTURE

In the beginning, God gave us the best diet possible. Today, scientists are discovering more and more about the amazing benefits of eating a diet that closely resembles the diet of Eden. Our nutrition is one of the most powerful tools we have to promote health. By improving our nutrition, we can substantially increase disease prevention[1] and be healthier, happier, and more energetic.

Think Positive

A mill worker was one hundred pounds overweight and wanted to lose weight but was too embarrassed to attend the nutrition classes his employer was offering. So he met with the presenter in her office to ask if she would be willing to help him individually. She agreed.

For the first week, all she asked him to do was write down everything he ate each day. He did, and brought his list to her the next week. She looked it over and then asked him to eat one piece of fruit every day in the coming week. He said to her, "But what about the pound of fudge I eat every day?" She encouraged him not to worry about it because it would take care of itself. And it did! The next week she asked him to add one vegetable (he had none on his list). He continued adding week by week until he was eating six-plus servings of fruits and vegetables daily. He took small steps and focused on the positive instead of the negative. This gave him the courage to gradually begin changing his diet and exercise patterns, and eventually he was successful in achieving his weight loss goals.

The important principle from this story is to focus on the positive. Add the positive to your life,

> "To eat is a necessity,
> but to eat intelligently is an art."
> ~ LA ROCHEFOUCAULD

and pretty soon the negative will be left behind because of lack of room. When looking at your diet, look at something good that you could do. Maybe you could add one fruit each day, an apple, perhaps? Maybe you want to increase your water intake in order to help your brain and body function better. Maybe you would like to start eating breakfast regularly. Or maybe you could choose to eat two cruciferous vegetables, like broccoli, cauliflower, brussels sprouts, kale, or cabbage every week in order to help your body clean out the toxins. Then, later, when that has gone well, you can add another healthy and nutritious habit to your diet.

The point is to choose to add something good to your diet, and not beat yourself up over the "bad." Research shows that dwelling on and highlighting the good is beneficial for your body, mind, and spirit. If you choose to think about this positively and make positive additions, YOU WILL SUCCEED!

We Are What We Eat

Getting back to the basics is essential for good nutrition. Simple, wise decisions about nutrition can have rich health rewards. Remember, food is your body's fuel. If you give your body good fuel, it will run better. Human blood cells have a life span of only three months. This means your body is constantly making new blood cells. Giving your body the highest quality food will allow it to make stronger, healthier blood cells. Thousands of other cells throughout your body are also being regenerated every day, so the importance of a healthy diet is easy to see: we really are what we eat.

Eat a variety of foods prepared in different ways. Don't be fooled by the latest trendy diet. Look carefully at it and ask yourself how different it is from what you know to be a balanced diet. Don't believe everything you hear. Ask critical questions about the food or dietary practice being promoted. When you see attractive headlines or advertisements, it is wise to make a habit out of asking critical questions. Ask yourself how this food will affect your overall health. Stand back and take a look at the big picture. Look deeper. Ask for perspective from a knowledgeable nutritionist. Get answers from reliable sources that have nothing to gain from your purchase of their product.

For healthy people, changes may best be made slowly, after careful consideration, in a way that fits into a balanced lifestyle and based on foundational principles.

A Special Word for People with Serious Diseases

People with serious diseases such as diabetes, heart disease, hypertension, and cancer may benefit from making rapid and dramatic changes in lifestyle practices. Apparently, amazing changes have resulted from carefully applied but aggressive lifestyle changes in people with significant illness. If you find yourself in this category, you might want to consider getting special help from health care professionals with experience in this area. There are several suggestions in Additional Resources at the end of this section.

> *"We are indeed much more than what we eat, but what we eat can nevertheless help us to be much more than what we are."*
> ~ ADELLE DAVIS

The Fiber Factor

In the Garden of Eden, God gave us a plant-based diet for our enjoyment and blessing. One of the most important aspects of this plant-based diet is fiber. High-fiber foods include beans, legumes, whole grains, pasta, vegetables, fruits, and nuts. Fiber satisfies without excess calories, which is great for achieving and maintaining a healthy weight. High fiber intakes are associated with lower serum cholesterol concentrations, lower risk of coronary heart disease, reduced blood pressure, enhanced weight control, better glycemic control, reduced risk of certain forms of cancer, and improved gastrointestinal function.[2] In fact, plant-based diets give us the lowest risk of cancer.[3] Foods high in fiber provide a slower rise in blood sugar, requiring less insulin to process a meal.[4] They also slow the emptying of food from the stomach, which slows the absorption of simple sugars into the small intestine.[5]

Studies also support the benefits of a plant-based diet for children. Researchers reported on changing the nutritional content of school lunches served to 1.1 million New York City public school students to a more wholesome, healthy diet. After just one year, a 16% increase in academic performance and a 41% decrease in the number of learning-disabled children were reported.[6]

You might be surprised to know that fruits and vegetables are an incredible promoter of harmonious living. In a study of eight thousand teenagers at nine juvenile correctional facilities, researchers arranged to have diets high in sugar and other refined carbohydrates replaced with diets high in fruits, vegetables, and whole grains. Amazingly, during the year in which the diets were changed, violent and antisocial incidents in the institutions decreased by almost half.[7]

The First Fast Foods

Fruits and vegetables are the original fast foods and are packed with fiber and nutrients. The color in fruits and vegetables is created by flavonoids, which science is discovering are amazing promoters of health. Different colors represent different nutrients and benefits. Colorful fruits and vegetables are wonderful. For example, purple, red, and blue fruits or vegetables are rich in phytochemicals called anthocyanins, which help get rid of free-radical damage in the body and the brain. Orange, yellow, and green vegetables are rich in stress-lowering carotenoids. One study found that some of these carotenoids, such as beta-carotene, when consumed on a regular basis, have a stress hormone-lowering effect,[8] so enjoy eating your fruits and vegetables in a rainbow of colors every day.

Fruits and vegetables are truly lifesaving. The World Health Organization states that up to 2.7 million lives could be saved annually with sufficient fruit and vegetable consumption. Low fruit and vegetable intake is among the top ten risk factors attributable to early mortality, according to evidence presented in the World Health Report 2002.[9]

There are many benefits from eating vegetables, and science is discovering more all the time. A study was done on Chinese women in Singapore, a city in which pollution levels are often high. This pollution creates extra stress on the cleaning capacity of people's lungs. The study found that in nonsmokers, eating cruciferous vegetables lowered their risk of lung cancer by 30%. In smokers, regularly eating cruciferous vegetables reduced lung cancer risk an amazing 69%.[10] This study clearly illustrates cruciferous vegetables' amazing ability to help protect the body.

Many studies have been done on specific fruits and, as with vegetables, more benefits are continually being discovered. For example, one fruit that has received great attention is the grape. Much of this attention has come from the apparent positive effects that drinking wine has on heart disease. The great news is that beneficial flavonoids that fight heart disease are found in the grape itself. By drinking grape juice, you can get the benefits from the grapes and avoid the damaging effects of alcohol, such as

addiction, cirrhosis, and increased risk of cancers. A study published in *The Lancet* found that high intakes of flavonoids predicted lower mortality from coronary heart disease and lower incidence of heart attacks.[11]

The latest research reveals that the old saying, "An apple a day keeps the doctor away," is fact, not folklore. Some of the nutritional stars in the apple – fiber and flavonoids – translate into the apple's ability to keep us healthy. A large review, including over eighty-five studies, found that regularly eating apples is the strongest association with a reduced risk of cancer, heart disease, asthma, and type 2 diabetes when compared to other fruits and vegetables. Additionally, apple intake was associated with increased lung function and increased weight loss.[12]

> *"You don't have to cook fancy or complicated masterpieces – just good food from fresh ingredients."*
> ~ JULIA CHILD

Another reason apples are so good for you is they are an excellent source of antioxidants. When compared to other commonly consumed fruits in the United States, they were found to have the second highest level of antioxidant activity (cranberries have the highest).[13] Apples can also help protect you from radiation. Researchers have found that the phenols in the skin of sun-kissed Braeburn apples provide a hefty dose of UV-B protection.[14] It's best to eat the whole apple, including the peel. Beneficial nutrients are lost when an apple is peeled.

"An apple a day keeps the doctor away."

~ Benjamin Franklin

Nut Cases

Healthy fats are essential to a good diet. And the best place to get those fats is from natural sources. Basically, the closer your food is to the way it came from nature, the better it is for you. Researchers found that when people on the Standard American Diet (SAD) were given an avocado-rich diet, their total cholesterol dropped an average of 8.2% with no change in HDL, high density lipoprotein cholesterol ("good cholesterol").[15] Another good source of healthy fat is found in nuts and seeds.

You have probably heard that eating too many nuts may lead to weight gain because they are so high in fat. But nuts impact our satiety in a positive way; they fill us up and help satisfy our hunger. In a review of the literature looking at the association between nut consumption and energy balance, clinical trials reveal little or no weight change with inclusion of various types of nuts in the diet over six months. Studies indicate this is largely attributable to the high satiety property of nuts, meaning people tend to eat less of other foods.

While the weight connection may still be debated in some circles, it is understood that the fat in nuts is a healthier fat. Nuts contain mostly mono- and polyunsaturated fats. These fats are more heart friendly. The Adventist Health Study, which included 26,473 people over a twelve-year period, found that people who ate nuts five or more times per week cut their risk of having heart attacks by 51% and had a 48% reduction in death from heart attacks as compared to those who ate nuts less than once a week.[16]

The Nurses' Health Study, lasting fourteen years and involving more than 86,000 women, found that those who consumed more than five ounces of nuts weekly cut their risk of coronary heart disease by 35%, compared to the women who ate less than one ounce per month. They found similar reductions in the risk of death from coronary heart disease (CHD) and nonfatal heart attacks.[17] Then, too, the seventeen-year Physicians' Health Study, which involved more than 21,000 men, found that those who ate nuts at least twice a week cut their risk of sudden cardiac death by 53% when compared with men who rarely ate nuts.[18]

Not only are nuts good for your heart, they are also an excellent "brain food." Researchers have credited them with helping to fight Alzheimer's disease and depression. Two studies published in the *Journal of the American Medical Association* suggested that the antioxidant vitamin E and other antioxidants in nuts, leafy green vegetables, and other foods might reduce the risk of Alzheimer's.[19-20] Another study found that a walnut extract helped with Alzheimer's.[21] The essential fatty acids found in flaxseed oil brought significant improvement to depression symptoms.[22]

Nuts are also a good source for choline, a brain-boosting chemical that is the precursor to acetylcholine – one of the crucial brain chemicals involved in memory.[23] Omega-3 fatty acids found in seeds and nuts affect the brain in a good way as well.

A Purdue University study showed that children low in dietary omega-3 essential fatty acids are significantly more likely to be hyperactive, have learning disorders, and display behavior problems. Those that had lower total blood omega-3 fatty acids also reported a greater number of behavior problems, temper tantrums, sleep problems, and had more learning and health issues, too.[24]

Science has demonstrated a wide range of problems associated with omega-3 deficiencies. Nuts high in omega-3 polyunsaturated fatty acids are not only heart and body healthy but also have powerful anti-inflammatory effects.[25] Flaxseeds, walnuts, and pumpkin seeds are good sources of omega-3. Other sources include dark green leafy vegetables and soybeans.

Walnuts also supply a helpful dose of one of the body's key factors for restful sleep, melatonin. In one study, researchers not only quantified the amount of melatonin present in walnuts (between 2.5 and 4.5 ng/gram) but also documented that eating walnuts can triple blood levels of serum melatonin, leading to an increase in the antioxidant activity in the bloodstream of animals.[26]

> "The wise man should consider that health is the greatest of human blessings. Let food be your medicine."
>
> ~ HIPPOCRATES

Seeds of Change

Seeds have great health benefits. Their high nutrient content shouldn't be surprising because seeds are "eggs" that contain the nutrients needed to nourish a new plant. We often use these nutritional wonders as an occasional snack. Making them a regular part of our diet has the potential of benefiting us even more.

Sesame seeds are a source of the bone-building mineral calcium. This is wonderful news for those who have trouble tolerating dairy products or who avoid them completely due to health concerns.

Flaxseeds provide several positive dietary factors. They are rich in omega-3 fatty acids, antioxidants such as lignan, and other fibers, all of which are good for our bodies. Ground flaxseeds have the potential to help with heart disease,[27] cancer,[28] high cholesterol,[29-30] blood pressure,[31] diabetes,[32] rheumatoid arthritis,[33] ADHD,[34] memory loss,[35] weight problems,[36] inflammation,[37] eczema,[38] acne, itchy dry skin, hives,[39] constipation,[40] menopause/PMS,[41-42] and even depression.[43]

Very little benefit is obtained from eating whole flaxseed because it passes right through the intestinal tract without being broken down enough to release many of the beneficial elements contained within.[44] Adding freshly ground flaxseed is the best way to include it in your diet. It can be sprinkled on cereal or used in baking. A coffee grinder works nicely to physically break the seeds down and release the beneficial components. Flaxseed oil and ground flaxseed get rancid quickly and require special care to maintain some of the healthy components. They should be refrigerated in dark, airtight containers for the longest shelf life. It is also recommended that an individual limit his or her intake of ground flaxseed to two tablespoons per day because it contains small amounts of cyanide. A small amount of this element will not cause any problems, but large amounts can significantly interfere with oxygen binding to hemoglobin in your blood. If you stick with the recommended amounts there will be no problems, and you can enjoy its many health benefits.

Beans and Whole Grains

"Legumes" is another name for beans. Beans are another example of a food that is packed with health benefits. They are low in calories and fat, a great source of folate and fiber, and contain a large amount of complex carbohydrates and many other important nutrients. Beans are a wonderful source of protein with about the same amount of protein per serving as most meats but without the unhealthy fats. Beans, in comparison to muscle meats, are low in fat, high in fiber, and much better for you.

Beans come in many colors, sizes, and flavors. Adding a few beans to your breakfast will mean you will not be as hungry at lunchtime and will choose to eat less throughout the day. Beans are great at helping to maintain a steady supply of energy for the brain and muscles throughout the day. Eating beans can reduce your risk of heart disease and strokes, and help prevent cancer, too.[45-46] They are good for diabetics because they have a low glycemic index. One study found that increased pinto bean intake lowered "bad" cholesterol (LDL-C), which should reduce the risk of heart disease.[47] Another study found that drinking soy milk more than once a day decreased the risk of prostate cancer by an amazing 70%.[48]

Some people have problems with intestinal gas (technically called flatus) from beans. Canned beans are usually treated in such a way to minimize this problem. If you prepare your own, you can minimize the gas-forming elements by bringing a pot of beans to a boil and then letting them sit overnight. The next morning, pour off the water and replace it with fresh water. Much of the gas-forming substances from the beans float off with the water. Then complete the cooking process. If the beans still cause gas problems, they can be cooked or eaten with papaya (or papain, a digestive enzyme from papaya), kiwi, uncooked pineapple (the bromelain enzyme in pineapple is destroyed by cooking), or meat tenderizer.

Whole grains were part of the original creation diet and are especially beneficial. "Whole grain foods are valuable sources of nutrients that are lacking in the American diet, including dietary fiber, B vitamins, vitamin E, selenium, zinc, copper, and magnesium. Whole-grain foods also contain phytochemicals, such as phenolic compounds that together with vitamins and minerals play important roles in disease prevention."[49]

Benefits of Water

Water is one of the most important elements of life. It's wonderfully refreshing, calorie free, and packed full of benefits. A large percentage of the human body is water. It is widely recognized as one of the seven basic constituents of food (along with fiber, carbohydrate, fat, vitamins, proteins, and minerals). "All of the body's important chemical reactions take place in water, and it has a vital role in the absorption of nutrients, removal of waste and control of temperature. Water's part in many other physical functions is becoming better understood, and the effects of water shortage upon the body is being measured in terms of under-performance, disease, and premature death."[50]

Lack of sufficient water can result in dehydration. In mild dehydration, the skin might appear flushed, dry, and loose, with a loss of elasticity.[51-52] Loss of skin elasticity is associated with aging as well.[53]

Dehydration also negatively affects mental performance. The symptoms of mild dehydration in adults include light-headedness, dizziness, tiredness, irritability, and headache, as well as reduced alertness and ability to concentrate.[54-56] At dehydration levels of more than 2%, people often report feeling more tired.[57]

Dehydration can also adversely affect a child's mental performance. Schools who took part in the Sandwell Children's Fund project to increase hydration among school children reported that since the beginning of the project, children showed improved concentration levels and were less tired and lethargic. Another study looked at the relationship between voluntary dehydration and cognitive performance in elementary school children ages ten to twelve years in southern Israel. It found that at the beginning of the day, there were no significant differences in mental performance between the hydrated and dehydrated children. But by midday the hydrated group performed better in four of the five cognitive tests compared to the dehydrated group, especially on a short-term memory task.[58]

Maintaining good levels of hydration is reported to decrease the risk of fatal coronary heart disease by 46% in men and 59% in women.[59] The risk of developing cancer is high. The most common types of cancer are lung, breast, bronchus, prostate, colon, rectum, and pancreatic.[60] Research into the relationship between hydration and incidences of cancer indicates a protective role for water. Research suggests that drinking enough water every day will reduce the risk of developing cancer of the breast, large bowel, and prostate.

Research has found that drinking water is associated with weight loss independent of diet and activity.[61] Drinking water fifteen to thirty minutes before a meal fills you up, and fewer calories are eaten. This is true for both obese[62] and normal weight individuals.[63-64] A population study of the water and food intake in the United States found that on a daily basis, those who drink water regularly intake 9% fewer calories than those who do not drink water regularly.[65]

So go ahead and drink plenty of good water. Keep well hydrated. Your body will function much better and properly metabolize the fat that you eat.

A note of caution is warranted. It is possible to drink too much water and wash out the body's sodium. This can lead to fatigue and even dangerous heart and brain dysfunction. Drink enough water to keep your urine a light straw color. For most people it would be reasonable to take ten to sixteen cups of water a day. Unless one is sweating a lot in hot weather, it is probably best not to drink more than 1-1/2 gallons a day. Recommendations may be lower for those with certain kidney, liver, or heart conditions. If a person has a chronic illness, it is usually best to follow a doctor's recommendations for water intake.

Breakfast for the Brain

Breakfast is especially important because the body has had a fast during the night. The brain's basic fuel is glucose, and so regularly supplying it with a new source of energy is essential. In 1995, the Pediatrics Department at the University of California at Davis hosted a group of psychologists, neuroscientists, nutritionists, and physiologists to review the scientific research on breakfast. The researchers concluded that the "eating of breakfast is important in learning, memory, and physical well-being in both children and adults."[66] The classic, much-quoted Alameda County Study found that those who ate breakfast almost every day or did not often eat between meals reported better physical health and tended to live longer than those who skipped breakfast or ate between meals.[67]

A good breakfast is essential for maximum efficiency of the body and mind, especially during the later morning hours. Breakfast eaters demonstrate more efficient problem solving, increased verbal fluency, an improved attention span, better attitudes and scholastic scores. A recent study, directed by Harvard psychologist Michael Murphy, included four thousand elementary school children. Half ate breakfast; half did not. Across the board, those who ate breakfast exhibited better scores on a battery of attention tests, which included a short-term memory test where they repeated a series of digits, and a verbal fluency test where they were asked to name all of the animals they could think of in sixty seconds.[68]

What kind of breakfast is the best? The answer is food with a low glycemic load. The glycemic index is a measure of how quickly the carbohydrates in food are absorbed into our bodies and converted to fuel. When it comes to sustained brain power, Terrill Bravender, professor of pediatrics at Duke University, explains that foods that are low on the scale – such as whole grains – are preferable. Even though a bowl of oatmeal and a bowl of sugary cereal may have the same number of carbohydrates, they have very different glycemic loads.[69] Beans, as noted earlier, have an even lower glycemic load and may work even better at supplying a steady, stable supply of good brain food.

The evidence is more than abundant. Our diet is very important to our health. By choosing to make positive changes we can each enjoy the health benefits that come from a good, balanced diet.

Childhood Obesity

The childhood obesity epidemic is destroying children's lives, draining family resources, and pushing America dangerously close to a total health care collapse – but parents can work to avert the coming crisis by taking control of the weight challenges facing every member of their family.

For the first time in American history, a new epidemic is killing our kids. In 1960, only 4% of American children were considered obese. That number has skyrocketed to 15% today and is almost triple that number in certain ethnic groups.

"Staggering" is the word the U.S. Surgeon General uses to describe the potential health care costs of childhood obesity. "We are seeing Generation Y growing into Generation XL," he declares.

Being overweight is robbing kids of both their quality and quantity of life. Medical problems that doctors once saw only in adults aged fifty or older are now striking children: heart disease, stroke, high blood pressure, asthma, joint problems, arthritis. One in three children born in 2000 is expected to develop type 2 diabetes, with the risk of blindness, loss of kidney function, and early death associated with it.

This is the first generation in American history whose life expectancy may actually decrease. Fad diets and self-focused weight loss plans have proven ineffective. "An overweight child cannot be effectively treated in isolation of the family," insisted one recent study stating, "surprisingly few intervention programs include multiple family members."

Authors of the book *SuperSized Kids*, Walt Larimore and Sherri Flynt, share with families how to cure this crisis. The book outlines a step-by-step, medically sound, and eminently doable lifestyle change program designed for the whole family. It also includes practical suggestions for impacting school and community programs as well. To learn more, visit: supersizedkids.com.

"One should eat to live, not live to eat."

~ MOLIERE

REINFORCE THE MESSAGE

SKILL BUILDERS

Choose the Skill Builders below that you would like to experience in your own life, then write a response on how they impacted you. Last, write further actions, if any, that you would like to take as a result of doing the Skill Builders.

 Skill Builder I | **Recipe Transformation**

Choose a recipe that you like and experiment with it to make it healthier. Pay attention to the details such as taste, calories, fat, presentation, content of whole foods, etc.

Ideas:

A. Substitute some or the entire amount of refined flour with whole-grain flour (for example, use light, whole-grain wheat instead of white flour)

B. Substitute sweeteners (for example, use dried fruit instead of sugar)

C. Substitute fats (for example, use applesauce or an oil substitute instead of oil)

DESCRIBE HOW THIS IMPACTED YOU:

....
....
....

FURTHER ACTION:

....
....
....

Skill Builder 2 | Plan Ahead

Make a basic list of the meals you typically eat.

Then make a grocery list from those meals.

Make a weekly or monthly meal plan.

Use this to introduce variety.

Now, look at the meal plan and the grocery list.

Take a few moments to see if you can make healthier substitutions.

DESCRIBE HOW THIS IMPACTED YOU:

....

....

....

....

FURTHER ACTION:

....

....

....

....

A. Set apart a specific time to go shopping and spend time looking at health food items.

B. Pay attention to the number of ingredients in the foods you buy. As noted above, the foods with the least ingredients and least processed are generally the healthiest. Read and understand the ingredients in your packaged food and know what they are.

DESCRIBE HOW THIS IMPACTED YOU:

....
....
....

FURTHER ACTION:

....
....
....
....

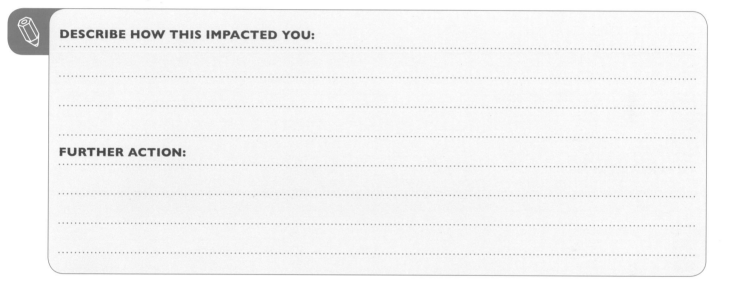

"Be not anxious for what you shall eat, or what you shall drink... isn't life more than food?"

~ LUKE 12:22

"Step back" and take a tour of your own kitchen.

A. Note things that help you in planning, preparing, and cleaning food items

For example, the following items are helpful:

- Large cutting board

- Chef's knife – learn how to use it and you will cut down considerably on preparation time

B. Note things that slow down your meal preparation.

C. Note things that you could buy to speed the process of food preparation and cleanup.

D. Note things that you want to buy that would aid in the presentation of your meals.

DESCRIBE HOW THIS IMPACTED YOU:
....
....
....
....

FURTHER ACTION:
....
....
....
....

NUTRITION

Skill Builder 5 | **Save Precious Time**

Take a favorite meal or recipe and make a double portion and freeze the rest for a quick, stress-free meal, or as a starter to a meal.

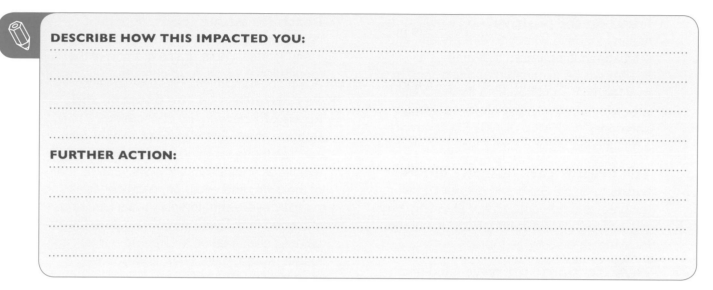

DESCRIBE HOW THIS IMPACTED YOU:

FURTHER ACTION:

 Skill Builder 6 | **Take Time to Explore How Food Can Help You**

Explore how food can help prevent disease or heal an existing health problem.

Research for yourself how eating specific foods can help with an ailment you might have or a disease you are genetically susceptible to. For example, if you are diabetic or have a genetic predisposition to diabetes, consider adding more fiber to your diet in order to help with blood sugar. There is amazing research that shows this will make a powerful difference. Another example is, if you are having problems with your memory or brain function, then do some research and consider including food items that will help you with this problem, such as nuts and seeds, especially walnuts and flaxseeds. If you have high incidences of cancer in your family, consider eating plenty of cruciferous vegetables.

DESCRIBE HOW THIS IMPACTED YOU:

FURTHER ACTION:

NUTRITION

TIPS FOR SUCCESS

POWER TIPS: IMPROVE YOUR OVERALL NUTRITION

- **Focus on the positive.** Add wholesome, healthy foods to what you already eat, and pretty soon the choices that are not as healthy will be eliminated and replaced by new foods. If you choose to think about your food positively and make positive additions, YOU WILL SUCCEED at having a healthy, nourishing diet.

- **The Creator gave us many different foods** to enjoy. Savor the different tastes, textures, and nutrients. Enjoy planning, buying, preparing, and eating. Food is our fuel for living, and so much more.

- **Pay attention** to our innate (God-given) internal signals to help us determine what and how much to eat. Allow your eating to be guided by internal signals of hunger, appetite, and satiety.

- **For best results** eat mainly a plant-based diet, God's diet given in the Garden of Eden. These are the most nutrient rich foods with numerous benefits that science continues to uncover.

- **Variety is a key to healthy eating.** Enjoy something "different" on a regular basis, or enjoy something you like but fixed in a different manner. A great way to add variety is with ethnic food. If you "tweak" a recipe just a little, you might like something that you had not enjoyed in the past. For example, you might not typically eat Indian cuisine because it's too spicy for you. Take a recipe, "tone it down," and then enjoy the new variety in your diet.

- **Color your diet.** A different color means different nutrients are present. Make it a goal to eat five or more fruits and vegetables a day.

- **Reach for whole foods.** Important nutrients and fiber are found in the skins of many foods. Whole grains are one of the foundational whole food choices.

- **Pay attention to the amount and kinds of fats** you are consuming. Replace "bad" fats with more healthy fats, such as those found in nuts, seeds, and avocados. Include healthy oils such as that of the olive, and avoid unhealthy ones like partially hydrogenated oils (trans fats) and saturated fats. Even "good" fats have lots of calories and, if taken in large amounts, can lead to weight gain. Thus, limit yourself to moderation with these as well.

- **Experiment with more natural sweeteners,** such as using dried fruit as a sweetener in a recipe rather than using sugar. Sugar can add extra calories and has a negative effect on your brain function and on your immune system. Overall, watch and limit the amount of sugar in your diet. For example, one easy way to do this is to buy canned fruit sweetened only with fruit juice and not any type of sugar, or to buy juice that is 100% juice and sweetened with only fruit juice. Read labels and be educated on what sweeteners are in your food.

- **Be a savvy consumer.** Look at the big picture of how a food will impact your overall health. Don't get caught up in the latest craze or diet. Choose to eat sensibly.

- **Choose to eat nuts and seeds daily** for great returns in healthy fats, powerful disease fighting potential, and other great nutrients.

- **Have fun with recipes.** Take "old favorites" and see how you can make them more healthy and appealing.

- **Over time, your tastes will change.** You can learn to like healthier foods. But please give yourself and others time to adjust. If you want to introduce a healthier option, sometimes it is helpful to change gradually by mixing the old item with the new in order to gradually get used to the new taste.

- **Enjoy experimenting** with flavorful herbs and spices. Add them to recipes for wonderful flavor options and nutrients.

- **Get back to the basics.** Foods with less processing and fewer ingredients are, generally, the healthiest for you, and the closest to the way the Creator made them. Look at the ingredients. It's really good when you can actually read and understand the ingredients on a label and know what they are. It is a good rule of thumb that the fewer the ingredients on the label, the better for you the product is likely to be.

- **Whenever possible, buy produce grown locally.** Fresh food has more nutritional content; and buying fresh food boosts the local economy and lessens the ecological impact of processing and shipping the food to a market that is far away. To take it a step further: grow your own. Plant your own vegetable and fruit garden and gain not only the nutritional benefits but also the many other benefits of tending to and taking care of a garden (fresh air, sunshine, exercise, etc.).

- **Take a walk** ten minutes after your meal to help your body more efficiently use the calories you just ingested.

- **Keep a clear mind** by not overeating at any one meal or eating too much fat or sugar. This will slow down the movement of your blood and will compromise your decision-making ability and brain function for several hours after that meal.

- **Drink plenty of pure water** for a host of healthful benefits.

- **Practice moderation** in all of your dietary habits. For example, remember fat is not an "enemy." The healthy fats, such as those found in nuts, seeds, and avocados, are essential to good health. Remember, "good" fats have the same number of calories as "bad" fats and, if taken in large amounts, can lead to weight gain. Thus, limit yourself to moderation of these as well.

- **Start each day off** with a power breakfast! Eat a well-balanced, healthy breakfast for benefits that will last the whole day.

- **Explore how foods can help you** prevent disease and heal from an illness. Research for yourself how eating specific foods can help with an ailment you might have or a disease that you are genetically susceptible to. For example, if you are diabetic or have a genetic predisposition to diabetes, consider adding more fiber to your diet in order to help with blood sugar. There is amazing research that shows this can make a significant difference. Memory or brain function may be helped by including foods such as nuts and seeds, especially walnuts and flaxseeds which contain larger amounts of omega-3 fats. If you have a high incidence of cancer in your family, eat extra cruciferous vegetables for their preventive qualities.

- **Plan your meals ahead of time.** This dramatically saves time and reduces stress. Planning ahead is a great way to introduce variety into your diet. Before you go to the grocery store, know what you want to buy.

- **When dining out,** make things healthier by asking for the vegetable of the day, or having your dressing put on the side, or asking the chef what healthy alternative he/she can make for you.

- **Try substituting** applesauce for the oil in baked good recipes that call for large amounts of oil. This can be done on a measure for measure basis. You can also purchase other commercial "oil substitutes" made from prune or plum sauces that are higher in fiber and very low in fat.

SMALL GROUP DISCUSSIONS

Directions: Review the discussion questions and choose one you would like to discuss first. Proceed through the rest of the questions as time allows.

1. Are there changes to your diet that you want to make? Why is it so important for you to start making these changes? Go around the group and have each person talk about what changes are most important to them.

....

....

2. How much do you enjoy your mealtimes? Are they stressful or relaxing? What can you do, right now, to make the experience more enjoyable? What do others do to make their mealtime experience pleasant?

....

....

3. Go around the group and ask each person to discuss what some of their favorite healthy foods are. Then talk about ways you can start adding these healthy choices to your diet. Then do the same with favorite unhealthy foods and talk about how you can start eliminating them from your diet.

....

....

4. What are some practical ways to get yourself into the habit of drinking more water, if you need to?

....

....

5. Some folks overeat as a response to stress or depression. What have you learned from this seminar that can help you control the amount of food you eat?

....

....

ADDITIONAL RESOURCES

Books:

SuperSized Kids, by Walt Larimore, MD and Sherri Flynt, MPH, RD, LD

Choices: Quick and Healthy Cooking, by Cheryl Thomas Peters

More Choices, by Cheryl D. Thomas Peters & James A. Peters

Websites:

supersizedkids.com
(A family plan to help your child control their weight and strengthen family ties)

childparenting.about.com/od/recipestips/a/healthyeaters_2.htm
(Children and healthy eating website)

kidshealth.org/parent/nutrition_fit/nutrition/habits.html (Ideas on helping kids eat healthfully)

nlm.nih.gov/medlineplus/vegetariandiet.html (Information about a vegetarian diet)

mypyramid.gov/tips_resources/vegetarian_diets.html (Information about a vegetarian diet)

vegweb.com/index.php?action=recipes (Vegan and vegetarian recipes)

cancer project.org (Online resource for those wanting to change their diet to prevent cancer or maximize their treatment by making dietary changes)

drmcdougall.com (Access to a large number of resources and educational experiences focusing on the dietary treatment of chronic diseases)

sdachip.org (Coronary Health Improvement Project in the church site. Training events and certification for those wanting to run a program in their church)

chiphealth.com (Coronary Health Improvement Project website run by Hans Diehl. The health of the whole town of Rockford, Illinois, was changed by this program – books and DVD-based program available)

Songs to Inspire Good Nutritional Choices:

Living Water (Hymn)

Breathe (Praise and worship)

Smart & Tasty (CD-songs for children)

Bon Appetite (CD-songs for children)

Groovin' Foods (CD-songs for children)

Smart Fruit & Veggie Songs (CD-songs for children)

ADDITIONAL RESOURCES

Chronic Disease Resources:

The McDougall Program for a Healthy Heart, by John McDougall M.D.

Reversing Diabetes, by Julian Whitaker M.D.

30-Day Diabetes Miracle, by House M.D., Seale M.D., Newman

The China Study, by T. Colin Campbell PhD

Other Resources:

Vita-Mix Whole Foods Mixer: A wonderful kitchen assistant! vitamix.com

When you're eating mostly fresh, whole foods, you can say good-bye to dieting. Fruits and vegetables allow you to eat more. You'll look and feel better, too. Eating freely of whole foods such as fruits, vegetables, beans, and whole grains along with a moderate amount of nuts and seeds, is truly the dietary key to physical, emotional, and spiritual health.

Vita-mix offers the following: FAST SIXTY SECONDS to scrumptious, fiber-full whole food juice. FOUR MINUTES to hot, homemade soup from scratch. THIRTY SECONDS to rich-tasting, low-fat frozen treats. NINETY SECONDS to whole-grain flour for homemade bread. This really is healthy fast food! Source: vitamix.com

REFERENCES

1. Willett W. "Diet and Health: What Should we Eat?" *Science* Apr 22, 1994 264(5158): 532–537.

2. Anderson J, Smith B, et al. "Health Benefits and Practical Aspects of High Fiber Diets." *American Journal of Clinical Nutrition* May 1994 59(5suppl): 1242S–1247S.

3. Colditz G, Atwood K, et al. "Harvard Report on Cancer Prevention Volume 4: Harvard Cancer Risk Index." *Cancer Causes and Control* 2000 11: 477–488.

4. Tabatabai A, Li S. "Dietary Fiber and Type 2 Diabetes." *Clin Excell Nurse Practitioner* Sept. 2000 4(5): 272–6.

5. Schneeman B. "Dietary Fiber and Gastrointestinal Function." *Nutrition Research* 1998 18(4): 625–632.

6. Challem J. "Mean Streets or Mean Minerals." January 18, 2003. March 27, 2007, http://www.thenutritionreporter.com/nutrition_and_crime.html.

7. Schoenthaler S. "Diet and Delinquency: A Multi-State Replication." *International Journal of Biosocial Research* 1983 5: 70–78.

8. Hasegawa T. "Anti-Stress Effect of Beta-Carotene." *ANN NY Acad Sci* 1993 691: 281–3.

9. World Health Report, *Reducing Risks, Promoting Healthy Lives,* 2002, WHO.

10. Zhao B, Seow A, et al. "Dietary Isothiocyanates, Glutathione S-Transferase -M1, -T1 Polymor-Phisms and Lung Cancer Risk among Chinese Women in Singapore." *Cancer Epidemiology Biomarkers & Prevention* Oct. 2001 10(10): 1063–7. 2001. PMID: 11588132.

11. Hertog M, Michael G, et al. "Dietary Antioxidant Flavonoids and Risk of Coronary Heart Disease: The Zutphen Elderly Study." *The Lancet* October 23, 1993 342: 1007–11.

12. Boyer J, Liu R. "Apple Phytochemicals and their Health Benefits." *Nutrition Journal* 2004 3: 5.

13. Sun J, Chu Y, et al. "Antioxidant and Antiproliferative Activities of Common Fruits." *Journal of Agricultural and Food Chemistry* 2002 50: 7449–7454.

14. Solovchenko A, Eiberger M. "Significance of Skin Flavonoids for UV-B-Protection in Apple Fruits." *Journal of Experimental Botany* August 2003 54(389): 1977–1984.

15. Colquhoun D, Moores D, et.al. "Comparison of the Effects on Lipoproteins and Apolipoproteins of a Diet High in Monosaturated Fatty Acids Enriched with Avocado, and a High-Carbohydrate Diet." *American Journal of Clinical Nutrition* 1992 56: 671–677.

16. Fraser G, et al. "Nut Consumption and CHD Risk & Whole-Wheat Bread." *Archives of Internal Medicine* July 1992 152.

17. Hu F, Stampfer M, et al. "Frequent Nut Consumption and Risk of Coronary Heart Disease in Women: Prospective Cohort Study." *BMJ* 1998 317: 1341–1345.

18. Albert C, Gaziano M, et al. "Nut Consumption and Decreased Risk of Sudden Cardiac Death in the Physicians' Health Study." *Archives of Internal Medicine* 2002 162: 1382–1387.

19. Morris M, Evans D, et al. "Dietary Intake of Antioxidant Nutrients and the Risk of Incident Alzheimer Disease in a Biracial Community Study." *Journal of the American Medical Association* June 26, 2002 287(24): 3230–3237.

REFERENCES

20. Engelhart M, Geerlings M, et al. "Dietary Intake of Antioxidants and Risk of Alzheimer Disease." *Journal of the American Medical Association* June 26, 2002 287(24): 3223–3229.

21. Chauhan N, Wang K, Weigel J, Malik M. "Walnut Extract Inhibits the Fibrillization of Amyloid Beta-Protein, and also Defibrillizes its Preformed Fibrils." *Current Alzheimer Research* 2004 1: 183–188.

22. Stoll A, Locke C, Marangell L, Severus W. "Omega-3 Fatty Acids and Bipolar Disorder: A Review." *Prostagladins, Leukotrienes and Essential Fatty Acids* 1999 60 (5&6): 329–337.

23. Zeisel S. "Nutritional Importance of Choline for Brain Development." *Journal of the American College of Nutrition* 2004 23(6): 621s–626s.

24. Burgess J, Stevens L, Zhang W, Peck L. "Long-Chain Polyunsaturated Fatty Acids in Children with Attention-Deficit Hyperactivity Disorder." *American Journal of Clinical Nutrition* 2000 71 (suppl): 327S–30S.

25. James M, Gibson R, Cleland L. "Dietary Polyunsaturated Fatty Acids and Inflammatory Mediator Production." *American Journal of Clinical Nutrition* 2000 71(suppl): 343S–8S.

26. Reiter R, Manchester L, Tan D. "Melatonin in Walnuts; Influence on Levels of Melatonin and Total Antioxidant Capacity of Blood." *Nutrition* Sep 2005 21(9): 920–4.

27. Houston M, Sparks W. "Latest Findings on Essential Fatty Acids and Cardiovascular Health." *The Original Internist*, June 2008: 65–68.

28. Donaldson M. "Nutrition and Cancer: A Review of the Evidence for an Anti-Cancer Diet." *Nutrition Journal* 2004 3: 19.

29. Marlett J, McBurney M, Slavin, J. "Position of the American Dietetic Association: Health Implications of Dietary Fiber." *Journal of the American Dietetic Association* Jul 2002 102: 7.

30. Cunnane S, Hamadeh, Mazen J, Liede, Andrea C, et al. "Nutritional Attributes of Flaxseed in Healthy Young Adults." *American Journal of Clinical Nutrition* Jan 1995 61(1): 6.

31. Katsuyuki M, et al. "Relationship of Dietary Linoleic Acid to Blood Pressure: The International Study of Macro-Micronutrients and Blood Pressure Study." *Hypertension*, 2008 52: 408.

32. Dahl W, Lockert E, Cammer A, Whiting S. "Effects of Flax Fiber on Laxation and Glycemic Response In Healthy Volunteers." *Journal of Medicinal Food* Dec. 2005 8(4): 508–511.

33. James M, Gibson R, Cleland L. "Dietary Polyunsaturated Fatty Acids and Inflammatory Mediator Production." *American Journal of Clinical Nutrition* 2000 71(suppl): 343S–8S.

34. Burgess J, Stevens L, Zhang W, Peck L. "Long-Chain Polyunsaturated Fatty Acids in Children with Attention-Deficit Hyperactivity Disorder." *American Journal of Clinical Nutrition* 2000 71 (suppl): 327S–30S.

35. Das U. "Long-Chain Polyunsaturated Fatty Acids in Memory Formation and Consolidation: Further Evidence and Discussion." *Nutrition* 2003 19: 988–993.

36. Marlett J, McBurney M, Slavin J. "Position of the American Dietetic Association: Health Implications of Dietary Fiber." *Journal of the American Dietetic Association* Jul 2002 102: 7.

37. James M, Gibson R, Cleland L. "Dietary Polyunsaturated Fatty Acids and Inflammatory Mediator Production." *American Journal of Clinical Nutrition* 2000 71(suppl): 343S–8S.

38. Ross S. "An Integrative Approach to Eczema (Atopic Dermatitis)." *Holistic Nursing Practice* 2003 17(1): 56–62.

39. Horribin D. "Essential Fatty Acids in Clinical Dermatology." *Journal of the American Academy of Dermatology* Jun 1989 20(6): 1045–53.

40. Marlett J, McBurney M, Slavin J. "Position of the American Dietetic Association: Health Implications of Dietary Fiber." *Journal of the American Dietetic Association*; July 2002 102: 7.

41. Lewis J, Nickell L, Thompson L, Szalai J, et al. "A Randomized Controlled Trial of the Effect of Dietary Soy and Flaxseed Muffins on Quality of Life and Hot Flashes During Menopause." *Menopause* Jul/Aug 2006 13(4): 631–42.

42. Sigurdson K. "The Natural Choice for PMS." *Total Health* Mar/Apr 2002 24: 1.

43. Stoll A, Locke C, Marangell L, Severus W. "Omega-3 Fatty Acids and Bipolar Disorder: A Review." *Prostagladins, Leukotrienes and Essential Fatty Acids* 1999 60(5&6): 329–37.

44. Austria J, et al. "Bioavailability of Alpha-Linolenic Acid in Subjects after Ingestion of Three Different Forms of Flaxseed." *Journal of the American College of Nutrition* Apr 2008 27(2): 214–21.

45. Bazzano L, et al. "Legume Consumption and Risk of Coronary Heart Disease in US Men and Women, NHANES I Epidemiologic Follow-Up Study." *Archives of Internal Medicine* 2001 161.

46. Kolonel L., et al. "Vegetables, Fruits, Legumes and Prostate Cancer: A Multiethnic Case-Control Study." *Cancer Epidemiology, Biomarkers & Prevention* Aug 2000 9: 795–804.

47. Winham D, Hutchins A, Johnston C. "Pinto Bean Consumption Reduces Biomarkers for Heart Disease Risk." *Journal of the American College of Nutrition* 2007 26(3): 243–9.

48. Jacobsen B, Knutsen S, Fraser G. "Does High Soy Milk Intake Reduce Prostate Cancer Incidence? The Adventist Health Study (United States)." *Cancer Causes and Control* 1998 9: 553–557.

49. Slavin J, Jacobs D, Marquart L, Wiemer K. "The Role of Whole Grains in Disease Prevention." *Journal of the American Dietetic Association* Jul 2001 101(7): 780.

50. *"Water for Health Conference Report: The Importance of Drinking Water to Public Health Policy."* BMA House, London WC1, May 12, 2005, p. 7. http://www.water.org.uk/home/policy/reports/health/water-for-health-conference-2005-output?s1=water&s2=for&s3=health&s4=report. Retrieved 4/20/09.

51. Eastwood M. *Principles of Human Nutrition*. Chapter 18: "Water, Electrolytes, Minerals and Trace Elements." London: Blackwell Publishing 2003 314.

52. Kleiner S. "Water: An Essential but Overlooked Nutrient." *Journal of the American Dietetic Association* Feb. 1999 99(2): 200–207.

REFERENCES

53. Eisenbeiss C, Welzel J, et al. "Influence of Body Water Distribution on Skin Thickness: Measurements Using High-Frequency Ultrasound." *British Journal of Dermatology* 2001 144: 947–951.

54. Kleiner S. "Water: An Essential but Overlooked Nutrient." *Journal of the American Dietetic Association* 1999 99: 201–207.

55. Rogers P, Kainth A, et al. "A Drink of Water Can Improve or Impair Mental Performance Depending on Small Differences in Thirst." *Appetite* 2001 36: 57–58.

56. Sherriffs S. unpublished data, as quoted in Maughan RJ. "Impact of Mild Dehydration on Wellness and on Exercise Performance." *European Journal of Clinical Nutrition* 2003 57 (Suppl 2): S19–23.

57. Cian C, Koulmann N, Barraud P, Raphel C, Jimenez C, Melin B. "Influence of Variations in Body Hydration on Cognitive Function: Effect of Hyperhydration, Heat Stress, and Exercise-Induced Dehydration." *International Journal of Psychophysiology* 2000 14: 29–36.

58. Bar-David Y, Urkin J, Kozminsky E. "The Effect of Voluntary Dehydration on Cognitive Functions of Elementary School Children." *Acta Paediatrica* 2005 94: 1667–73.

59. Chan J, Knutsen SF, et al. "Water, Other Fluids, and Fatal Coronary Heart Disease." *American Journal of Epidemiology* 2002 155: 827–33.

60. American Cancer Society. *Cancer Facts & Figures 2008*. Atlanta: American Cancer Society 2008.

61. Stookey J, Constand F, Popkin B, Gardner C. "Drinking Water is Associated with Weight Loss in Overweight Dieting Women Independent of Diet and Activity." *Obesity* 16(11).

62. Davy B, Dennis E, et al. "Water Consumption Reduces Energy Intake at a Breakfast Meal in Obese Older Adults." *Journal of the American Dietetic Association* 2008 108: 1236–1239.

63. Van Walleghen EL, Orr JS, Gentile CL, Davy BM. "Pre-Meal Water Consumption Reduces Meal Energy Intake in Older but Not Younger Subjects." *Obesity (Silver Spring)* 2007 15: 93–99.

64. Lappalainen R, Mennen L, van Weert L, Mykkanen H. "Drinking Water with a Meal: A Simple Method of Coping with Feelings of Hunger, Satiety and Desire to Eat." *European Journal of Clinical Nutrition* 1993 47: 815–819.

65. Popkin B, Barclay D, Nielsen S. "Water and Food Consumption Patterns of U.S. Adults from 1999 to 2001." *Obesity Research* 2005 13: 2146–2152.

66. Matthews R. "Importance of Breakfast to Cognitive Performance and Health." *Perspectives in Applied Nutrition* 1996 3(3): 204–212.

67. Belloc N, Breslow L. "Relationship of Physical Health Status and Health Practices." *Preventive Medicine* Aug 1972 1(3): 409–421.

68. Aubrey A. "A Better Breakfast Can Boost a Child's Brainpower." NPR Script aired on Aug. 31, 2006. http://www.npr.org/templates/story/story.php?storyId=5738848. Retrieved Aug. 31, 2006.

69. Ibid.

NOTES

NOTES

NOTES

QUESTIONS
& ASSESSMENTS

valuable tools to foster growth and renewal

creation®
H E A L T H

CONTENTS

OUTLOOK

NUTRITION

ADDITIONAL ASSESSMENTS

ARE YOU LIVING CREATION HEALTHY?

Directions: Utilizing the scale below, rate yourself on the following statements, based on the past year.
5 = Excellent   4 = Above Average   3 = Average   2 = Below Average   1 = Poor

CHOICE

___GOALS – I regularly set and write down goals for myself in the most important areas of my life.

___DISCIPLINE – I am good at delaying gratification until I achieve the goals I set.

___HABITS – I am able to curb unhealthy habits and replace them with more beneficial alternatives.

___BALANCE – I recognize when my life is out of balance and minimize or eliminate stressful situations to bring my life back in to balance.

___MISSION – I have a personal written mission statement that describes my values and guides the decisions I make on a daily basis.

CHOICE Total _____

REST

___SLEEP – I sleep soundly 7-9 hours in a 24-hour period.

___WORK – I minimize excessive work hours. Before my work shift, I determine the time I will go home and stick to it.

___MEDIA BREAK – At least once a week, I dedicate an evening to minimizing the use of TV, video games, social media, the Internet, etc.

___REST DAY – Once a week, I take a day of rest in which I don't do my regular work and instead focus on rest, relationships, inspiration, and attitude.

___VACATION – At least once a year, I take a vacation that allows me to "slow down" or "get away from it all" and experience relaxation and rejuvenation.

REST Total _____

ENVIRONMENT

___HOME – The décor and atmosphere of my home improves my attitude and gives me a sense of well-being.

___SIGHT – I have added beautiful sights to my personal world. This may include plants, photographs, nature scenes, art, or other things that bring me joy.

___SOUND – I have found ways to make my home and work environment more peaceful and relaxing through the use of music, nature sounds, and sometimes just silence.

___SMELL – I regularly incorporate fragrances that are enjoyable and relaxing in my home or work environment.

___NATURE – At least once a week, I engage in an outdoor activity that allows me to enjoy nature.

ENVIRONMENT Total _____

ACTIVITY

___AEROBIC – I get at least 30 minutes of aerobic exercise (such as walking, running, cycling, swimming, etc.) 3-6 days a week.

___STRENGTH – I have a muscle development routine (such as weightlifting, resistance training, core strengthening, etc.) that challenges me at least 3 times a week.

___STRETCHING – I perform a stretching routine at least 3 times a week.

___MOVEMENT – I take every opportunity to increase my daily movement (i.e. taking stairs instead of the elevator, walking instead of driving, etc.).

___SUPPORT – I have family or friends that support my activity goals and encourage me to follow through with my commitments. This may include an exercise partner who helps keep me accountable and makes the activity more enjoyable.

ACTIVITY Total _____

TRUST

___FAITH – I believe there is a Creator ultimately in control of the universe.

___PRAYER – I talk honestly with God about my life including my hopes, fears, desires, and needs. I believe God hears my prayers.

___ACCEPTANCE – I know God accepts me and is with me. As a result, I have hope.

___CONTEMPLATION – I regularly set aside time for personal spiritual development. Such time might include study, meditation, prayer, praise, journaling, etc.

___FELLOWSHIP – I participate in a faith fellowship that supports my spiritual growth.

TRUST Total _____

INTERPERSONAL RELATIONSHIPS

___FAMILY – I have a good relationship with my immediate family in which I give and receive love.

___FRIENDSHIP – I have friends I enjoy and with whom I can be myself. I share my true thoughts and feelings with at least one close friend.

___PRIORITIES – I do whatever it takes to nurture and grow the most important relationships in my life.

___FORGIVENESS – When someone hurts me, I forgive them. When I hurt someone else, I am quick to seek forgiveness.

___SERVICE – I am involved in volunteer activities where I can serve others. This may include charity work, community service, mission trips, spiritual outreach, etc.

INTERPERSONAL RELATIONSHIPS Total _____

OUTLOOK

___ATTITUDE – I am generally optimistic with a positive attitude that impacts the way I view life, the world, and the people I interact with.

___ACCEPTANCE – I accept myself despite my faults and limitations. I do not expect perfection in my life.

___RESPONSIBILITY – I take responsibility for my feelings and actions and do not blame others.

___MENTAL FITNESS – I keep my mind alert through continuous learning. Mental challenges are regular and rewarding experiences for me.

___SERVICE – I am involved in non-work activities where I serve others. This may include charity work, community service, mission trips, spiritual outreach, etc.

OUTLOOK Total _____

NUTRITION

___FRESH – I eat at least 5 servings of fresh fruits and vegetables every day.

___COLORS – I choose a wide variety of fruits and vegetables from all parts of the color spectrum.

___PROCESSED FOOD – I avoid processed and fast food whenever possible.

___WATER – I drink at least 6-8 glasses of water every day.

___WEIGHT – My Body Mass Index (BMI) and my weight are within healthy guidelines.

NUTRITION Total _____

See the next page for scoring and assessment

CREATION HEALTH SCORING AND ASSESSMENT

Directions: Write the total score for each principle below and add them together to discover your CREATION Health score.

_____ Choice

_____ Rest

_____ Environment

_____ Activity

_____ Trust

_____ Interpersonal Relationships

_____ Outlook

_____ Nutrition

_____ **TOTAL**

3 Highest Score Letters

LETTER   SCORE

(_____) = _____

(_____) = _____

(_____) = _____

3 Lowest Score Letters

LETTER   SCORE

(_____) = _____

(_____) = _____

(_____) = _____

What is your CREATION Health Score?

200 (Excellent)
Congratulations! Your score indicates that you keep healthy living a priority in your life. Keep up the great work!

160 – 199 (Above Average)
Your experience of life is rewarding and well balanced. Keep up the good work and promise yourself to continue on this "healthy" path.

120 – 159 (Average)
While "good" is acceptable to most, you're so much better. By reviewing your individual CREATION letter scores, you'll discover the principles you can start improving on today. Commit to becoming a better you!

80 – 119 (Below Average)
Your candid analysis of yourself and your health behaviors is an excellent first step to making changes. Review your letter scores and make a list of opportunities you have to improve your health.

40 – 79 (Poor)
It is hard for us to realize that bad choices may be the reason we aren't living life to the fullest. The good news is that you can make the choice today to start anew. Remember that small changes can bring BIG results!

NOTES

LOCUS OF CONTROL ASSESSMENT

Generalized locus of control – that is, the perceived ability to control life circumstances – is assessed with the following questionnaire, which has been used extensively in studies in eastern Europe[1] and in the INTERHEART study, which included over 24,700 participants, from fifty-two countries.[2]

A = Strongly Disagree
B = Disagree
C = Neutral
D = Agree
E = Strongly Agree

Directions: Please circle the answer that most reflects how you feel about the statement.

1. At work, I feel I have control over what happens in most situations. (Mark here if not applicable: i.e., no longer working ____)

   A B C D E _____

2. I feel what happens in my life is often determined by factors beyond my control.

   A B C D E _____

3. Over the next 5–10 years, I expect to have more positive than negative experiences.

   A B C D E _____

4. I often have the feeling I am being treated unfairly.

   A B C D E _____

5. In the past ten years my life has been full of changes without my knowing what will happen next.

   A B C D E _____

6. I gave up trying to make big improvements in my life a long time ago.

   A B C D E _____

Scoring:

1. For items 2, 4, 5, & 6 score:
5 points for "A" answers
4 points for "B" answers
3 points for "C" answers
2 points for "D" answers
1 point for "E" answers

2. For items 1 & 3 score:
1 point for "A" answers
2 points for "B" answers
3 points for "C" answers
4 points for "D" answers
5 points for "E" answers

3. Sum all items to obtain your total score for the assessment.

Your Total Score: _____   **4. Divide the total score by 6 and write that number here:** _____

Interpretation:

Low internal locus of control = 3 or less
Moderate internal locus of control = above 3 to 3.3
Medium locus of control = above 3.3 to 3.7
High locus of control = above 3.7

Write your category here: _____

Sources:
1. Bobak M, Pikhart H, et al. "Socioeconomic Factors, Material Inequalities, and Perceived Control in Self-Rated Health: Cross-Sectional Data from Seven Post-Communist Countries." *Social Science and Medicine* 2000; 51: 1343–50. **2.** (Also source for this assessment) Rosengren A, Hawken S, et al. "Association of Psychosocial Risk Factors with Risk of Acute Myocardial Infarction in 11, 119 Cases and 13, 648 Controls from 52 Countries (the INTERHEART study): Case-Control Study." *The Lancet* 2004; 364: 953–62.
Used with Permission

SATISFACTION WITH LIFE SCALE

Developed in 1980 by University of Illinois psychologist Edward Diener, a founding father of happiness research. Since then the scale has been used by researchers around the world.[1]

Directions: Read the following five statements and circle a number from 1 to 7 to rate your level of agreement.

1. In most ways my life is close to my ideal

1	2	3	4	5	6	7
Not at all true			Moderately True		Absolutely true	

2. The conditions of my life are excellent

1	2	3	4	5	6	7
Not at all true			Moderately True		Absolutely true	

3. I am satisfied with my life

1	2	3	4	5	6	7
Not at all true			Moderately True		Absolutely true	

4. So far I have gotten the important things I want in life

1	2	3	4	5	6	7
Not at all true			Moderately True		Absolutely true	

5. If I could live my life over, I would change almost nothing

1	2	3	4	5	6	7
Not at all true			Moderately True		Absolutely true	

Total Score: _____

Scoring:

31-35	You Are Extremely Satisfied with Your Life
26-30	Very Satisfied
21-25	Slightly Satisfied
20	Neutral Point
15-19	Slightly Dissatisfied
10-14	Dissatisfied
5-9	Extremely Dissatisfied

Sources:
1. Claudia Wallis, "The New Science of Happiness." *Time* (165)3 Jan. 17, 2005. **Source For Scale:** Ed Diener, Robert A. Emmons, Randy J. Larsen, and Sharon Griffin. "The Satisfaction of Life Scale." *Journal of Personality Assessment* (49)1 1985.
Public Domain

MY SMART HEALTH ACTION PLAN

Good health doesn't just happen. It is the result of healthy living each day. Review your Personal Wellness Profile™ to determine where you would like to make changes in your life. Then follow these three simple steps in designing your SMART Health Action Plan.

STEP 1

List areas in which you would like to see improvement.

Select the one area you are most interested in improving and most likely to complete.

....

....

....

STEP 2

WRITE A SMART GOAL FOR ACHIEVING THIS. SMART GOALS ARE . . .	FOR EXAMPLE . . .
Specific. Be specific in what you want to accomplish and the action steps you will take.	**Specific:** I will get 20-30 minutes of moderate activity, 3-5 days every week.
Measurable. If you can't measure it, you can't manage it.	**Measurable:** I will log my daily activity and accumulate 120+ minutes of activity/week.
Attainable. Set goals you can realistically accomplish in a few weeks or months.	**Attainable:** I will enlist the support of my neighbor as an exercise buddy.
Rewarded. Reward yourself when you reach your goal. Have something to look forward to.	**Reward:** If I meet my goal for six weeks, I will treat myself to a relaxing massage.
Timeline based. Set time expectations. Have a start date and finish date by which you expect to reach your goal. This gives you a clear target to work toward.	**Timeline:** After eight weeks, I'll reevaluate my goals and adjust as needed to meet my long-term goal of three hours of exercise/week.

250

STEP 3

MY SMART PERSONAL HEALTH ACTION PLAN

SPECIFIC:
....
....
....

MEASURABLE:
....
....

ATTAINABLE:
....
....

REWARD:
....
....

TIMELINE:
....
....
....

Tips to Help You Reach Your Goals

1. **Focus on one goal at a time.** Taking on too much can be overwhelming, leading to failure.

2. **Pick something you are ready to tackle** and have a genuine desire to improve.

3. **Start with small steps.** Set goals that challenge you but that you are confident you can accomplish.

4. **Take a class or join a support group or participate in a wellness challenge** for added knowledge, motivation, and support.

5. **Log your progress daily.** It helps keep you on track – and seeing progress is motivating!

6. **Reevaluate your progress often.** Do more of what is working. If something isn't working, try a new approach. Don't give up!

7. **Set new goals quarterly.** Tackle other areas of your life you want to change.

8. **Be optimistic.** Think positively. You can do it!

Commitment. I am committed to making healthy choices to improve my life. To the best of my ability I will follow my action plan as described above.

HEALTHSTYLE INDEX (HSI)

Based on Healthy People Goals

Directions: For each health indicator, check the box in the column that best describes you. Write score shown next to the check box in the score column to the right.

HEALTH INDICATORS	COLUMN A	COLUMN B	COLUMN C	SCORE
Physical Activity. Number of days you get 30+ min. of moderate to vigorous activity?	[ ] 0 No regular physical activity	[ ] 4 2-3 days/week	[ ] 10 4-7 days/week	__/10
Strength Training. Number of 15+ min sessions/week?	[ ] 0 No strength training	[ ] 1 Once/week	[ ] 3 Twice/week or more	__/3
Body Weight. BMI value, (See BMI chart.)	[ ] 0 BMI 30+	[ ] 5 BMI 25-29.9	[ ] 10 BMI less than 25	__/10
Fruits/Vegetables. # serv/day? 1 serv = 1 med. fruit, 1C fresh, 1/2 C chopped, 6 oz. juice	[ ] 0 0-2 serv/day	[ ] 2 3-4 serv/day	[ ] 5 5-9 serv/day	__/5
High Sat. Fat. How often do you eat tacos, fried chicken, steak, fries, rich desserts, hamburgers, hot dogs, cheese pizza?	[ ] 0 Often, or most days	[ ] 1 Occasionally, 2-3 times/week	[ ] 4 Seldom or never eat these foods	__/4
Nuts/Seeds. # serv/week? 1 serving = 1 oz or 2T nut butter	[ ] 0 Seldom/never eat nuts	[ ] 2 2-4 serv/week	[ ] 4 5+ serv/week	__/4
Whole Grains. # serv/day? 1 slice bread, 2/3 C dry cereal, 1/2 C cooked oats or brown rice	[ ] 0 Seldom eat whole grains	[ ] 1 1-2 serv/day	[ ] 3 3 serv/day	__/3
Breakfast. How often do you eat breakfast (more than just coffee and a roll)?	[ ] 0 Seldom or never	[ ] 1 3-4 days/week	[ ] 2 Daily or nearly so	__/2
Refined Food/Sugar. How often do you eat soda pop, pastry, cookies, chips, or candy?	[ ] 0 2+ times daily	[ ] 1 No more than once/day	[ ] 2 Limit to a few times/week	__/2
Legumes. # serv/week? 1 serving = 1/2 C peas, beans, tofu, lentils, etc.	[ ] 0 None	[ ] 1 1-2 serv/week	[ ] 2 3+ serv/week	__/2
High Calcium Foods. # serv/day? 1 serving =1C milk, cheese, yogurt, broccoli or collard greens, 1/2 C firm tofu, 1C Ca fortified OJ?	[ ] 0 less than one/day	[ ] 1 at least one/day	[ ] 2 two or more/day	__/2
Salt. Do you add salt to food and/or eat salty foods?	[ ] 0 Frequently	[ ] 1 Occasionally	[ ] 2 Seldom, limit salt and salty food	__/2
Water. How many glasses (8 oz.) of water do you drink daily?	[ ] 0 0-3 glasses/day	[ ] 1 4-5 glasses/day	[ ] 2 6-8+ glasses/day	__/2
Smoking. Do you smoke or are you a nonsmoker often exposed to secondhand smoke?	[ ] 0 Currently smoke	[ ] 4 Frequent secondhand smoke	[ ] 10 Nonsmoker	__/10
Sun. Are you careful to avoid excess sun by wearing protective clothing/sun screen?	[ ] 0 Sometimes	[ ] 1 Most of the time	[ ] 2 Always	__/2
Alcohol. Number drinks/week (1 drink = beer 12 oz., wine 3.5 oz., or liquor 1.5 oz.)	[ ] 0 3-5 or more/day	[ ] 3 Not more than 1-2/day	[ ] 4 Seldom or never drink	__/4

CONTINUED ON THE NEXT PAGE

HEALTH INDICATORS	COLUMN A	COLUMN B	COLUMN C	SCORE
Happiness/Mental Health. During the past month, how happy have you been?	[ ] 0 Very unhappy	[ ] 1 Pretty happy	[ ] 3 Very happy	___/3
Stress. How well are you coping with stress and pressures in your life?	[ ] 0 Very stressed out, anxious, or angry, not coping	[ ] 1 Often stressed or anxious, not coping too well	[ ] 3 Sometimes stressed but coping well	___/3
Social Support/Contact. How is your social support/contact with family and friends?	[ ] 0 Little/no contact or support, often lonely	[ ] 1 Occasional contact, limited social support	[ ] 3 Frequent contact, good social support	___/3
Community. Do you participate regularly in a faith community or other social group?	[ ] 0 Don't participate in any faith/social group	[ ] 1 Occasionally participate in a faith/social group	[ ] 3 Participate regularly in a faith/social group	___/3
Rest. Number of hours of sleep you usually get each day?	[ ] 0 Less than 6 hours	[ ] 1 6-6.9 hours	[ ] 3 7-8 or more hours	___/4
Safe Sex. Do you take precautions to avoid sexually transmitted disease (STDs) and unwanted pregnancy?	[ ] 0 Multiple sex partners and don't always use protection	[ ] 1 Multiple sex partners but always use protection	[ ] 3 Limit relations to one faithful partner or abstain	___/3
Seat Belts. How often do you wear your seat belts when riding in a car?	[ ] 0 Seldom or never	[ ] 1 Often	[ ] 2 Always	___/2
Helmet. Do you wear protective gear if biking or in-line skating?	[ ] 0 Seldom or never	[ ] 1 Often	[ ] 2 Always	___/2
Smoke Alarm. Do you have a working smoke alarm in your home?	[ ] 0 No or not sure	[ ] 1 Yes, but not tested recently	[ ] 2 Yes, and I know it works	___/2
Drink and Drive. Ever drive after drinking or ride with a driver who's been drinking?	[ ] 0 Frequently	[ ] 0 Once in a while	[ ] 2 Never	___/2
Access. Do you have a source for ongoing health/medical care (health plan, primary care doctor, etc)?	[ ] 0 Not presently	[ ] 1 Yes, but don't have a primary physician yet	[ ] 2 Yes, plus a good working relationship with my doctor	___/2
Preventive Exams/Immunizations. Are all recommended exams and immunizations current (see age/gender specific list)?	[ ] 0 No, seldom get health checkups	[ ] 2 Not sure but have had a health checkup in last 2 yrs	[ ] 4 Yes, get regular checkups and all preventive exams	___/4

Total number of checked boxes in columns A and B

[   ]

These checked boxes are your health improvement opportunities.

Total # of checked boxes in column C

[   ]

This is your HealthStyle Index score. Maximum score is 28

A score greater than 20 is desirable for good health

Total

___/100

Weighted Score
60-79 is good
80-100 is Excellent

PLEASE SEE SCORING DIRECTIONS ON NEXT PAGE.

HEALTHSTYLE INDEX (HSI) (continued)

Based on Healthy People Goals

Scoring Directions:

1. Add all of the individual scores in the right-hand column. Put total at the bottom. The total maximum **Weighted Score** is 100.

2. Total the number of checked boxes in columns A and B. Write total in the space provided (**Improvement Opportunities**).

3. Do the same for Column C. This is your **HealthStyle Index**.

Summary Scores and Explanations

DESCRIPTION	YOUR SCORE (FROM PREVIOUS PAGES)	EXPLANATIONS
Health Improvement Opportunities	Column A + B _____	These are items you can target for improving your health and longevity.
Your HealthStyle Index Score	Column C _____	The number of "Good Health" practices you currently follow from the above list of 28. The higher the score the better your HealthStyle!
Your Weighted Score (total weighted score of each individual health indicator listed above)	Total of right-hand column _____	The total possible weighted score is 100. The higher the score, the healthier the lifestyle. A score of 60 is the minimum score for good health. A score of 80+ indicates excellent health.

Making Changes

List those key areas of your HealthStyle that you would most like to improve. Consider which changes might make the most improvement in your health and which you are currently willing to change. Seek additional help and support in making these changes from health programs and resources in your community, reliable self-help study guides and websites, and health professionals and supportive family and friends.

Health Practices I Choose to Improve:

1. ....

2. ....

3. ....

4. ....

Date: _____

NOTES

SELF-TEST A: WHAT'S MY SLEEP IQ?

Directions: Please indicate True or False for the following statements:

T F   1. Newborns dream less than adults.

T F   2. Men need more sleep than women.

T F   3. Not everyone dreams every night.

T F   4. As you move from early to later adulthood you need less sleep.

T F   5. By playing audio during the night, you can learn while you sleep.

T F   6. Chocolate candies provided on your hotel pillow will help you sleep better.

T F   7. If you have insomnia at night, you should take a long nap during the day.

T F   8. Sleeping pills are very helpful for people who have had insomnia for months.

T F   9. Arousing a person who is sleepwalking can be very dangerous.

T F   10. A soft mattress is better than a hard one for obtaining good sleep.

T F   11. You are most alert when you first wake up.

T F   12. To promote optimal sleep the best time to exercise is early in the morning.

T F   13. A sound sleeper rarely moves during the night.

T F   14. A boring meeting, heavy meal, or low dose of alcohol can make you sleepy, even if you're not sleep deprived.

T F   15. Sleep before midnight is better than sleep that begins after midnight.

Scoring:

Self-Test A reveals your general knowledge of sleep. All but statement 15 are false.

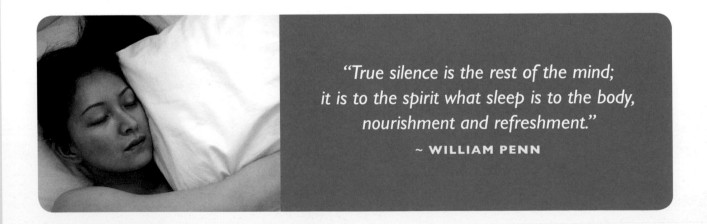

"True silence is the rest of the mind; it is to the spirit what sleep is to the body, nourishment and refreshment."

~ **WILLIAM PENN**

SELF-TEST B: AM I SLEEP DEPRIVED?

Directions: Please indicate True or False for the following statements:

T F   1. I need an alarm clock in order to wake up at the appropriate time.

T F   2. It's a struggle for me to get out of bed in the morning.

T F   3. Weekday mornings I hit the snooze button several times to get more sleep.

T F   4. I feel tired, irritable, and stressed out during the week.

T F   5. I have trouble concentrating and remembering.

T F   6. I feel slow with critical thinking, problem solving, and being creative.

T F   7. I often fall asleep watching TV.

T F   8. I often fall asleep in boring meetings or lectures in warm rooms.

T F   9. I often fall asleep after heavy meals or after a low dose of alcohol.

T F 10. I often fall asleep while relaxing after dinner.

T F 11. I often fall asleep within five minutes of getting into bed.

T F 12. I often feel drowsy while driving.

T F 13. I often sleep extra hours on weekend mornings.

T F 14. I often need a nap to get through the day.

T F 15. I have dark circles around my eyes.

Scoring:

Self-Test B checks to see if you are sleep deprived. If you answered true to three or more of the fifteen items, you are probably not getting enough sleep. You are not alone.

SELF-TEST C: HOW GOOD ARE MY SLEEP STRATEGIES?

Directions: Please indicate True or False for the following statements:

T F   1. I go to bed at different times during the week and on weekends, depending on my schedule and social life.

T F   2. I get up at different times during the week and on weekends, depending on my schedule and social life.

T F   3. My bedroom is warm or often noisy.

T F   4. I never rotate or flip my mattress.

T F   5. I drink alcohol within two hours of bedtime.

T F   6. I have caffeinated coffee, tea, colas, or chocolate after 6 p.m.

T F   7. I do not exercise on a regular basis.

T F   8. I smoke.

T F   9. I regularly take over-the-counter or prescription medication to help me sleep.

T F 10. When I cannot fall asleep or remain asleep I stay in bed and try harder.

T F 11. I often read frightening or troubling books or newspaper articles right before bedtime.

T F 12. I do work or watch the news in bed just before turning out the lights.

T F 13. My bed partner keeps me awake with his/her snoring.

T F 14. My bed partner tosses and turns or kicks/hits me during his/her sleep.

T F 15. I argue with my bed partner in bed.

Scoring:

Self-Test C examines your sleep strategies. If you answered true to one or more of the questions, it is likely that at least one aspect of your lifestyle is interfering with your sleep.

"Sometimes the most urgent and vital thing you can possibly do is take a complete rest."

~ ASHLEIGH BRILLIANT

SELF-TEST D: MIGHT I HAVE A SLEEP DISORDER?

Directions: Please indicate True or False for the following statements:

T F   1. I have trouble falling asleep.

T F   2. I wake up a number of times during the night.

T F   3. I wake up earlier than I would like and have trouble falling back to sleep.

T F   4. I wake up terrified in the middle of the night, but I don't know why.

T F   5. I fall asleep spontaneously during the day in response to high arousal, such as when I hear a funny joke.

T F   6. I have been told I snore loudly and stop breathing temporarily during sleep.

T F   7. I walk or talk in my sleep.

T F   8. I move excessively in my sleep.

T F   9. I have hurt myself or my bed partner while I was sleeping.

T F 10. I become very confused, afraid, and/or disoriented after sundown.

T F 11. I cannot fall asleep until very late at night or cannot wake up in the morning.

T F 12. I cannot stay awake early in the evening and I wake up before dawn.

T F 13. I feel mild pain or a tingling sensation in my legs just before falling asleep.

T F 14. I physically act out my dreams during the night.

T F 15. I am often too anxious, depressed, or worried to fall asleep.

Scoring:

Self-Test D probes for problems that could indicate you have a sleep disorder. Some sleep disorders are more serious than others and may require medical attention. If you answered true to any of these questions this may indicate that you have a sleep disorder. Consult your doctor about this matter.

Self-Test A-D, Adapted from and Used with Permission.

Maas, James B. *Power Sleep*. New York: Harper Collins, 1998.

HEALTHY HOME AND LIFESTYLE

Take a tour through your home with your family and talk about how each room impacts the health and well-being of you, your family, and those that come and visit you. Take your time and make sure everyone's thoughts and input is given and valued appropriately, especially when it is that particular person's room.

Below is a list of questions that you can ask as you go from room to room.

- Is the décor and coloring appealing to you and your family?
- Are furnishings comfortable and appealing to you and your family?
- Is the room well lighted?
- Is the room well ventilated, with fresh air available?
- Is the room typically organized and free of clutter?
- Is the room a comfortable temperature?
- Where applicable, are the closets, drawers, and storage spaces well organized and free of clutter?
- Overall, does being in this room feel inviting to you?

When you have completed this, answer the following questions about your observations and comments from your family.

- Do you want to change it?
- Can this be changed?
- Who will change it?
- How will they change it?
- When will they change it?

SYMPTOMS LOG

Directions: Keep this log for one week. Patterns are usually easier to identify if you record your log for one month. Record what symptoms you are experiencing and what you expect may have been the cause.

MONTH	DAY	TIME	SYMPTOMS	ACTIVITY/EXPOSURE	ACTION	OUTCOME

ARE YOU EXERCISE HESITANT?

People who do not exercise regularly are often thought of as lazy; the solution offered is "just do it," regardless of what is really going on. We need to remember that we were all born with a hunger for movement. If we choose not to move our bodies now, it is because something got in the way. Throw out the idea that you are too lazy and discover the real reasons you might be hesitant to be regularly active.

Directions: Start by checking any of the following that apply to you:

____ I "should" be exercising.

____ I need to exercise to look like society says I should.

____ I have been pushed into exercise by others who had their own agenda – for instance, they wanted me to "have fun" or to lose weight.

____ I felt pressure to perform in athletics as a child.

____ I am somewhat of a perfectionist and believe that "if I can't do it right, I won't do it at all."

____ I usually only exercise when I diet. When I quit dieting, I usually quit exercising.

____ I have been injured while exercising and the whole idea of it scares me.

____ I usually only exercise to manage and/or to lose weight.

____ I was almost always the last one picked for team sports growing up.

____ If I miss a day or two of my exercise routine, I usually feel like I've blown it and it is hard for me to get going again.

____ I often feel intimidated by exercise, the equipment, or the fancy moves in aerobics.

____ I often feel rejected by friends, family, or society because of the size or shape of my body and somehow feel that exercise might help that.

____ I feel bad about my body and on some level believe that the less I move, the less attention I call to my body.

____ I hate to sweat.

____ I have used exercise as an external measure of self-worth – I feel better about myself when I exercise because I am doing something good.

____ I have used exercise as a "punishment."

____ I count up the calories I have burned or weight I will lose while I exercise.

____ I have forced myself to exercise when I ate too much or didn't lose enough weight.

____ I have been sexually abused at some time in my life.

Review the comments with checkmarks to begin to understand why you might be hesitant to get moving. Each has negative connotations that can contribute to exercise resistance. Consider discussing these with a trusted friend to help sort out some of the issues. Sometimes this is enough to remove the barriers. In other cases, a skilled therapist might help. Also, consider how you might be able to alter your perceptions of physical activity to something that is your birthright!

© 2000 Karin Kratina, PhD, RD *Used with Permission* *NourishingConnections.com*

AEROBIC MILE CHART

Use the Aerobic Mile Chart to give you an estimate of your energy output in a number of different activities. The times shown for each activity are equivalent in energy to jogging one mile.

Mowing the yard (vigorous gardening) for 24 minutes equals one aerobic mile.

Playing moderate tennis for 15 minutes equals one aerobic mile.

Easy cross country skiing for 17 minutes equals one aerobic mile.

Bicycling at a moderate pace for 12 minutes equals one aerobic mile.

Aerobic Mile Chart © 1981-92. Donald R. Hall, DHSc Adapted from ACSM, Guidelines for Exercise Testing, Fourth Edition, Lea and Febiger, 1991

ACTIVITY	MINUTES TO EQUAL ONE AEROBIC MILE		
	EASY	MODERATE	VIGOROUS
Aerobic exercise to music	20	15	12
Backpacking	15	12	10
Basketball	20	12	10
Bicycling	18	14	10
Calisthenics/conditioning exercises	20	15	12
Canoeing/rowing	20	15	12
Cycling, stationary (4, 6, 8 METs)	24	16	11
Football, touch	20	15	12
Gardening, active	60	40	24
Golfing, carrying bag or pulling cart	30	25	20
Hiking, cross country & hills	20	15	12
Jogging/running (12-10-8 minute/mile pace)	12	10	8
Mountain climbing	15	12	10
Racquetball, handball, squash	20	15	10
Rope skipping	12	10	8
SCUBA diving	20	15	10
Skating	20	15	12
Skiing, cross country	17	12	8
Skiing, downhill	20	15	12
Soccer	15	12	10
Stair or bench stepping	15	13	11
Swimming	24	16	12
Table tennis	60	30	20
Tennis	20	15	11
Volleyball	30	20	15
Walking, (24, 20, 15 min/mile pace)	24	20	15
Water skiing	20	15	12
Weight training, circuit	20	15	12

ACTIVITY

PAR-Q & YOU

A Questionnaire for People Aged 15–69

Regular physical activity is fun and healthy, and increasingly more people are starting to become more active every day. Being more active is very safe for most people. However, some people should check with their doctor before they start becoming much more physically active. If you are planning to become much more physically active than you are now, start by answering the seven questions in the box below. If you are between the ages of fifteen and sixty-nine, the PAR-Q will tell you if you should check with your doctor before you start. If you are over sixty-nine years of age and you are not used to being very active, check with your doctor.

Directions: Common sense is your best guide when you answer these questions. Please read the questions carefully and answer each one honestly: circle YES or NO.

Y N   1. Has your doctor ever said that you have a heart condition and that you should only do physical activity recommended by a doctor?

Y N   2. Do you feel pain in your chest when you do physical activity?

Y N   3. In the past month, have you had chest pain when you were not doing physical activity?

Y N   4. Do you lose your balance because of dizziness or do you ever lose consciousness?

Y N   5. Do you have a bone or joint problem (for example, back, knee, or hip) that could be made worse by a change in your physical activity?

Y N   6. Is your doctor currently prescribing drugs (for example, water pills) for your blood pressure or heart condition?

Y N   7. Do you know of any other reason why you should not do physical activity?

If you answered YES to one or more of the questions, talk with your doctor by phone or in person BEFORE you start becoming much more physically active or BEFORE you have a fitness appraisal. Tell your doctor about the PAR-Q and which questions you answered YES.

- You may be able to do any activity you want – as long as you start slowly and build up gradually. Or, you may need to restrict your activities to those that are safe for you. Talk with your doctor about the kinds of activities you wish to participate in and follow his/her advice.

- Find out which community programs are safe and helpful for you.

If you answered NO to all of the questions, you can be reasonably sure that you can:

- Start becoming much more physically active – begin slowly and build up gradually. This is the safest and easiest way to go.

- Take part in a fitness appraisal – this is an excellent way to determine your basic fitness so that you can plan the best way for you to live actively. It is also highly recommended that you have your blood pressure evaluated. If your reading is over 144/94, talk with your doctor before you start becoming much more physically active.

Delay becoming much more active:

- If you are not feeling well because of a temporary illness such as a cold or a fever – wait until you feel better; or

- If you are or may be pregnant – talk to your doctor before you start becoming more active.

> PLEASE NOTE: If your health changes so that you then answer YES to any of the above questions, tell your fitness or health professional. Ask whether you should change your physical activity plan.

© Canadian Society for Exercise Physiology

NOTES

FLEXIBILITY ASSESSMENT

Pretest: Participant should perform a short warm-up prior to this test and include some stretches. It is also recommended that the participant refrain from fast, jerky movements, which may increase the possibility of injury. The participant's shoes should be removed.

1. Sit on the floor with the legs straight out in front of you, about 8 to 10 inches apart. Put a yardstick or tape measure on the floor between your legs and line up your heels with the 15-inch mark (the zero mark should be toward the body). Straighten your arms and put the tips of your middle fingers on top of each other. Keeping the fingers in contact with the yardstick, exhale, drop your head, and gradually stretch (without bouncing) to touch the farthest point possible on the yardstick. Take your best of three tries.

2. Your knees should stay extended. Breathe normally during the test and do not hold your breath at any time.

Flexibility (in inches) by Age Groups and Gender

RATING	% RANKING	AGE 18-25		AGE 26-35		AGE 36-45		AGE 46-55		AGE 56-65		OVER 65	
		M	F	M	F	M	F	M	F	M	F	M	F
Excellent	100	28	29	28	28	28	28	26	27	24	26	24	26
	95	23	24	22	24	22	23	20	22	19	21	19	22
	90	22	24	21	23	21	22	19	21	17	20	17	20
Good	85	21	22	19	22	19	21	18	20	16	19	16	19
	80	20	22	19	21	19	21	17	20	15	19	15	18
	75	20	22	19	21	18	20	16	19	15	18	14	18
Above Average	70	19	21	17	20	17	19	15	18	13	17	13	17
	65	18	20	17	20	17	19	15	18	13	17	12	17
	60	18	20	17	20	16	18	14	17	13	16	12	17
Average	55	17	19	16	19	15	17	13	16	11	15	11	16
	50	17	19	15	19	15	17	13	16	11	15	10	15
	45	16	19	15	18	15	17	12	16	11	15	10	15
Below Average	40	15	18	14	17	13	16	11	14	09	14	09	14
	35	15	18	14	17	13	16	11	14	09	13	09	13
	30	14	17	13	16	13	15	10	14	09	13	08	13
Poor	25	13	16	12	15	11	14	09	13	08	12	07	12
	20	13	16	11	15	11	14	09	12	07	11	07	11
	15	12	16	11	14	09	13	08	12	06	10	06	10
Very Poor	10	11	14	09	13	07	12	06	10	05	09	04	09
	05	09	12	07	12	05	10	04	08	03	07	03	07
	00	02	07	02	05	01	04	01	03	01	02	00	01

Reprinted with permission from the YMCA Fitness Testing and Assessment Manual, Fourth Edition.

STRENGTH: PUSH-UP ASSESSMENT

1. The push-up test is administered with male subjects starting in the standard "down" position (hands pointing forward and under the shoulder, back straight, head up, using the toes as the pivotal point) and female subjects in the modified "knee push-up" position (legs together, lower leg in contact with mat with ankles plantar-flexed, back straight, hands shoulder width apart, head up, using the knees as the pivotal point).

2. The subject must raise the body by straightening the elbows and return to the "down" position, until the chin touches the mat. The stomach should not touch the mat.

3. For both men and women, the subject's back must be straight at all times and the subject must push up to a straight arm position.

4. The maximal number of push-ups performed consecutively without rest is counted as the score.

5. The test is stopped when the client strains forcibly or is unable to maintain the appropriate technique within two repetitions.

Push-ups Fitness Categories by Age Groups and Gender

RATING	AGE 20-29		AGE 30-39		AGE 40-49		AGE 50-59		AGE 60-69	
	M	F	M	F	M	F	M	F	M	F
Excellent	≥ 36	≥ 30	≥ 30	≥ 27	≥ 25	≥ 24	≥ 21	≥ 21	≥ 18	≥ 17
Very Good	29-35	21-29	22-29	20-26	17-24	15-23	13-20	11-20	11-17	12-16
Good	22-28	15-20	17-21	13-19	13-16	11-14	10-12	07-10	08-10	05-11
Fair	17-21	10-14	12-16	08-12	10-12	05-10	07-09	02-06	05-07	02-04
Needs Improvement	≤ 16	≤ 09	≤ 11	≤ 07	≤ 09	≤ 04	≤ 06	≤ 01	≤ 04	≤ 01

Source: Canadian Physical Activity, Fitness & Lifestyle Approach:
CSEP-Health & Fitness Program's Health Related Appraisal & Counseling Strategy, Third Edition. ©2003.
Reprinted with permission from the Canadian Society for Exercise Physiology.

ACTIVITY

NOTES

BODY MASS INDEX AND WAIST CIRCUMFERENCE ASSESSMENT

The Body Mass Index (BMI) is used to assess weight relative to height and is calculated by dividing weight in pounds by height in inches squared and then multiply by 703. For most people, obesity-related health problems increase beyond a BMI of 25. Because of the relatively large standard error of estimating percent fat from BMI ($\pm 5\%$ fat), other methods of body composition assessment should be used to predict body fatness during a fitness assessment.

The pattern of body fat distribution is recognized as an important predictor of the health risks of obesity. The waist circumference can be used alone as an indicator of health risk because abdominal obesity is the issue. Android obesity, which is characterized by more fat on the trunk (abdominal fat), provides an increased risk of hypertension, type 2 diabetes, dyslipidemia, coronary artery disease, and premature death compared with individuals who demonstrated gynoid obesity (fat distributed in the hips and thighs).

Procedures:

$$\text{BMI} = \frac{\text{weight in pounds}}{(\text{height in inches})^2} \times 703$$

Waist Circumference = With the subject standing upright and relaxed, a horizontal measurement with a cloth tape measure at the greatest anterior extension of the abdomen, usually at the level of the umbilicus. The average of two measures is used provided each measure is within 5 mm.

Body Mass Index and Waist Circumference Classification of Disease Risk

CLASSIFICATION	BMI	DISEASE RISK* RELATIVE TO NORMAL WEIGHT & WAIST CIRCUMFERENCE	
		MEN, ≤ 40 in WOMEN, ≤ 35 in	MEN, > 40 in WOMEN, > 35 in
Underweight	<18.5	—	—
Normal	18.5-24.9	—	—
Overweight	25.0-29.9	Increased	High
Obesity, Class I	30.0-34.9	High	Very high
Obesity, Class II	35.0-39.9	Very high	Very high
Obesity, Class III	≥40	Extremely high	Extremely high

*Disease risk for type 2 diabetes, hypertension, and cardiovascular disease. Dash (—) indicates that no additional risk at these levels of BMI were assigned. Increased waist circumference can also be a marker for increased risk in persons of normal weight.

American College of Sports Medicine, ACSM's Guidelines for Exercise Testing and Prescription, Lippencott Williams and Wilkins, 7th Edition, May 2005.

THE SPIRITUAL HEALTH INVENTORY FOR PAIN

Directions: For each question, circle the answer that best applies to your life.

PART 1: SOURCES OF HOPE, MEANING, COMFORT, STRENGTH, PEACE, LOVE, AND CONNECTION

	No/Never	Rarely	Sometimes	Usually	Yes/Always
1. Do you believe in God or a Supreme Power?	1	2	3	4	5
2. Do you feel you have a personal relationship with God?	1	2	3	4	5
(3-10) Does your faith or trust in God give you:					
3. A pervasive sense of HOPE?	1	2	3	4	5
4. A pervasive sense of LOVE?	1	2	3	4	5
5. A pervasive sense of INNER PEACE?	1	2	3	4	5
6. A pervasive sense of COMFORT?	1	2	3	4	5
7. A pervasive sense of MEANING?	1	2	3	4	5
8. A pervasive sense of STRENGTH?	1	2	3	4	5
9. A pervasive sense of CONNECTION with God?	1	2	3	4	5
10. A pervasive sense of CONFIDENCE in the future?	1	2	3	4	5
11. During your chronic pain, do you turn to God for comfort?	1	2	3	4	5
12. During stressful and hard times, do you feel God's peace?	1	2	3	4	5
13. Does prayer result in you feeling relaxed and at peace?	1	2	3	4	5
14. Do you feel loved and unconditionally accepted by God?	1	2	3	4	5
15. Do you often feel close to God?	1	2	3	4	5

PART 2: ORGANIZED RELIGION

	No/Never	Rarely	Sometimes	Usually	Yes/Always
16. Are you a member of a particular church, synagogue, mosque, or other religious group?	1	2	3	4	5
17. Do you attend religious services weekly?	1	2	3	4	5
(18-20) Does your religion generally cause you to be:					
18. Less judgmental (critical) than most people?	1	2	3	4	5
19. Less irritated with others of different beliefs?	1	2	3	4	5
20. More loving toward people in general?	1	2	3	4	5

PART 2: ORGANIZED RELIGION (continued)

	No/Never	Rarely	Sometimes	Usually	Yes/Always
21. Do you have close relationships with people within your particular place of worship?	1	2	3	4	5
22. Do you participate in any organized fellowship groups with those in your religious community?	1	2	3	4	5
23. When you're around people from your religious community are you generally honest and open discussing your feelings and personal issues (versus quiet or pretending all is okay)?	1	2	3	4	5
(24-30) Do the teachings of your organized religion tend to:					
24. Make you feel UNBURDENED (versus obligated and heavy)?	1	2	3	4	5
25. Make you feel FORGIVEN (versus guilty)?	1	2	3	4	5
26. Make you feel FREE (versus under pressure)?	1	2	3	4	5
27. Make you feel ENCOURAGED (versus discouraged)?	1	2	3	4	5
28. Make you feel LOVED by God (versus judged)?	1	2	3	4	5
29. Make you feel HOPEFUL about the future (versus fearful)?	1	2	3	4	5
30. Make you feel CONCERNED with others (versus angry)?	1	2	3	4	5

PART 3: PERSONAL SPIRITUALITY AND PRACTICES

	No/Never	Rarely	Sometimes	Usually	Yes/Always
31. Do you have an active faith in God?	1	2	3	4	5
32. Is your faith PERSONAL (versus abstract, impersonal)?	1	2	3	4	5
33. Is your faith GROWING (versus stagnant or diminishing)?	1	2	3	4	5
34. Is your faith VITAL to you (versus going through the motions)?	1	2	3	4	5
35. Is your faith in God IMPORTANT to you?	1	2	3	4	5
(36-40) What is your view of God?					
36. God is patient and difficult to anger.	1	2	3	4	5
37. God is kind and generous to me personally.	1	2	3	4	5
38. God is concerned about me individually.	1	2	3	4	5
39. God is loving and He loves me unconditionally.	1	2	3	4	5
40. God is forgiving and He forgives me quickly.	1	2	3	4	5

TRUST

TRUST

PART 3: PERSONAL SPIRITUALITY AND PRACTICES (CONTINUED)

	No/Never	Rarely	Sometimes	Usually	Yes/Always
41. Is your faith more important to you NOW than in the past?	1	2	3	4	5
42. Do you engage in personal confession frequently?	1	2	3	4	5
43. Do you engage in private prayer frequently?	1	2	3	4	5
44. Do you ever pray corporately or in groups?	1	2	3	4	5
45. Do you usually pray about OTHERS' needs (versus your own)?	1	2	3	4	5
46. When you pray, do you believe God is actually listening?	1	2	3	4	5
47. Do you engage in private meditation or reflection about God?	1	2	3	4	5
48. Do you think more about what God thinks of you (versus what others think about you)?	1	2	3	4	5
49. In general, do you rely heavily on God to live out each day?	1	2	3	4	5
50. Do you find that you are quick to forgive others?	1	2	3	4	5

PART 4: EFFECTS OF SPIRITUALITY ON YOUR MENTAL CONDITION

	No/Never	Rarely	Sometimes	Usually	Yes/Always
51. Has your struggle with chronic pain generally ENHANCED your spirituality and personal beliefs?	1	2	3	4	5
52. When you have pain, do you often ask others to pray for you?	1	2	3	4	5
53. Despite your pain, have you been able to take steps or do things that help you spiritually?	1	2	3	4	5
54. Are you now looking (or thinking about looking) for ways that might help you reconnect with your spiritual community?	1	2	3	4	5
55. Are you now looking (or thinking about looking) for ways that might help you reconnect with God?	1	2	3	4	5

TOTAL SCORE _____ **(275 possible)**

Interpretation:

<100:   You may be in SIGNIFICANT Spiritual DISTRESS
100-165:   You may be in MODERATE Spiritual DISTRESS
166-230:   You may have MODERATE Spiritual HEALTH
>230:   You may be enjoying SIGNIFICANT Spiritual HEALTH

NOTES

SOCIAL HEALTH ASSESSMENT (ISEL-12)

This scale is made up of a list of statements, each of which may or may not be true about you. For each statement circle true or false.

Directions: Circle T for all True answers and F for False answers for each question:

T F   1. I would have a hard time finding someone to come with me for a day at the beach.

T F   2. I don't have someone I feel I could share my greatest worries or fears with.

T F   3. Should I badly need $100 on short notice, I don't have anyone to go to and ask for help.

T F   4. I haven't contacted my family members in over a month.

T F   5. I'm not married and/or have no one with whom I feel close enough to express love, concern, and close companionship.

T F   6. I belong to and attend a church regularly, or some other group with caring, supportive values.

T F   7. If I needed someone to pick me up at the airport, I have friends I feel comfortable enough to call to help me.

T F   8. I invite friends over or go out with friends at least once or twice a month.

T F   9. I often (at least weekly) contact friends or family by phone, email, or visiting face to face.

T F   10. I have people who are interested in my success and take pride in my accomplishments.

Scoring:

There are ten possible points. Add up your score using the following: give yourself one point for each false response in questions one through five, and one point for each true response in questions six through ten. The higher the score, the stronger your social support network and generally the happier you'll be.

Your Total Score: _____

> *"There is no physician like a true friend."*
> **~ AUTHOR UNKNOWN**

Interpretation:

8–10   You have a strong support system – a positive health trait.

6–7   You probably have adequate social support to protect your health.

5   Take note. You would likely benefit from improved social contact.

4   A score of four or lower indicates that you definitely need to reach out. Get help from your pastor or a counselor in order to help improve this aspect of your life. If social intimacy isn't your strong point, join a church or other caring group you can associate with and do things with other people.

Source:
(Interpersonal Support Evaluation List) Dr. Sheldon Cohen – author, http://www.psy.cmu.edu/~scohen/index.html
Adapted and Used with Permission.

NOTES

NOTES

> *"Dance like no one is watching.*
> *Sing like no one is listening.*
> *Love like you've never been hurt,*
> *and live like it's heaven on Earth."*
> **~ ALFRED D. SOUZA**

NOTES

OUTLOOK

DEPRESSION ASSESSMENT

This depression assessment was developed by the Center for Epidemiological Studies (Radloff, 1977). This self-reporting questionnaire measures symptoms of depression and is intended for the general population.

Directions: Below is a list of the ways you might have felt or behaved recently. Using the scale below as a guide, write a number beside each statement that best describes how you felt, behaved, and the frequency of these feelings during the past week.

0 = Rarely or none of the time (less than 1 day)
1 = Some or a little of the time (1–2 days)
2 = Occasionally or a moderate amount of time (3–4 days)
3 = Most or all of the time (5–7 days)

During the Past Week:

____1. I was bothered by things that usually don't bother me.

____2. I did not feel like eating; my appetite was poor.

____3. I felt that I could not shake off the blues even with help from my family or friends.

____4. I felt that I was just as good as other people.

____5. I had trouble keeping my mind on what I was doing.

____6. I felt depressed.

____7. I felt that everything I did was an effort.

____8. I felt hopeful about the future.

____9. I thought my life has been a failure.

____10. I felt fearful.

____11. My sleep was restless.

____12. I was happy.

____13. I talked less than usual.

____14. I felt lonely.

____15. People were unfriendly.

____16. I enjoyed life.

____17. I had crying spells.

____18. I felt sad.

____19. I felt that people dislike me.

____20. I could not get "going."

> **Remember this great piece of news:**
> *Optimism and pessimism are learned behaviors. We can learn how to be more optimistic and how to be less pessimistic.*

OUTLOOK

Scoring:

1. Reverse code items 4, 8, 12, and 16 prior to scoring.

That is,

3 points for a score of "0"
2 points for a score of "1"
1 point for a score of "2"
0 points for a score of "3"

2. Add items to obtain your total score for the assessment.

Your Total Score: _____

Interpretation:

Total CES-D scores range from 0–60, with high scores reflecting greater symptoms of depression.

Please Note: Before you interpret your score, you should know that a high score is not the same thing as a diagnosis of depression. Some individuals who get a high score are not in fact depressed, and people with a low score may in fact be depressed. A score ≥ 16 suggests a clinically significant level of psychological distress. It does not necessarily mean that you have a clinical diagnosis of depression. A diagnosis of depression depends on other things, such as the duration of symptoms and whether they have another primary source other than depression. A diagnosis of depression can only be made after a through interview with a qualified psychologist or psychiatrist.

0–9 Non Depressed
10–15 Mildly Depressed
16–24 Moderately Depressed
24+ Severely Depressed

Regardless of your score on this measure, if you are experiencing depressive symptoms that you feel are affecting your life, please contact a mental health professional.

Source of Center for Epidemiologic Studies Depression Scale (CES-D), NIMH: Radloff, L. "The CES-D scale: A Self Report Depression Scale for Research in the General Population." *Applied Psychological Measurement* 1977 1: 385–401. Public Domain.

OUTLOOK

GENERALIZED ANXIETY DISORDER (GAD) SELF-TEST

For further information go to nimh.nih.gov/HealthInformation/anxietymenu.cfm or adaa.org

Directions: Check the box in the column that best describes how you feel. When finished, add the numbers shown by each box to arrive at your total score.

OVER THE LAST TWO WEEKS, HOW OFTEN HAVE YOU BEEN BOTHERED BY THE FOLLOWING PROBLEMS?	NOT AT ALL	SEVERAL DAYS	MORE THAN HALF THE DAYS	NEARLY EVERY DAY
Feeling nervous, anxious, or on edge	( ) 0	( ) 1	( ) 2	( ) 3
Not being able to stop or control worrying	( ) 0	( ) 1	( ) 2	( ) 3
Worrying too much about different things	( ) 0	( ) 1	( ) 2	( ) 3
Trouble relaxing	( ) 0	( ) 1	( ) 2	( ) 3
Being so restless it's hard to sit still	( ) 0	( ) 1	( ) 2	( ) 3
Becoming easily annoyed or irritable	( ) 0	( ) 1	( ) 2	( ) 3
Feeling afraid as if something awful might happen	( ) 0	( ) 1	( ) 2	( ) 3
ADD COLUMNS		+	+	+

Your Total Score: _____

If you checked any problems, how difficult have these problems made it for you to do your work, take care of things at home, or get along with other people?

____ Not difficult at all   ____ Very difficult

____ Somewhat difficult   ____ Extremely difficult

Mark your total score with an X on the Generalized Anxiety Scale below.

0	Minimal	5	Mild	10	Moderate	15	Severe	21

Interpretation:

On the scale above, a total score of ten or higher indicates you may be experiencing generalized anxiety disorder (GAD) and need further evaluation by a doctor or mental health counselor. This is especially true if your anxiety has been interfering with work and daily living requirements for a month or more.

* Based on research by Robert Spitzer, et al. "A Brief Measure for Assessing Generalized Anxiety Disorder." *Archives of Internal Medicine* 166:1092–97, May 22, 2006.

OUTLOOK

Understanding Your GAD-7 Score[1]

This self-assessment of GAD was developed by the Department of Psychiatry at Columbia University as a self-scoring screening tool.

- Scores less than ten indicate normal or mild symptoms of anxiety.

- Scores of ten or higher indicate you may be experiencing generalized anxiety disorder and you need further evaluation by a mental health professional and therapy if indicated.

Compare your score on the generalized anxiety self-test to the following norms.

Score	Rating
0–4	Minimal anxiety
5–9	Mild anxiety
10–14	Moderate anxiety, need further evaluation
15–21	Severe anxiety, need further evaluation and follow-up

Understanding Anxiety[2]

Everyone becomes anxious from time to time. That's normal. Briefly "getting the jitters" before making a presentation, taking a test, or having a first date is stressful and produces anxiety, but it's normal. Being a little anxious about an upcoming speaking engagement helps you prepare and do a better job.

Generalized anxiety disorder is much more than the normal anxiety people experience day to day. It's chronic and fills your day with exaggerated worry and tension even though there is little or nothing to provoke it. Having GAD means always anticipating disaster, and often worrying excessively about health, money, family, or work. Sometimes the source of the worry is hard to pinpoint. Just the thought of getting through the day provokes anxiety.

People with GAD can't seem to shake their concerns, even if they realize their anxiety is more intense than the situation warrants. Their worries are accompanied by physical symptoms such as fatigue, headaches, muscle tension, muscle aches, difficulty swallowing, trembling, twitching, irritability, sweating, hot flashes, feeling light-headed or out of breath. They also may feel nauseated or have to go to the bathroom frequently.

Individuals with GAD seem unable to relax, and they may startle more easily than other people.

They tend to have difficulty concentrating, too. Often, they have trouble falling or staying asleep.

About four million adult Americans are affected by GAD and about twice as many women as men. The disorder comes on gradually and can occur across the life cycle, although the risk is highest between childhood and middle age.

GAD is diagnosed when someone spends at least six months worrying excessively about a number of everyday problems.

Dealing with Anxiety[2]

Anxiety that is constant and disabling needs professional treatment. Get help from your doctor or a professional mental health counselor. The most effective treatments are medications or "talk therapy" such as cognitive behavior therapy or both.

Anxiety rarely occurs alone. It is often accompanied by depression and substance abuse. These other disorders also need treating along with anxiety to see good results.

There are things you can do, however, that may also be helpful in dealing with this problem.

- Join a self-help or support group and share problems and achievements with others.

- Talk over problems with a trusted friend or member of the clergy, although this isn't a substitute for mental health care.

- Enlist the help and understanding of your family. Their understanding, support, and encouragement is important for recovery.

- Learn new stress management techniques, for example meditation and relaxation skills.

- Get regular aerobic exercise such as brisk walking. It helps you relax, relieves tension, and improves mental outlook. Invite a friend to join you.

- Alcohol, caffeine, and illicit drugs can aggravate the symptoms of anxiety.

National Institute of Mental Health
nimh.nih.gov

Anxiety Disorders Association of America
adaa.org

References:
1. Robert Spitzer et al. "A Brief Measure for Assessing Generalized Anxiety Disorder." *Archives of Internal Medicine* 2006;166:1092–97.
2. National Institute of Mental Health. Anxiety Disorders, 2006.

OUTLOOK

VALUES LIST FOR MY LIFE

By Daniel Roberts   *Used with Permission*   *For directions go to wisedecisions.com*

1. Abundance
2. Accountability
3. Achievement
4. At Ease with Uncertainty
5. Balance (Home/Work)
6. Balance (Physical/ Emotional /Mental/ Spiritual)
7. Beauty
8. Being Liked
9. Being the Best
10. Belonging
11. Caring
12. Caution
13. Commitment
14. Common Good
15. Community Service
16. Compassion
17. Conflict Resolution
18. Control
19. Cooperation
20. Counseling
21. Courage
22. Courtesy
23. Creativity
24. Determination
25. Discovery
26. Diversity
27. Education
28. Efficiency
29. Empowered
30. Enthusiasm
31. Environmental Awareness
32. Equality

33. Ethics
34. Excellence
35. Fairness
36. Family
37. Fellowship
38. Financial Health
39. Flexibility
40. Forgiveness
41. Freedom
42. Future Generations
43. Generosity
44. Health
45. Honesty
46. Humility
47. Humor/Fun
48. Image
49. Independence
50. Innovation
51. Integrity
52. Interdependence
53. Intuition
54. Joy
55. Justice
56. Knowledge
57. Learning
58. Logic
59. Love
60. Loyalty
61. Making a Difference
62. Material Assets
63. Meaning
64. Mercy
65. Mission Focus
66. Nature Loving

67. Open Communication
68. Passion
69. Patience
70. Peace
71. Perseverance
72. Personal Fulfillment
73. Personal Growth
74. Personal Relationships
75. Power
76. Pride
77. Professional Growth
78. Prosperity
79. Reason
80. Reliability
81. Respect
82. Responsibility
83. Risk Averse
84. Risk Taking
85. Safety
86. Security
87. Self-Expression
88. Self-Improvement
89. Self-Worth
90. Spirituality
91. Status
92. Success
93. Tolerance
94. Trust
95. Values Awareness
96. Versatility
97. Vision
98. Wealth
99. Wholeness
100. Wisdom

THE 25 PIECES OF MY IDEAL LIFE

By Daniel Roberts　　　*Used with Permission*　　　　　　　*For directions go to wisedecisions.com*

THE 25 PIECES OF MY IDEAL LIFE	IMPORTANCE IN MY LIFE * = LOWEST ***** = HIGHEST	% ACHIEVED SO FAR	EFFORT I AM CURRENTLY EXPENDING (1-10 SCALE)	I WANT TO FOCUS ON THIS NOW / LATER

MEASURED CRITERIA TABLE

By Daniel Roberts   *Used with Permission*   *For directions go to wisedecisions.com*

QUESTION:

CRITERIA	POSSIBLE POINTS	CHOICE #1	CHOICE #2	CHOICE #3
TOTAL:				

WEIGHTED CRITERIA TABLE

By Daniel Roberts   *Used with Permission*   *For directions go to wisedecisions.com*

QUESTION:

CRITERIA	WEIGHT 1-10	OPTION #1	OPTION #2	OPTION #3
TOTAL:				

BEN FRANKLIN LEDGER

By Daniel Roberts   *Used with Permission*   *For directions go to wisedecisions.com*

WHAT ARE THE PROS AND CONS OF:

PRO	CON

> "A happy person is not a person
> in a certain set of circumstances,
> but rather a person with
> a certain set of attitudes."
>
> ~ **HUGH DOWNS**

OUTLOOK

MENTAL OUTLOOK ASSESSMENT

Directions: Using the scale below as a guide, for each question write a number beside each statement to indicate how you most typically think or feel.

2 = Fully Agree
1 = Partially Agree
0 = Don't Agree

____1. I expect much from life.

____2. I do not look forward to what lies ahead of me in the years to come.

____3. My days seem to pass slowly.

____4. My life is full of plans.

____5. I expect things to work out well for me.

____6. I blame myself if things go wrong.

____7. I believe that something positive can be found in most negative situations.

____8. I see change in life as difficult and annoying.

____9. I see change as opportunity for growth and improvement.

Scoring:

1. Reverse code items 2, 3, 6, and 8 prior to scoring.

That is,

if you scored a "2," give yourself a "0."
if you scored a "1," give yourself a "1."
if you scored "0," give yourself a "2."

2. Sum items to obtain your total score for the assessment and then mark your score with an X on the Optimism Scale below.

Your Total Score: _____

Optimism Scale:

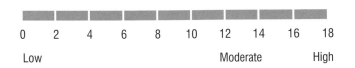

| 0 | 2 | 4 | 6 | 8 | 10 | 12 | 14 | 16 | 18 |

Low   Moderate   High

Interpretation:

0–9   Indicates low optimism
10–16 Indicates moderate optimism
17–18 Indicates high optimism

Based on the following research: Giltay EJ, et al. *Archives of Internal Medicine*. February 27, 2006.
Assessment developed by LifeLong Health. Adapted and Used with Permission.

OUTLOOK

NOTES

HEALTHY EATING SELF-TEST

Directions: How healthy are your eating habits? Take this quick nutrition self-test to see. Mark the box in each row that best describes your usual eating pattern. Write the score beside that box in the far right column.

EATING PRACTICES	COLUMN A	COLUMN B	COLUMN C	SCORE
Breakfast How often do you eat breakfast?	[ ] 0 Occasionally or never	[ ] 3 Most days (5 or more times/week)	[ ] 10 Every day	
Whole-Grain Bread/Cereal Number of servings you eat daily? (serv = 1 slice bread, 3/4 C dry cereal, 1/2 C cooked cereal or brown rice)	[ ] 0 0-2/day	[ ] 5 At least 3/day	[ ] 10 4 or more/day	
Fruits and Vegetables Number of servings you eat daily? (serving = 1 fruit, 1 C fresh, 1/2 C cooked, 2/3 C juice)	[ ] 0 0-4 serv/day	[ ] 5 5-6 serv/day	[ ] 10 7 or more serv/day	
Spreads and Other Fats What kinds do you usually eat?	[ ] 0 Primarily use butter or stick margarine and shortening	[ ] 5 Primarily use soft tub margarine and vegetable oils	[ ] 10 Only use vegetable oils and trans fat-free margarine	
Meats/Protein Foods What kinds of protein foods do you typically eat?	[ ] 0 Regularly eat red meat including steak, hot dogs, hamburger, and/or sausage	[ ] 5 Seldom eat meat or limit it to only lean meat, skinless poultry, or fish	[ ] 10 Eat primarily peas, beans, lentils, nuts, soy proteins, tofu, and other plant-based protein foods	
Dairy Products What kind of dairy products do you typically use?	[ ] 0 Use regular milk, cheese, cottage cheese, and yogurt	[ ] 3 Use only lowfat milk, cheese, cottage cheese, or yogurt	[ ] 5 Use only nonfat milk, cheese, or yogurt or use soy milk	
Legumes, Dry Beans/Peas How often do you eat them?	[ ] 0 0-2 times/week	[ ] 3 3-6 times/week	[ ] 5 Daily	
Nuts, Seeds, Nut Butters How often do you eat them?	[ ] 0 0-3 times/week	[ ] 5 4-5 times/week	[ ] 10 Daily	
Salt and Salty Foods How much do you eat?	[ ] 0 Always salt food at mealtime and often eat salty foods	[ ] 3 Occasionally add additional salt to food or eat salty foods	[ ] 5 Use salt sparingly and limit intake of salty foods	
High Glycemic Foods How often do you eat white bread, white rice, sugary dry cereals, pastry, and snack foods?	[ ] 0 Eat some of these foods most every day	[ ] 3 Limit these foods, only eat them a few times in a week	[ ] 5 Seldom eat high glycemic foods or eat in small amounts	
Sodas/Sweets How often do you eat/drink soda pop, punch, ice cream, candy, sugar, jam, and other sweets?	[ ] 0 Love sweets, eat them every day	[ ] 3 Limit sweets, only eat sweets occasionally or in small amounts	[ ] 5 Seldom eat sugar-rich foods, and eat primarily fresh fruit and pure fruit juices	

CONTINUED ON THE NEXT PAGE

EATING PRACTICES	COLUMN A	COLUMN B	COLUMN C	SCORE
Body Mass Index (BMI) Mark your BMI value or waist girth (refer to BMI chart in this section).	[ ] 0 BMI 30 or higher Waist 35"+ women, 40"+ men	[ ] 5 BMI 25-29.9 Waist 32–35" women, 37–40" men	[ ] 10 BMI 18.5-24.9 Waist <32" women, <37" men	
Physical Activity Level How often do you get 30+ min. of physical activity in a day? Ex: jog, walk, bike, dance, garden, hike.	[ ] 0 Never or seldom exercise	[ ] 3 3-4 days/week	[ ] 5 5-7 days/week	
Water Number of glasses of water you normally drink each day?	[ ] 0 Less than 5 glasses /day	[ ] 3 5-7 glasses/day	[ ] 5 8-10 glasses/day	

Scoring: Sum all of the scores in the right-hand column to arrive at your total score or Nutrition Index. Compare your results with the norms on the right. Put an "X" on the Nutrition Scale that corresponds with your score.

Nutrition Scale: (0–100) a high score is ideal

```
0   10   20   30   40   50   60   70   80   90   100
```
Needs Improving   Doing Well   Excellent

Your Nutrition Index (0–100) [   ]

INTERPRETING YOUR NUTRITION INDEX SCORE		
	Nutrition Index	**% of Population**
Excellent	80-100	18%
Doing Well	54-79	22%
Needs Improving	35–53	43%
Poor Eating Habits	less than 35	17%

DIABETES RISK PROFILE

Directions: For each risk factor, check the box in the column that best describes you. Write score shown next to the check box in the score column to the right.

RISK FACTORS	COLUMN A	COLUMN B	COLUMN C	SCORE
1. Age. Indicate your age range.	[ ] 0 Less than 45	[ ] 4 45-64	[ ] 6 65 or older	
2. Race. Indicate your race.	[ ] 0 Caucasian, other	[ ] 1 African-American, Hispanic, Asian	[ ] 2 Pacific Islander, Native American	
3. Family History. Number of parents, brothers, or sisters with diabetes	[ ] 0 None	[ ] 1 One	[ ] 2 Two or more	
4. Pregnancy History. Women with gestational diabetes or delivered a baby weighing 9 pounds or more	[ ] 0 Men	[ ] 0 Women, no	[ ] 1 Women, yes	
5. Symptoms. How many do you have? Excessive thirst, frequent urination, unusual weight loss, extreme hunger, increased fatigue, blurry vision	[ ] 0 None	[ ] 1 One symptom	[ ] 5 Two or more symptoms	
6. Body Weight. Indicate your weight range (refer to BMI chart in this section)	[ ] 0 Healthy weight BMI < 25	[ ] 3 Overweight BMI 25-29.9	[ ] 6 Very overweight, BMI 30+ or high waist girth 35+ women, 40+ men	
7. Physical Activity. Number of days you get 30+ minutes of moderate to vigorous physical activity.	[ ] 0 4-7 days/week	[ ] 1 2-3 days/week	[ ] 3 No regular physical activity program	
8. High Glycemic Index Foods. How often do you eat the following foods: soda pop, pastry, cookies, candy, chips, desserts, potatoes, french fries	[ ] 0 Only eat these foods occasionally (no more than once/day)	[ ] 1 Eat these foods regularly, usually 2-3 times most days	[ ] 2 Eat these foods often, usually 4-5 or more times most days	
9. Breads and Cereals. What kind do you usually eat?	[ ] 0 Eat whole-wheat bread, oatmeal, brown rice, and other whole grains	[ ] 1/2 Half the time eat white bread, white rice, and sweetened cereals	[ ] 1 Usually eat white bread, white rice, and typical sweetened cereals	
10. Fruits and Vegetables. How many servings of fruits and vegetables do you usually eat daily?	[ ] 0 5 or more serv/day	[ ] 1/2 3-4 serv/day	[ ] 1 0-2 serv/day	
11. Fats Eaten. What kinds of fats do you usually eat?	[ ] 0 All vegetable oils, no animal or solid fats	[ ] 1/2 Use both kinds of fats	[ ] 1 Mostly solid fats, butter, or hard stick margarine	
12. Smoking. Indicate your present smoking status	[ ] 0 Never smoked	[ ] 1/2 Ex-smoker	[ ] 1 Current smoker	

CONTINUED ON THE NEXT PAGE

RISK FACTORS	COLUMN A	COLUMN B	COLUMN C	SCORE
13. Blood Pressure. Indicate your present range. If you don't know, skip the question but get it checked.	[ ] 0 Normal blood pressure, less than 120/80	[ ] 1 Pre-hypertension, 120/80-139/89	[ ] 2 High blood pressure 140/90 or higher	
14. Blood Triglyceride and HDLs (mg/dL). Indicate your status. Skip if not known. If age 45+, sedentary, and overweight, you are likely at risk (mark Col. B)	[ ] 0 Normal blood fat levels Trig.<150, and HDLs 45+ men, 55+ women	[ ] 1 High blood fat level Trig. 150-199, or HDLs men 40-44, women 40-54	[ ] 2 Very high blood fat level Trig. 200+, or HDLs <40	
15. Blood Glucose Level. Indicate your blood sugar level. If you don't know, mark normal. If age 45+ get it checked regularly. You need to know!	[ ] 0 Normal blood sugar Fasting <100 mg/dL Non-fasting <140 mg/dL	[ ] 8 Pre diabetes Fasting 100-125 mg/dL Non-fasting 140-199	[ ] 15 High or diabetic, Fasting 126+ mg/dL Non-fasting 200+ mg/dL	

Diabetes Risk Score*: a low score is ideal. Mark your score with an "X" on the scale.

Add scores in right column to determine your personal diabetes score.

0	6	12	16	24	+
Low Risk		Increased Risk		High Risk or Diabetes	

*A score of 12+ indicates increased risk, 16–20+ is high risk or diabetes is present

PREVENTING DIABETES

Current Trends

Diabetes is increasing at a rapid rate in the United States. In the last ten years, rates are up 33%. Currently there are 18.2 million people with diabetes in the U.S. and unfortunately, some 5.2 million don't even know they have the problem. Another forty-five million people have pre-diabetes! Over one million people will be diagnosed with diabetes this year.[1]

Recent studies indicate that diabetes is largely preventable by adopting a healthy lifestyle. In the Nurses' Health Study (84,000 women followed for sixteen years) the researchers concluded that 90% of all new cases of diabetes could have been prevented by a healthier lifestyle.[2]

Preventive Actions You Can Take

Here are seven key steps you can take based on this large population study and other research, to help you prevent diabetes.

1. **Achieve and maintain a healthy weight.** Excess body fat, measured as body mass index (BMI), is the primary risk factor for diabetes. Compared to lean women (BMI <23), moderately overweight women (BMI of 25-29) were 7.6 times more likely to develop diabetes. A BMI over 30 increased the risk by twenty times, and a BMI of 35+ jumped the risk by thirty-nine times! Risks are similar for men. Check your BMI in the chart below (height in inches, weight in pounds).

HEIGHT	HEALTHY BMI 23	OVERWT BMI 25	OBESE 1 BMI 30+	OBESE 2 BMI 35+
4' 10"	110	119+	143+	167+
5' 0"	118	128+	153+	179+
5' 2"	126	136+	164+	191+
5' 4"	134	145+	174+	204+
5' 6"	142	155+	186	216+
5' 8"	151	164+	197+	230+
5' 10"	160	174+	209+	243+
6' 0"	169	184+	221+	258+
6' 2"	179	194+	233+	272+
6' 4"	189	205+	246+	287+

Source: NIH, NHLBI, National Obesity Initiative, 2003

2. **Get regular physical activity.** Exercise acts much like insulin in the body and is a key therapeutic action for both treatment and prevention of diabetes. Regular activity also helps weight control, normalizing of blood pressure and blood fats, and reduces insulin resistance that is so closely linked to type 2 diabetes. The national guideline for fitness states, "Every US adult should accumulate 30 minutes or more of moderate intensity physical activity on most, preferably all, days of the week."[3] Walking is one of the best activities nearly everyone can do safely. Regular activity can reduce the risk of diabetes by 25%–50%.

3. **Not smoking.** Smoking increases the risk of diabetes. Nonsmokers had a 34% lower risk of getting diabetes.[4]

4. **Limit sweets, refined foods, and high glycemic index foods.** Highly refined foods are absorbed more quickly, resulting in a higher insulin response. Eating heavily of these foods, termed "high glycemic index" foods, increases the risk of developing diabetes. Eat these foods sparingly.

    Foods of high glycemic index include:

    *   Sugar, sweets, most desserts
    *   Soda pop and sugar-sweetened punch
    *   White rice
    *   Refined cereals rich in sugar
    *   Potatoes such as french fries
    *   Pastry, cookies, and most snack foods
    *   White bread, rolls, pancakes, etc.

5. **Eat more high-fiber foods.** Unrefined foods, high in dietary fiber, slow the absorption of carbohydrates and decrease the insulin demand. These foods protect against diabetes. It's recommended that you eat at least 15 grams of dietary fiber per 1,000 calories eaten per day. That's generally 30+ grams of dietary fiber daily.

Good sources of high-fiber foods include:

- Whole-grain breads, oatmeal, brown rice, cereal

- Fruits: apples, bananas, berries, melons, citrus

- Vegetables: salads, greens, squash, broccoli,

- Cabbage, tomatoes, peppers, peas, stir fry

- Legumes: peas, lentils, beans, garbanzos, soy

- Nuts and seeds

Limiting refined and high glycemic foods and eating more fiber can cut the risk of diabetes in half.

6. **Choose healthy fats.** The Nurses' Health Study showed that reducing trans fats (found in foods with partially hydrogenated vegetable oils) by only 2% of calories and replacing them with polyunsaturated fats resulted in a 40% decreased risk of getting diabetes. Avoiding saturated fat and cholesterol is also important for heart health.

7. **Regular checkups.** The American Diabetic Association recommends testing for diabetes (a fasting blood glucose test) in all persons age forty-five and older, at least once every three years. This test should be started at a younger age and checked more often in high-risk persons.

Summary

Take preventive steps now. By following these positive guidelines you can lower your chances of ever developing diabetes by as much as 90%, even if you have a family history of diabetes.[2] You will also certainly look and feel your best. Get help from your doctor, a dietitian, or health counselor as needed in making therapeutic lifestyle changes.

More Information? Visit Diabetes.org

References:
1. American Diabetes Association website: diabetes.org, Facts and Figures, 2005. **2.** Hu FB, et al, "Diet, Lifestyle, and the Risk of Type 2 Diabetes Mellitus in Women," *New England Journal of Medicine* 345:790–7, Sept. 13, 2001. **3.** NIH, and ACSM, "Physical Activity and Public Health," *JAMA* 273:402–7, 1995. **4.** Hu FB, et al., "Diet, Lifestyle, and the Risk of Type 2 Diabetes."

OSTEOPOROSIS – ARE YOU AT RISK?

Directions: Take this Osteoporosis Self-test to find out if you are at risk. Put an "X" in the column that best describes you for each risk factor.

RISK FACTORS	COLUMN A	COLUMN B	COLUMN C
1. Gender	[ ] Male, female pre-menopause	[ ] Female, uterus removed or not menstruating for other reasons	[ ] Female, post-menopausal
2. Race	[ ] African-American	[ ] Hispanic	[ ] White, Asian, Native American
3. Age	[ ] Less than 60	[ ] 60-64	[ ] 65 or older
4. Weight/BMI	[ ] Overweight Weight 154+, BMI greater than 25	[ ] Normal weight Weight 127-153, BMI 18.5-24.9	[ ] Very lean Weight less than 127, BMI < 18.5
5. Fracture History	[ ] No family or personal history of broken bones from a fall	[ ] Family history of broken bones from falls	[ ] Personal history of broken bones from falls
6. Physical Activity	[ ] Weight-bearing exercise 4+ times a week and do weight training	[ ] Moderate activity such as walking, no weight or resistance training	[ ] Sedentary, little or no regular physical activity
7. Smoking	[ ] Never smoked	[ ] Ex-smoker	[ ] Current smoker
8. Alcohol	[ ] Never drink alcoholic beverages	[ ] Have up to 1-2 alcoholic drinks/ day	[ ] Often have 3+ alcoholic drinks/ day
9. Calcium Intake	[ ] Eat 2 or more 8 oz. servings of milk or yogurt or calcium equivalent daily OR calcium supplement (500-600 mg/day)	[ ] Eat only 1 serving of calcium-rich food daily and no calcium supplement	[ ] Seldom or never drink milk or other calcium-fortified foods and take no calcium supplement
10. Protein Source	[ ] Eat primarily plant protein foods, seldom or never eat animal foods	[ ] Eat animal protein foods daily (meats, poultry, or fish)	[ ] Get most of my protein from animal foods (meats, poultry, or fish)
11. Blood Pressure	[ ] Normal: less than 120/80	[ ] High normal: 120/80-139/89	[ ] High: 140/90 or higher
12. Medications anti-convulsants steroids, drugs for hyperthyroidism	[ ] Have never used these medications on a regular basis	[ ] Have used these medications for a few months	[ ] Have used these medications for many months or years
13. Vitamin A (Retinol)	[ ] Do not take vitamin supplements with vitamin A (retinol)	[ ] Take vitamin supplements but less than 500 mcg/day of vitamin A	[ ] Take vitamin A supplements of 700 mcg/day or higher

CONTINUED ON THE NEXT PAGE

RISK FACTORS	COLUMN A	COLUMN B	COLUMN C
14. Folate and Vitamin B-12	[ ] Have adequate intake: 400+ mcg folate or 2.5 mcg vitamin B-12 daily	[ ] Have marginal intake of folate and vitamin B-12 daily	[ ] Have a low intake of folate and vitamin B-12 daily
15. Vitamin D	[ ] Get 400 IU vitamin D/day (700-800 if over age 70) in diet or from sun	[ ] Get less vitamin D from sun and in diet than recommended	[ ] Get very little sun and very little vitamin D in diet
16. Vitamin K	[ ] Eat foods high in vitamin K 5+ times/week	[ ] Eat foods high in vitamin K 2-4 times/week	[ ] Eat foods high in vitamin K less than once a week
YOUR SCORE	# OF CHECKS IN COLUMN A _____	# OF CHECKS IN COLUMN B _____	# OF CHECKS IN COLUMN C _____

Scoring Your Results: Count the number of checked boxes in each column. Add columns B and C and write total in the overall risk score box.

- Any checks in Column A indicate "Low Risk" for that specific risk factor.

- Checks in Column B indicate "Moderate Increased Risk."

- Checks in Column C indicate "High Risk."

Overall Risk Score: (number of checks in column C). The greater the number of risks you have, the higher your overall risk for osteoporosis. Review the explanations and suggestions on the next page for enhancing bone health.

OSTEOPOROSIS – PREVENTION GUIDELINES

Risk Factor Explanations

1. **Gender.** Women are more likely to develop osteoporosis than men and at an earlier age.

2. **Race.** Caucasians (whites) have the highest risk for osteoporosis. It is common in Asians and Native Americans, lower in Hispanics, and lowest in African-Americans.

3. **Age.** Men and women lose bone tissue as they age. Some have stronger bones to start with. Others lose it more slowly. See preventive actions that follow.

4. **Weight/BMI.** Lean individuals (less than 154 lb) are at high risk. Maintaining a healthy weight is important, but being too lean (BMI <18.5) is not desirable.

5. **Fracture history.** If your parents had vertebral or other fractures due to osteoporosis, you may have inherited a similar tendency. If you have fallen and broken a bone yourself, you are at high risk for future problems.

6. **Physical activity.** Active people generally have stronger bones than inactive people. Bones grow stronger when stressed. Weight-bearing activities and weight lifting are best for increasing bone strength.

7. **Smoking.** To stop smoking is a positive way to build stronger bones and overall health.

8. **Alcohol.** A high intake of alcohol weakens bones and increases the risk of falls. Avoid or limit alcohol.

9. **Dietary calcium.** If calcium intake is low, bone strength is also likely low. One thousand mg of calcium/day is recommended for adults, 1200 mg/day for persons seventy or older.

10. **Dietary protein.** Adequate protein is essential for all healthy tissue, including bones. Recent research shows that a high ratio of vegetable to animal protein protects bones, slows the loss of calcium, and reduces fractures. Good sources of vegetable protein include beans, lentils, split peas, soybeans, garbanzos, tofu, nuts, whole grains, soy milk, and gluten/soy-based meat alternatives.

11. **Blood pressure.** High blood pressure (140/90 or higher) can increase the loss of bone in elderly individuals. Lowering blood pressure may reduce your risk of osteoporosis and heart problems.

12. **Medications.** Certain medications increase bone loss, for example, corticosteroids, excess thyroid hormone, anticonvulsants, hormone- and immune-suppression drugs. Ask your doctor for guidance regarding medication use.

13. **Retinol.** Beta-carotene does not increase risk, but a total intake of 1.5+ mg/day of vitamin A or retinol increases risk.

14. **Folic Acid/Vitamin B-12.** Folic acid and vitamin B-12 reduce hip fractures. Recommendations: vitamin B-12: 2.5 mcg/day; folic acid: 400 mcg/day. Spinach and other leafy greens and lentils and other legumes are high in folate. Only animal foods or fortified foods have vitamin B-12.

15. **Vitamin D.** Adequate vitamin D comes from sunshine and diet. Adults need 400 IU daily, persons seventy and older need 700-800 IU daily. One glass of milk = 100 IU of vitamin D. Sunlight's contribution varies by season and by exposure.

16. **Vitamin K.** In one study, women who ate 250 mcg/day had half the fracture rates of those eating 60 mcg/day. Good sources: dark leafy greens, broccoli, cabbage. The recommended intake is 90 (women), 120 mcg/day (men).

Preventive Actions for Bone Health

If you are at increased risk, be sure to take preventive actions as soon as possible. The national Osteoporosis Foundation recommends four important actions:

1. **Eat a balanced diet.** Get adequate calcium, folate, and vitamins D, B-12, and K. Good sources of calcium include lowfat milk and yogurt, lowfat cheese, dark leafy greens, calcium-enriched soy milk and tofu, calcium-enriched orange juice, and V-8 vegetable juice. If needed, take a calcium and vitamin D supplement. Emphasize vegetable proteins in your diet. Limit intake of salt or sodium.

2. **Do weight-bearing exercises regularly.** The best activities are those that stress the bones: jog, jump rope, climb stairs, dance, play tennis, and weight lift (to build strength of bones in arms as well). Get guidance from your doctor or a knowledgeable fitness trainer on how best to start an exercise program.

3. **Follow a healthy lifestyle.** Avoid smoking, alcohol, and caffeine. They all increase bone loss. Be active in the sunlight, eat well, get adequate rest, and be positive on life.

4. **Get help from your doctor as needed.** Your doctor can check your bone mineral density. If needed there are also medications that can be taken to go along with a healthy lifestyle to prevent excessive bone loss. Discuss these and other options with your doctor.

Sources:
1. National Osteoporosis Foundation, www.nof.org, 2005. **2.** NIH Consensus Panel, "Osteoporosis Prevention, Diagnosis, and Therapy," *JAMA* 285:785–95, Feb. 14, 2001. **3.** "Screening for Osteoporosis," *NEJM* 353:164–71, Jul 14, '05. **4.** Surgeon General's Report on Bone Health & Osteoporosis, www.surgeongeneral.gov, 2004.

"I know of no more encouraging fact than the unquestionable ability of man to elevate his life by a conscious endeavor."

~ **HENRY DAVID THOREAU**

CORONARY RISK PROFILE

Directions: Check the box in each row that best describes you. Write the score next to the box you checked in the score column on the far right.

RISK FACTORS	COLUMN A	COLUMN B	COLUMN C	SCORE
1. Age. Indicate your age range.	[ ] 0 men <40, women <50	[ ] 4 men 40-44, women 50-54	[ ] 10* men 45+, women 55+	
2. Family History of Early Heart Disease in a brother, sister, or parent. They had a heart problem before 55 in men or 65 in women.	[ ] 0 No	-------	[ ] 10* Yes	
3. Personal History. Has a dr. told you you have coronary heart disease, or have you had a heart attack (MI) or stroke?	[ ] 0 No	-------	[ ] 20* Yes	
4. Physical Activity. Number of days you get 30+ minutes of moderate to vigorous physical activity.	[ ] 0 4-7 days/week	[ ] 4 2-3 days/week	[ ] 10* No regular physical activity program	
5. Smoking. Indicate your present status.	[ ] 0 Never smoked regularly	[ ] 4 Stopped smoking	[ ] 10* Current smoker	
6. Blood Pressure. Do you have high blood pressure?	[ ] 0 Normal blood pressure, less than 120/80	[ ] 5 Pre-hypertension 120/80-139/40	[ ] 10* High, 140/90+ or taking medication for high BP	
7. Total Cholesterol (mg/dL). Do you have high blood cholesterol levels or high LDL? (If you don't know, skip for now but find out.)	[ ] 0 Low chol., less than 200 or LDL less than 130	[ ] 10* Elevated chol. 200-239 or LDL 130-159	[ ] 12* High chol. 240 or higher or LDL of 160 or higher	
8. HDL Cholesterol (mg/dL). Do you have low HDL chol. levels? (If you don't know, skip for now but find out.)	[ ] 0 High HDL levels, 60+	[ ] 2 Average HDL 40-59	[ ] 10* Low HDL, less than 40	
9. Diabetes. Are you a diabetic or have high blood sugar levels?	[ ] 0 No diabetes. Normal blood sugar. Fasting <100 mg/dL Non-fast. <140 mg/dL	[ ] 5 Pre diabetes Fasting 100-125 mg/dL Non-fast 140-199	[ ] 20* Diabetic, or Fasting 126+ mg/dL Non-fast 200+ mg/dL	
10. Body Weight. Indicate your weight range (refer to BMI chart in this section).	[ ] 0 Healthy weight BMI <25	[ ] 5 Overweight BMI 25-29.9	[ ] 10* Obese, BMI 30+ or waist girth 35+ women, 40+ men	
11. Breads and Cereals. What kind do you usually eat?	[ ] 0 Eat whole-wheat bread, oatmeal, brown rice, and other whole grains	[ ] 1 Half the time eat white bread, white rice, and refined cereals	[ ] 3 Usually eat white bread, white rice, and refined cereals	
12. Fruits and Vegetables. How many servings of fruits, vegetables, and legumes do you usually eat daily?	[ ] 0 5-9 or more serv/day	[ ] 1 3-4 serv/day	[ ] 2 0-2 serv/day	
13. Fats Eaten. What kinds of added fats do you usually eat?	[ ] 0 All vegetable oils, no animal or solid fats	[ ] 1 Use some of both kinds of fats	[ ] 2 Mostly solid fats, butter, or hard stick margarine	
14. High Saturated Fat Foods. How often do you eat sausage, steak, french fries, rich desserts, hamburgers, cheese, etc.?	[ ] 0 Seldom or never eat these foods, 0-2 times/week	[ ] 1 Occasionally, 3-5 times/week	[ ] 4 Often, 1-2 times/day or more	
15. Nuts/Seeds. How many servings do you eat weekly? 1 serving = 1 oz or 2T nut butter (peanut butter etc).	[ ] 0 5+ serv/week	[ ] 1 2-4 serv/week	[ ] 3 Seldom or never eat nuts	
16. Water. How many glasses (8 oz.) of water do you drink daily?	[ ] 0 5+ glasses/day	[ ] 1 1-4 glasses/day	[ ] 2 less than 1 glass/day	

Scoring:

YOUR NUMBER OF MAJOR RISKS (COUNT ONE FOR EACH MAJOR RISK*)	
Add answers from numbers 1-10 (in column C from the chart to the left)	———
COMPARE YOUR ANSWER TO THE RISK RATING BELOW	

RISK RATING	NUMBER OF RISKS
Ideal	None
Low Risk	0-1 risks
Increased Risk	2-3 risks
High Risk	4 or more

OVERALL CORONARY RISK SCORE	
Sum scores (columns A, B, and C) to see your overall risk.	———
If your total score adds to at least 12 points and you exercise 30+ minutes five or more days/week, or if your HDLs are 60+, subtract 10 points from the total.	———
FINAL SCORE **MARK AN (X) ON THE RISK SCALE BELOW.**	———

MAJOR RISK FACTORS
Obesity, BMI 30+
Early family history CHD
Cholesterol 200+
Blood pressure 140/90+
Smoker
Inactive (if very active, - 1)
Age, men 45+, women 55+
HDL <40 (60+, minus one)
Diabetes or Hx MI

```
0      10     20     30     40     50     60     +
Low Risk            Increased Risk         High Risk
```

* A score of 20+ indicates increased risk. A score of 40+ is high risk. Use the coronary risk score to track progress on repeat tests.

PREVENTING HEART DISEASE
Practical Guidelines for Reducing Risk

Current Trends

Heart disease is the leading cause of death in America.[1] This year some 1.1 million people will suffer a heart attack, and 530,000 will die from it (about 45%). Half of those dying from a heart attack have no warning (63% in women). This is why prevention is so important. Don't wait for a problem to develop; take preventive action now.

The good news is that recent studies demonstrate that heart disease is largely preventable by adopting a healthy lifestyle. In the MRFIT heart study and others, researchers conclude that 76–92% of heart disease (in men and women) can be prevented by a healthy lifestyle if there are no modifiable risk factors.[2]

Preventive Actions You Can Take

Refer to your Risk Profile to identify any risks you have. Then use these seven key steps to reduce your risk of a heart attack.

1. **Achieve and maintain a healthy weight.**[3] Excess body fat, measured as body mass index (BMI), is a primary risk factor for heart health. Obesity, a BMI of 30 or higher, contributes to high blood pressure, high cholesterol, low HDL, sedentary lifestyle, and increased risk for diabetes. These are all major factors that cause heart disease. Check your BMI in the chart below (height in inches, weight in pounds). Maintain a healthy weight – a BMI less than 25. Even a 10–15 pound weight loss reduces risk substantially.

HEIGHT	LEAN BMI 23	OVERWT. BMI 25-29	OBESE 1 BMI 30-3	OBESE 2 BMI 35+
4' 10"	110	119-142	143-166	167+
5' 0"	118	128-152	153-178	179+
5' 2"	125	136-163	164-190	191+
5' 4"	134	145-173	174-202	203+
5' 6"	142	155-185	186-215	216+
5' 8"	151	164-196	197-229	230+
5' 10"	160	174-208	209-242	243+
6' 0"	169	184-220	221-257	258+
6' 2"	179	194-232	233-271	272+
6' 4"	189	205-245	246-286	287+

Note: "Healthy Weight" is defined as a BMI of 18.5-24.9. A BMI of 20-23 is ideal for most women; 21-24.9 for most men.

2. **Get regular physical activity.**[4] Exercise is a key therapeutic action for both treatment and prevention of heart disease. Regular activity helps control weight, high blood pressure, blood fats, and insulin resistance that is closely linked to diabetes and increased coronary risk. Get your doctor's guidance if you have existing health problems.

   U.S. guidelines state, "Every U.S. adult should accumulate 30 minutes or more of moderate-intensity physical activity on most, preferably all, days of the week."[5] Walking is one of the safest activities nearly everyone can do. It may cut your risk of heart disease by half when done regularly.

3. **Not smoking.**[6] Smoking is a major cause of heart attacks. If you stop smoking you greatly reduce your risk! Ask your doctor for guidance and about medications that can double your chances of stopping successfully.

4. **Limit animal fats and cholesterol.**[7] Foods that raise the cholesterol levels the most are those highest in saturated fat and trans fats (hydrogenated vegetable oils).

Limit these foods:

- High-fat meats: sausage, hot dogs, hamburger, steak, fried chicken, bacon, etc.

- High-fat dairy: whole milk, cream, cheese, ice cream

- Solid fats: butter, lard, shortening, hard stick margarine

- Baked goods using solid or hydrogenated fats (most cakes, pies, pastry, snack crackers, microwave popcorn)

- Deep fat-fried foods: fries, doughnuts, etc.

- Rich desserts

5. **Choose healthy fats.**[8] Foods rich in vegetable oils that have not been hydrogenated are the safest to use. They actually help reduce cholesterol and heart disease.

Examples include:

- Olive oil, canola and soy oils, olives, and avocados

- Trans fat-free margarines, especially the type with added plant sterols/stanols which can lower cholesterol directly

- Nuts, seeds, peanut butter and almond butter, flaxseeds or meal, and tahini (sesame butter). Nuts are especially protective to the heart. The Nurses' Health Study and others showed that those who ate five or more ounces of nuts weekly cut their risk of heart disease by one-third to one-half.

6. **Eat more high-fiber foods.**[9] Unrefined foods, high in dietary fiber, help trap cholesterol and rid it from the body. High-fiber foods also slow the absorption of carbohydrates and decrease the insulin demand protecting against the development of diabetes. Aim to eat at least three or more servings of whole-grain foods daily while limiting white bread, snacks, sugar, and other refined foods. This could cut your risk of heart disease in half.

Eat at least 15 grams of dietary fiber per 1000 calories eaten per day. That's generally 30+ grams of dietary fiber daily. Good sources of high-fiber foods include:

- Whole-grain breads, oatmeal, brown rice, cereal

- Fruits: apples, bananas, berries, melons, citrus

- Vegetables: salads, greens, squash, broccoli, cabbage, tomatoes, peppers, peas, stir fry

- Legumes: peas, lentils, beans, garbanzos, soy

- Nuts and seeds

7. **Regular checkups.**[10] Get your weight, blood pressure, blood sugar, and cholesterol levels checked regularly.

Summary

Take preventive steps now. By following these positive health guidelines you can lower your chances of ever developing heart disease. Some studies document as much as 80–90% decreased risk. You will also certainly look and feel your best. Get help from your doctor, a dietitian, or health counselor as needed in making therapeutic lifestyle changes.

More Information? Visit myllh.org

References:
1. AHA, 2005 Heart and Stroke Statistical Update, AmericanHeart.org. **2.** Jeremiah Stamler, et al, "Low Risk-Factor Profile and Long-Term Cardiovascular Mortality and Life Expectancy," *JAMA* 282(21):2012–2018, Dec. 1, 1999. **3.** NIH, NCEP, Adult Treatment Panel III Report, 2001, NCEP website. **4.** Ibid. **5.** "CDC and the American College of Sports Medicine." *JAMA*, 273 (5). **6.** NIH, NCEP, Adult Treatment Panel III Report, 2001, NCEP website. **7–10.** Ibid.

NOTES

BLOOD PRESSURE PROFILE

High blood pressure is a major cause of heart disease, stroke, kidney disease, congestive heart failure, and eye disease. The CDC estimates that high blood pressure is the primary or contributing cause of 270,000 deaths yearly in America. About one-third of the people with high blood pressure are unaware they have a problem. Take this blood pressure self-test to see how you can lower your risk of developing high blood pressure.

Directions: Mark the column that best describes you for each risk factor.

RISKS	COLUMN A	COLUMN B	COLUMN C
1. Race	[ ] 10 African-American	[ ] 5 Asian-American	[ ] 0 White
2. Age	[ ] 10 60 years or older	[ ] 5 40-59 years of age	[ ] 0 Younger than 40 years of age
3. Family History	[ ] 10 Two family members with high blood pressure	[ ] 5 One family member with high blood pressure	[ ] 0 No family history of high blood pressure
4. Alcohol	[ ] 10 Often have 3 or more alcoholic drinks/ day	[ ] 5 Drink alcoholic beverages, but no more than 1-2 drinks/day	[ ] 0 Rarely or never drink alcohol
5. Weight/BMI	[ ] 15 Excessively overweight BMI greater than 30	[ ] 10 Overweight BMI 25-29.9	[ ] 0 Normal weight 18.5-24.9
6. Physical Activity	[ ] 10 Seldom or never get regular physical activity	[ ] 5 30 minutes of physical activity at least 2-3 days/week	[ ] 0 30 minutes or more of physical activity on most days of the week
7. Vegetable and Fruit Intake	[ ] 15 Eat few fruits and vegetables daily or none	[ ] 10 Eat fruits and veggies daily but less than recommended, less than 2 C fruit, 2.5 C veggies daily	[ ] 0 Eat lots of fruits and veggies, at least 2 C of fruit and 2.5 C vegetables daily
8. Salt	[ ] 10 Eat plenty of chips, pretzels, pickles, or other salty foods and freely salt food at the table	[ ] 10 Eat average amount of salt and salty foods	[ ] 0 Eat sparingly of salt or salty foods
9. High Saturated Fat Diet	[ ] 10 Eat red or processed meats regularly such as beef, pork, sausage, hot dogs, bacon, hamburgers	[ ] 5 Eat only fish, skinless poultry, or small amount of lean meat	[ ] 0 Eat all vegetable protein foods such as legumes, soy, tofu, nuts, veggie burgers
	HIGH RISK _____	MODERATE RISK _____	LOW RISK
Blood Pressure Norms	**High blood pressure** 140/90+ or take BP medicine	**Pre-hypertension** 120–139/80–89	**Normal** Less than 120/80

Risk Rating: Total of Columns A and B _____ Put an "X" on the line below corresponding with your present score. The higher the score, the higher your risk.

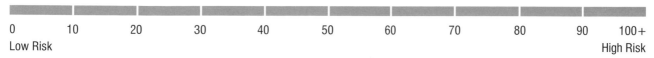

0	10	20	30	40	50	60	70	80	90	100+
Low Risk										High Risk

BLOOD PRESSURE RISK AND PREVENTION GUIDE

Blood Pressure and Your Health

High blood pressure (also called hypertension) is one of the nation's most common health problems. When blood pressure remains high, it makes the heart work too hard, causing heart damage and heart failure. It also damages the arteries, kidneys, and eyes.

Prevalence

- 65 million Americans (30%), or one in three adults, has high blood pressure.

- Another 59 million (28%) have prehypertension, an early stage of high blood pressure that also damages the arteries, heart, and brain.

- Even if your blood pressure is OK now, you still have a 90% chance of developing high blood pressure sometime in your life.

Prevention

- Get your blood pressure checked yearly. Know your blood pressure numbers!

- Learn what causes high blood pressure and take steps to lower or prevent high blood pressure.

BLOOD PRESSURE STANDARDS	
Normal (Healthy)	Less than 120/80
Prehypertension	120/80 – 139/89
Hypertension, stage 1	140-159/90-99
Hypertension, stage 2	160/100 or higher

Factors Affecting Blood Pressure – Risks

There are many causes of high blood pressure, including genetic conditions, medical conditions such as kidney disease, thyroid or parathyroid disease, and steroids and certain other drugs. That's why it's important to have your doctor rule out any medical causes of high blood pressure.

Unchangeable Risks. Other common unmodifiable risks related to high blood pressure include:

- **Age.** Risk increases as we get older. By age sixty-five, one in two Americans has high blood pressure.

- **Race.** African-Americans are more likely to get high blood pressure than whites and at an earlier age.

- **Family history.** If you have parents, brothers, or sisters with high blood pressure, you may have inherited a similar tendency.

Modifiable Risks. Most cases of high blood pressure, however, are linked to modifiable risk factors:

- **Excess body weight.** As weight goes up, so does the risk of hypertension.

- **Physical inactivity.** The arteries need regular physical activity to remain elastic, relaxed, and healthy. Regular physical activity is one positive step you can take to lower blood pressure or help prevent high blood pressure from developing.

- **Alcohol.** A high intake of alcohol is strongly related to high blood pressure. A high intake of alcoholic beverages can also damage the heart muscle.

- **Medications.** Certain drugs can raise blood pressure, including: steroids, anti-inflammatories, some antidepressants, and St. John's Wort.

- **Poor diet.** What you eat can also affect your blood pressure. A diet high in sodium (salt), high in saturated fat (e.g. meats and high-fat dairy products), and low in fruits and vegetables is linked to increased risk of high blood pressure.

Lowering/Preventing High Blood Pressure

The National High Blood Pressure Education Program (NHBEP) recommends the following guidelines for lowering or preventing the development of high blood pressure.

1. **Follow a healthy eating plan.** The DASH diet is especially helpful in lowering high blood pressure. It emphasizes fruits and vegetables (7–9 servings daily), low-fat dairy, and a diet low in saturated fat and cholesterol. It also includes whole grains, poultry, fish, and nuts, and reduced amounts of red meats, sweets, and sugared beverages.

2. **Reduce sodium (salt) in the diet.** All Americans are encouraged to eat less than 2,300 mg of sodium daily. For best results in blood pressure, aim for less than 1,500 mg of sodium daily. Processed foods (read food labels) are the primary source of sodium in the diet (about 80%). Limit salt and salty foods (e.g. chips, sauces, canned foods, snack foods, convenience or packaged foods).

3. **Maintain a healthy weight.** Losing even ten pounds can lower your blood pressure. Learn to like lower calorie foods. Begin by limiting foods high in calories but low in nutrition such as snack foods, candy, cake, and soft drinks. Also watch portion size and seconds!

4. **Be physically active.** Aim for 30–60 minutes of moderate physical activity daily on at least most days each week. Good activities for blood pressure include brisk walking, bicycling, swimming, and active gardening. It's OK to break your time into two or three 15–20 minute sessions if it fits into your schedule better.

5. **Maintain adequate intake of potassium (3,500 mg/day).** Potassium is a mineral found in fresh fruits and vegetables that is protective against high blood pressure. That's another reason why the DASH diet recommends 7–9 servings of fresh fruits and vegetables daily.

6. **Avoid or limit alcohol intake.** If you choose to drink, NIH recommends no more than one drink/day for women and no more than two drinks/day for a man. A drink is defined as twelve ounces of beer or five ounces of wine or one ounce of liquor.

7. **Medications.** If needed, your doctor may prescribe medications that can help lower your blood pressure. Medications don't replace the need for lifestyle change but can provide additional help when needed. Follow your doctor's instructions faithfully for best results.

References:
1. NIH, National Heart, Lung, and Blood Institute, JNC-7 Report,. Available at www.nhlbi.nih.gov/prevent. Accessed Oct 2006.

CANCER – FACTORS ASSOCIATED WITH RISK

No one can predict if you'll get cancer, but this self-assessment can help you focus your prevention efforts. The best way to fight cancer is to create an internal environment hostile to cancer and favorable to your health, to be watchful and screen appropriately, and to treat early if necessary.

Directions: Mark the column that best describes you for each risk factor.

RISK AREAS	COLUMN A	COLUMN B	COLUMN C
1. Gender	[ ] Male	[ ] Female	---
2. Race	[ ] African-American	[ ] White	[ ] Asian
3. Age	[ ] 60 or older	[ ] 25-59	[ ] Younger than 25
4. Smoking	[ ] Current smoker	[ ] Ex-smoker	[ ] Never smoked
5. Alcohol	[ ] Often have 3+ alcoholic drinks/day	[ ] Have up to 1-2 alcoholic drinks/day	[ ] Never drink alcoholic beverages
6. Physical Activity	[ ] Very little daily physical activity at work or during leisure time	[ ] 30-minutes daily of physical activity outdoors at work or at leisure	[ ] 1 hour or more of daily physical activity at work or at leisure
7. Weight/BMI	[ ] Obese or overweight; BMI greater than 25	[ ] Underweight BMI <18.5	[ ] Normal weight BMI 18.5-24.9
8. Vegetable and Fruit Intake	[ ] Eat as few vegetables and fruits as possible, other than potatoes	[ ] Eat 2-3 fruits and vegetables daily, usually cooked or prepared	[ ] Eat 5 or more servings of fruits and vegetables daily
9. Meat/Legume Consumption	[ ] I eat more red meats, bacon, and cold cuts than legumes/beans	[ ] I eat more poultry and fish than either red meat or legumes/beans	[ ] I eat more legumes/beans than animal meats, poultry, fish
10. Fat Intake	[ ] Usually cook with or eat animal fat as part of meat or in baked products	[ ] Eat animal fats or vegetable oils without attention to which is used	[ ] Regularly eat mostly vegetable oils in cooking and in baked products
11. Radiation/Ultraviolet	[ ] Was earlier or am often sunburned	---	[ ] Browned, but not sunburned
12. Occupational Exposure	[ ] Heavy metals, cutting oils, benzene, polycyclic aromatic hydrocarbons, etc.	[ ] Regular pesticide or herbicide application. Blood contact	[ ] Little exposure to chemicals at work, in the house, or at leisure
13. Previous Cancer	[ ] Had cancer in the past	---	[ ] Have never had cancer
14. Family History or Genetic Risks	[ ] Parents, brothers, sisters, aunts, uncles, or cousins on maternal or paternal side have cancers	---	[ ] Almost no one on either side of my family has cancer for several generations back
15. Unsafe Sex	[ ] Had multiple sex partners, had or continue to have unprotected sex	[ ] No longer have unprotected sex or multiple sex partners	[ ] Both partners have always been monogamous
RISK AREAS	GREATEST RISK _____	SOME RISK _____	LEAST RISK _____

Scoring Your Risk Areas: Count the number of checked boxes in each column. Except for 1–3, you may be able to lower each risk in column A or B.

© 2016 LifeLong Health. Permission given to copy for educational purposes only.

CANCER RISK AND PREVENTION GUIDELINES

The more risks you have, the greater your potential impact on lowering them with lifestyle changes. Review the explanations and suggestions below to begin reducing your cancer risks.

- Checks in Column A indicate areas of Greatest Risk.
- Checks in Column B indicate areas of Some Risk.
- Checks in Column C indicate areas of Least Risk.

1. **Gender.** Men get cancer (incidence) and die of cancer (mortality) at a higher rate than women, largely due to smoking.

2. **Race.** African-Americans have the highest rates of getting or dying from cancer, Asians the lowest, whites are in between. Hispanic rates are similar to whites below age thirty-five and somewhat higher than Asians at age thirty-five and over.

3. **Age.** Death rates are in the single digits below age thirty in most race categories (fewer below age twenty in Asians), but almost double with each successive decade. Incidence is lowest in all race categories between ages five and ten.

4. **Smoking.** A long history of tobacco research shows smoking to be the strongest medical risk factor for cancer. Quitting lowers risks measurably.

5. **Alcohol.** High intake of alcohol increases the risk for several cancers. Avoid or limit alcohol to lower risks.

6. **Physical activity.** Physical inactivity is associated with increased risk for several cancers. Activity may lower risk.

7. **Weight/BMI.** Excessive weight or being underweight puts a person at risk for cancer, but risk varies with the cancer.

8. **Vegetable & fruit intake.** Research on the diet-cancer connection is in its infancy, especially compared to tobacco research. Many areas remain unstudied. But we have discovered that whole foods lower risk.

9. **Meat/legume consumption.** Red and processed meat has been shown to increase the risk of cancer with inadequate folate intake (from veggies, oranges). Fish may be protective. Legumes (beans, peas) provide protein, folate, and many other nutrients that strengthen the body.

10. **Fat intake.** Animal fat increases cancer risk separately from the risk associated with red or processed meats. Milk fats do not have the same effect.

11. **Radiation/ultraviolet.** Sunburned skin and artificial tans increase cancer risk, whereas tanning without burning is being found to be beneficial.

12. **Occupational exposure.** Work with cutting oils, heavy metals, and carcinogenic chemicals increases a person's risk of cancer. Applying pesticides regularly is also a risk.

13. **Previous cancer.** Therapy poses a risk, but sometimes the risk of the first cancer is greater than the risk of the second.

14. **Family history/genetic risks.** Regular exams and knowing your family history can help you be alert for early signs. Medical interventions are increasingly available.

15. **Unsafe sex.** Like other personal history risks, keeping alert and not continuing unsafe practices can lower risks.

Take Action against Cancer

Rates of new cancers at most sites vary widely among different population groups and in different regions of the world. The American Cancer Society lists sixty-nine different cancers on its 2005 website, each with a different incidence and mortality rate.

The National Cancer Institute defines prevention as lowered cancer mortality through reduced incidence. In practice this means avoiding carcinogens (tobacco, many occupational exposures), using lifestyle and diet to modify cancer-causing factors or genetic predispositions, and using medical intervention to successfully treat precancerous lesions (for example, colon polyps). The following recommendations for prevention summarize what we know for sure.

1. **Avoid tobacco and alcohol.** You can quit! Others have. Get help. Keep trying. Success will come.

2. **Be physically active each day.** The best activities are outdoors. Aim for an hour a day as often as possible. Get guidance from your doctor or a knowledgeable fitness trainer on how best to start an exercise program.

3. **Eat a "whole" diet daily.** Get five or more servings of vegetables and fruits daily. Eat mostly whole-grain cereals and breads. Avoid refined cereals, breads, and baked products as much as possible. Avoid beverages/foods without nutrients – choose fruit juices or vegetable juices. Include legumes or beans in as many meals as possible, preferably daily.

4. **Get regular medical check-ups.** The best lifestyle cannot prevent all cancer. Medical interventions may help.

Sources:
1. American Cancer Society Statistics, 2005; NCI guidelines, 2005. **2.** Polednak AP. "Trends in Incidence Rates for Obesity-Associated Cancers in the U.S. Cancer Detection and Prevention." 2003; 27(6):415–421. **3.** Norat T, et al. "Meat, Fish, and Colorectal Cancer Risk: The European Prospective Investigation into Cancer and Nutrition." *J Natl Cancer Inst.* 2005 Jun 15;97 (12):906–16. **4.** Nothlings U, et al. "Meat and Fat Intake as Risk Factors for Pancreatic Cancer: The Multiethnic Cohort Study." *J Natl Cancer Inst.* 2005 Oct 5;97(19):1458–65. **5.** Mahabir S, et al. "Physical Activity and Renal Cell Cancer Risk in a Cohort of Male Smokers." *Int J Cancer.* 2004 Feb 10;108(4):600–5. **6.** Macera CA. "Past Recreational Physical Activity and Risk of Breast Cancer." *Clin J Sport Med.* 2005 Mar;15(2):115–6. **7.** United States Cancer Statistics: 2001 Incidence and Mortality.

NOTES

> "Life is an opportunity, benefit from it.
> Life is beauty, admire it.
> Life is a dream, realize it.
> Life is a challenge, meet it.
> Life is a duty, complete it.
> Life is a game, play it.
> Life is a promise, fulfill it.
> Life is sorrow, overcome it.
> Life is a song, sing it.
> Life is a struggle, accept it.
> Life is a tragedy, confront it.
> Life is an adventure, dare it.
> Life is luck, make it.
> Life is too precious, do not destroy it.
> Life is life, fight for it."
> ~ MOTHER TERESA

NOTES

PLEASE READ THIS IMPORTANT MESSAGE

The work contained in this CREATION Health seminar series has been produced over a long period of time and represents hundreds of hours of labor and a significant financial investment. Please honor the terms of our agreement included in this package, and respect these materials by not duplicating or sharing them. ALL MATERIALS COPYRIGHT © 2016 FLORIDA HOSPITAL.

IMPORTANT: PLEASE READ THIS AGREEMENT CAREFULLY BEFORE USING THESE SEMINAR MATERIALS

FLORIDA HOSPITAL OWNS OR CONTROLS ALL INTELLECTUAL PROPERTY AND OTHER RIGHTS CONTAINED IN THE MATERIALS YOU WILL RECEIVE RELATING TO THE CREATION HEALTH SEMINAR PROGRAM (COLLECTIVELY, THE "CONTENT"). FLORIDA HOSPITAL LICENSES TO YOU, THE LICENSEE ("YOU") THE LIMITED RIGHT TO USE THE CONTENT SUBJECT TO THE TERMS AND CONDITIONS SET FORTH IN THIS LICENSE AGREEMENT. BY USING, AND/OR INSTALLING ANY OR ALL OF THE CONTENT ON A COMPUTER, WHETHER PERMANENTLY OR TEMPORARILY, YOU INDICATE THAT YOU ACCEPT AND AGREE TO ABIDE BY THE TERMS AND CONDITIONS SET FORTH IN THIS LICENSE AGREEMENT. AS A RESULT, YOU SHOULD CAREFULLY READ THIS LICENSE AGREEMENT BEFORE EITHER READING, USING, OR INSTALLING THE CONTENT ON A COMPUTER. IF YOU DO NOT ACCEPT THE TERMS AND CONDITIONS OF THIS LICENSE AGREEMENT, YOU SHOULD MAKE NO USE OR COPY OF THE CONTENT AND SHOULD RETURN THE CONTENT TO FLORIDA HOSPITAL AT THE FOLLOWING ADDRESS: **FLORIDA HOSPITAL MISSION DEVELOPMENT, 496 WEST CENTRAL PARKWAY, ALTAMONTE SPRINGS, FLORIDA 32714.**

LICENSE GRANT

In consideration of your purchase fee, Florida Hospital grants to You, and You accept, a limited, nonexclusive, non-transferable license for the term of this License Agreement permitting You to read and use the Content for personal use and/or in a local seminar or small group. The Content is licensed, not sold, to You. You agree that You will not assign, sublicense, transfer, pledge, lease, rent, or share your rights under this License Agreement, except as indicated in the instructions in this leader's guide. You acknowledge and agree that You may not, and may not permit any other person or entity to, assemble, decompile, or otherwise recast, translate, or reformat the Content, create works derived from the Content, or install, distribute, provide access to, or use the Content on or by means of an intranet, extranet, or Internet system, or by means of networked computers. You may not use, or authorize another to use, the CREATION Health logo or the Florida Hospital logo.

OWNERSHIP OF CONTENT

The Content is protected by copyright law and international treaties. You acknowledge and agree that Florida Hospital retains ownership or control of the Content and all subsequent copies of the Content, regardless of the media in which such copies may exist including, without limitation, any and all copyright, trademark, trade secret, and other proprietary rights arising under the United States, state, and international laws, treaties, or conventions. You further acknowledge and agree that all right, title, and interest in and to the Content, including associated intellectual property rights, are and shall remain with Florida Hospital. This License Agreement does not convey to You an interest, ownership or otherwise, in or to the Content, but only a limited right of use revocable in accordance with the terms of this License Agreement. Unauthorized reproduction or distribution may result in severe civil or criminal liability and will be prosecuted to the fullest extent allowed under the law.

TERM

This License Agreement is effective upon your opening the Content for your personal use or for leading a local seminar or small group. Florida Hospital may terminate this license at any time for any reason on written notice to you. You may terminate this License Agreement at any time by destroying the Content and ensuring that all users of the Content have uninstalled the Content and destroyed all copies of the Content in any form. This License Agreement will terminate automatically upon breach by You of any of the terms and conditions of the License Agreement. Upon such termination, You agree to (i) destroy the Content, ensure that all users of the Content have uninstalled the Content, and destroy all copies in any form, or (ii) upon demand by Florida Hospital, return the Content to: Florida Hospital Mission Development, 683 Winyah Drive, Orlando, Florida 32803, at your expense, within five (5) business days after receiving such demand.

LIMITATION OF LIABILITY

EXCEPT AS WARRANTED ABOVE, IN NO EVENT WILL FLORIDA HOSPITAL BE LIABLE TO YOU OR ANY OTHER PERSON OR ENTITY FOR CLAIMS OR DAMAGES ARISING FROM USE OF OR INABILITY TO USE THE CONTENT, COPYRIGHT OR TRADEMARK INFRINGEMENT, OR FOR CAUSES RELATED TO OR ARISING OUT OF THIS LICENSE AGREEMENT, INCLUDING BUT NOT LIMITED TO LOST REVENUE, LOST PROFITS, CONSEQUENTIAL, INCIDENTAL, INDIRECT, SPECIAL, PUNITIVE OR EXEMPLARY DAMAGES, LOSS OF DATA, OR INTERRUPTION OR LOSS OF USE, EVEN IF FLORIDA HOSPITAL HAS BEEN ADVISED OF THE POSSIBILITY OF SUCH DAMAGES AND REGARDLESS OF WHETHER SUCH CLAIMS OR DAMAGES ARE BASED ON CONTRACT, TORT, STRICT LIABILITY, OR ANY OTHER THEORY. SOME STATES DO NOT ALLOW THE LIMITATION OR EXCLUSION OF LIABILITY FOR INCIDENTAL OR CONSEQUENTIAL DAMAGES, SO THE ABOVE LIMITATION MAY NOT APPLY TO YOU. IN ANY EVENT, ANY LIABILITY OF FLORIDA HOSPITAL RESULTING FROM USE OF OR INABILITY TO USE THE CONTENT, OR RELATED TO THIS LICENSE AGREEMENT, WILL BE LIMITED TO REPLACEMENT OF THE CONTENT UPON YOUR RETURN OF THE DEFECTIVE CONTENT.

MISCELLANEOUS

This License Agreement shall be construed and governed in accordance with the laws of the State of Florida, without reference to its conflicts of law principles. You and Florida Hospital expressly agree that exclusive jurisdiction for any claim or dispute with Florida Hospital or arising from or relating to this License Agreement shall reside in a court of competent jurisdiction located in Orange County, Florida and You further consent to submit to personal jurisdiction in a court of competent jurisdiction located in Orange County, Florida in connection with such suit. The parties hereby waive any jurisdictional, venue, or inconvenient forum objections to such courts.

Should any part of this License Agreement be declared invalid, illegal, or otherwise unenforceable by any court of competent jurisdiction, such part will be treated as severable from every other part of this License Agreement, and the remainder of the License Agreement will remain valid, legal, and fully enforceable. The failure of either party to enforce any rights granted hereunder or to take action against the other party in the event of a breach hereunder shall not be deemed a waiver by that party as to subsequent enforcement of rights or subsequent actions in the event of future breaches.

This License Agreement may be modified or amended only in a writing signed by both parties. This License Agreement, and all the rights and duties herein, will be binding on, and inure to the benefit of, the parties' successors and assigns.

This License Agreement constitutes the complete and exclusive statement of all the terms, conditions, representations, and warranties between You and Florida Hospital with respect to the Content, and supersedes all other oral and written communications relating hereto. Florida Hospital expressly reserves all rights not expressly granted herein

Additional copies of the Content and books written by Florida Hospital as well as other publications offered by Florida Hospital, may be purchased directly from Florida Hospital.

For questions or more information, please contact:
Florida Hospital Mission Development
407-303-7789

PLEASE NOTE:

This CREATION Health seminar series is a personal growth seminar. Everyone is at a different stage in his or her growth, and we are never finished growing when it comes to improving the quality/quantity of our mental and physical activity.

There is no "perfect" exercise for our minds or bodies, nor is there an ideal training schedule we must adhere to. Improving our mental and physical activity is a journey that has no destination and will continue throughout eternity.

Topics and issues will be presented in this seminar that might touch very close to home such as the nature of the "activities" that occupy your mind and the nature of your regular physical activities. As we discuss these topics, you might feel uncomfortable or realize you need some help and would like to talk to someone. You may request contact information from the presenter of this seminar that will aid you in finding a qualified mental health professional, physician or pastor who can help you personally and confidentially. Please contact one of these professionals or one you may already know if you feel you need assistance. You will also find in the supplemental material, a list of books, internet sources and resources that you might find helpful in your personal growth efforts.

DISCLAIMER:

The information provided in this seminar is for educational purposes only and is not intended to be a substitute for professional medical or psychological advice nor is it intended to diagnosis or treat specific medical or psychological conditions. You should seek prompt professional medical attention if you have a concern about your physical or mental health, or are experiencing specific symptoms.